D0207488

MILITANT ISLAMISTS

MILITANT ISLAMISTS

TERRORISTS WITHOUT FRONTIERS

Nozar Alaolmolki

PRAEGER SECURITY INTERNATIONAL

Westport, Connecticut • London

Library of Congress Cataloging-in-Publication Data

Alaolmolki, Nozar
  Militant Islamists : terrorists without frontiers / Nozar Alaolmolki
    p. cm. —
  Includes bibliographical references and index.
  ISBN 978–0–313–37221–6 (hard copy : alk. paper) — ISBN 978-0-313-37222-3
  (ebook : alk. paper)
1. Terrorism—Religious aspects—Islam. 2.   Religious militants. 3.   Islam and world
politics. 4.   War on Terrorism, 2001- I. Title.
BP190.5.T47A55 2009
363.325—dc22   2009010073

British Library Cataloguing in Publication Data is available.

Library of Congress Catalog Card Number: 2009010073
ISBN: 978–0–313–37221–6

First published in 2009

Praeger Security International, 88 Post Road West, Westport, CT 06881
An imprint of Greenwood Publishing Group, Inc.
www.praeger.com

Printed in the United States of America

The paper used in this book complies with the
Permanent Paper Standard issued by the National
Information Standards Organization (Z39.48–1984).

10 9 8 7 6 5 4 3 2 1

Contents

Acknowledgments

This book began during my Fulbright Scholar appointment in Kyrgyzstan in 1995, specifically after my visit to the southern city of Osh, where I became aware of the existence Islamic movement. The Islamist resurgence in the region and in Andijan across the border in Uzbekistan, in addition to the proximity of the region to the ongoing development in Afghanistan motivated my interests in the subject. Then came the terrorist attacks of September 11, 2001, on New York and Washington, D.C., when I began to write and present papers at the International Studies annual conferences, Third World Studies, and other conferences, including those overseas. I would like to express my appreciation and thanks to Hiram College for its generous support and assistance in enabling me to conduct research, attend professional conferences, and complete the project. A special thanks to Cassandra Talerico-Kaplan, Ph.D., and Maureen Molloy at ABC-CLIO for their editorial role in the book manuscript as well as to my wife, Kathleen, for her continuous encouragement and support.

CHAPTER 1

Terrorism and Suicide Bombing

The violent twentieth century encompassed at least two devastating world wars in addition to numerous other armed conflicts. Militant Islamists, those that this author studies, began their terrorist campaigns with the bombings of U.S. embassies in Kenya and Tanzania in 1998, followed by bombings in Indonesia. Next they adopted suicide bombing as their principal tactic, which they carried out on September 11, 2001, by attacking the World Trade Center in New York City and the Pentagon in Washington, D.C. Americans woke up to the news that there are people who are willing to fly airplanes into buildings, killing thousands of people. Not long afterwards, terrorist attacks continued with train bombings in Madrid and London.

This book introduces the reader to the emergence of the Militant Islamists, and the use of terrorism, suicide, and other forms of violence to achieve their stated objectives. Particular emphasis is placed on the evolution of the Militant Islamist world view and its militant campaigns throughout the Islamic world. Foremost among the complex array of forces that have influenced such development are the terrorist actions and bombings since the 1990s. However, this book focuses on Militant Islamist activities since the overthrow of the Taliban regime in Afghanistan in the aftermath of September 11, 2001, and the Militant Islamists' responses to the invasion of Iraq (see Table 3.2). I contend that terrorism is a symptom rather than a cause of violence, and thus could easily be eradicated.

This work presents an historical overview as well as the current political and socioeconomic conditions and forces in the individual Muslim nations, in addition to the regional and international determinants that play major roles in the emergence and perpetuation of violent Militant Islamists. I contend that the invasion of Afghanistan resulted in setbacks for *al-Qa'ida* in Afghanistan, where it enjoyed total freedom to run camps and to attract recruits through Pakistan to those camps. However, the consequence of the Afghan invasion, which mobilized Afghan opposition and attracted the old as well as the new Militant Islamists recruits to the war against the invaders, has prevented the Kabul government from becoming a viable functioning state. Afghanistan can easily be characterized as a failed state, despite the direct involvement of the NATO-coalition forces. Moreover, this study contends that the U.S. invasion of Iraq in March 2003 has made the Militant Islamist ideology even more attractive and has led to the spread of Militant Islamist cells in the Muslims nations, Western Europe, Thailand, the Philippines, and the Caucasus region.

This book is not aimed at analyzing *al-Qa'ida* alone, but rather the spread of Militant Islamists and the consequences of its propagation. Thus, I contend the Militant Islamists will remain a challenge for some time as long as the root causes remain— regional, national and global conflicts—that continue to fuel the spread of *al-Qa'ida*. At the national level, many if not all Muslim nations suffer from a disparity of wealth, widespread poverty, and the absence of democracy. Next, the persisting Israeli-Palestinian conflict fuels regional polarization. The national and political interests of the United States and the Western European states compels these nations to support the Arab governments and side with Israel, which generates a perception of anti-Islam, especially among the *al-Qa'ida*. and other Militant Islamist organizations. All of these factors will continue to catalyze the spread of *al-Qa'ida* ideology as well as other Militant Islamist groups. Due to the nature of terrorism and the character of Militant Islamist cells, it is very difficult if not impossible to detect and prevent their growth, and thus they continue to present a new dilemma for the target nations.

It is very important to present an historical background and current analysis of terrorism using several definitions of the term because of a lack of agreement on a single definition. The suicide bombings that have become part of the terrorist's tactics in recent years were first carried out in Sri Lanka on July 5, 1987, by the Liberation Tigers of Tamil Eelam (LTTE), which killed 40 Sri Lankan troops in the Nelliyad army camp in the north of the country. Tamil Tigers, a separatist armed organization, in the past three decades has been using violence against Sri Lankans with the aim of establishing a Tamil independent state.

Terrorism, including suicide missions, has existed throughout the history of humanity, reaching back at least to the Old Testament. For example, Samson brought down the temple of *Deghon*, committing suicide and killing all the Philistine military and major dignitaries who were in attendance. Also of historical importance are the Assassins, an order founded in the eleventh century by Hassan al-Sabbah in the northern part of present-day Iran. Their actions fascinated people so much that it was widely believed for a long time that the Assassins were intoxicated by hashish when they carried out their suicide missions. Thus, they were known for a long time as *Hashishins* because people could not comprehend the blind commitment of the Assassins to their cause.[1]

In the nineteenth century, Russian anarchists included Mikhail Bakunin (1814–1876), Carl Pisacue (1818–1857), Pyotr (Peter) Kropotkin (1842–1921), and Sergei Nachaev (1847–1882) the foremost anarchist and coined the phrase "propaganda of the Deed, by the Deed." One of the foremost Russian anarchists, Bakunin, believed that "the passion for destruction is also a creative urge" for regenerating the society; in other words, through destruction of empires their ideal world would be created. In 1880 German anarchist Johann Most wrote a pamphlet called "Philosophy of the Bomb," in which he said, "Outrageous violence will seize the imagination of the public and awaken its audience to political issues." Spanish anarchists like Buenaventura Durruti and Francisco Ferrer conveyed their disregard for state authority through violence, assassinations, and the destruction of existing state institutions.[2]

Terrorists aim to frighten their targets in unimaginable ways in order to significantly impact the psyche and emotions of people as well as the political and economic sectors of a nation. Dan Mulvenna, a terrorism specialist at the Center for Counterintelligence and Security Studies, points out that, "Throughout history, terrorists have stepped out of the bounds of conventional moral thinking." The U.S. intelligence community is guided by the definition of terrorism contained in Title 22 of the US Code, Section 2656f (d):

- The term "terrorism" means premeditated, politically motivated violence perpetrated against noncombatant targets by sub-national groups or clandestine agents, usually intended to influence an audience.
- The term "international terrorism" means terrorism involving the territory or the citizens of more than one country.
- The term "terrorist group" means any group that practices, or has significant subgroups that practice, international terrorism.[3]

The U.S. Department of Defense defines terrorism as "the unlawful use of—or threatened use of—force or violence against individuals or property to coerce or intimidate governments or societies, often to achieve political, religious, or ideological objectives." It should be noted that the term "unlawful use of..." is prominent in the above definition, which appears to present a political angle to the definition. On the other hand, the United Nations High-Level Panel on Threats, Challenges and Change defines terrorism as "any action intended to kill or seriously harm civilians or noncombatants, with the purpose of intimidating a population or compelling action by a government or international organization."[4]

To add to the difficulty, the international community has not been able to formulate a definition for terrorism that is acceptable to all members. Defining terrorism is a delicate subject because in their quest to achieve political goals many governments often use numerous forms of violence that can easily be characterized as state-terrorism. Moreover, one group's freedom-fighter, hero, and martyr are another nation's terrorists. Thus, the absence of an acceptable definition or understanding of terrorism continues to hamper the development of a global framework by which nation-states can fight terrorism together.

Terrorism is a challenging concept, and in particular the psychology of the suicide bomber is a mystery. Nobody knows exactly what leads a Militant Islamist to accept self-sacrifice and carry out suicide bombing against the target that he or she believes to be a threat to Islam. As long as conflicts real or perceived continue to dominate the environment—in this case, the Western threat to Islam—terrorism will continue in some form.[5] Thus, it appears that terrorism cannot be stamped out, but there is still an immediate need to contain it.

Almost all terrorist activities are rooted in and sustained by some form of political conflict. Suicide bombing can be a sanctioned state military or armed effort, such as the Japanese state-supported *Kamikaze* pilots who were trained as a cadre to terrorize the American fleet in the Pacific in 1944 and 1945. Such suicide missions or other violent acts often are presented and justified as either sanctioned or rewarded by a supreme being. These particular Kamikaze suicide acts were not carried out to defend the homeland, but rather for the glory of the empire. Japanese atrocities against the Chinese and other conquered territories were justified on the basis of Japanese socialization at that time and an educational system that included the formal indoctrination of the Japanese in the adoration of the emperor. If soldiers were to die in battle, their souls would go to the *Yasukuni Jinja* shrine (built in 1869). Today, *Yasukuni Jinja* is a *Shinto* shrine in Tokyo that, according to tradition, is the repository of the souls of Japan's war dead. During the second World War, the Japanese military closely associated itself with this shrine; even a number of soldiers found guilty of war crimes are considered divine spirits of the shrine. However, the interpretation of the definition of state-terrorism is often broadened to include many other forms of military action that result in the large loss of civilian lives.[6]

Throughout human history soldiers in democratic and non-democratic states go to war either willingly or are ordered to do so. They are sent with messages that their heroic act is blessed and will be rewarded by the almighty, depending on religious belief, or is necessary for the defense of the motherland, depending on the ideology of the state.

Terrorism is an act of the powerless against the powerful. Termed asymmetrical, many of these conflicts are familiar and have been ongoing for decades, such as those between Palestinians and Israelis, between the Irish Republican Army (IRA) and Protestant armed groups in Ireland, as well as conflicts in Spain, Sri Lanka, and India, where the Basque E.T.A. (*Euskadi Ta Askatasuna* "Basque Homeland and Liberty"), the Liberation Tigers of Tamil Eelam, and Kashmiri Muslims in the Indian-administered Kashmir perpetrate terrorist acts against their respective governments. More recently, asymmetrical terrorist conflict has arisen between the Chechens and the Russian government, the Aceh and Philippine Muslim movements, and the governments of Indonesia and the Philippines, respectively. In Afghanistan and in Iraq, where such conflict is occurring between those who resist occupation and the imposition of dictatorship, it is not difficult to witness indiscriminate terrorism. For example, in Iraq "savage and barbarian" beheading of hostages, suicide bombings, car bombings, desecration of the enemy's corpses, and assassinations are used as weapons to counter the powerful; the aim is to inflict fear among the security and military forces and the public in general. Thus, the definition of terrorism requires one to zoom in on the methods and actions used in the attacks.

In March 2004, four American security guards were gunned down in Fallujah. Their cars were burned by a mob of Iraqis, who then dragged the charred bodies through the streets and hanged the corpses from a bridge on the Euphrates River.[7] The report by *Reuters* news services, which on February 16, 2005 obtained the videotape that is described, provides a vivid look into the psyche of a suicide bomber that would make it difficult if not impossible to stop him, even though the videotape could have been created for the purpose of propaganda.

A Saudi Militant Islamist smiles and points to a wire taped to 20 large artillery shells in the back of an ambulance. He then speeds to his death, ramming into a U.S. base in Iraq. The undated video, which shows the man with hand grenades and a bullet belt strapped to his body, is the latest example of just how determined Muslim militants are to drive American forces out of Iraq as part of a publicized holy war.

"I am going to serve God," he says to his mother on the video before going up in flames in the suicide bombing near the Syrian border. "I hope to see you there. I say goodbye to this life. All I ask is that you pray for me." Composed and soft-spoken, the man appealed to all Muslims and noted that more young men are taking up al-Qa'ida's cause. He condemned those who were not interested in fighting holy war. The video identified the militant, who appeared to be in his thirties, as Abu Mu'aad al-Janubee, a member of al-Qa'ida in Iraq, a group headed by Jordanian Abu Musab al-Zarqawi. As Iraq's most wanted man Zarqawi, with a $25 million U.S. bounty on his head, and his followers have carried out some of the deadliest bombings in postwar Iraq. Sitting against a backdrop of a map of Iraq and images of flames engulfing the sky, Janubee is one of scores of militants inspired by Zarqawi, who draws followers from across the Arab world. A relaxed Janubee stood beside the ambulance and pointed to the trigger mechanism attached to a wire that ran across the shells, which are abundant in Iraq. "This is the wire and this is where it is attached. Then you press this button," he said as he gently touched a switch attached to the ambulance steering wheel. "So what do you think of it?" Janubee asked, smiling into the camera. Then he covered the shells with a white cloth, climbed into the ambulance, and headed down the street, beeping and flashing his rear-light signal before striking the target. He goes on to ask, "Why do some Muslims fight and struggle while others just drink and eat?" Thus, it is the Militant Islamists like Janubee who pose perhaps the biggest security risk for Iraq's interim government and American troops, if not to other countries.[8]

However, as a spate of suicide bombings around the world in recent years has shown, the face of terror is involving female bombers. In 1991 a female Sri Lankan separatist killed herself and former Indian Prime Minister Rajiv Gandhi. Since then similar bombings have occurred in Turkey, Pakistan, Israel, Uzbekistan, and Iraq. In Russia at least 11 female Chechen bombers have struck, including the women who downed two Russian airliners and those who helped seize a Beslan middle school and kill over 330 hostages, many of them children. Moreover, one of the December 11, 2007, Algerian suicide bombers, a 63-year-old grandfather, has puzzled Algerians as well as others, who usually characterize terrorists and suicide bombers in particular as being malleable and impulsive youths. If the grandfather's suicide associate that day, a 30-year-old ex-convict who set off the second of two bombs, was described as a textbook case of a young radicalized man, the grandfather broke the usual stereotypes. As can be attested with the cases of a 64-year-old Palestinian grandmother in northern Gaza, Fatima Omar an-Najar— mother of 9 and grandmother of 41— and Muriel Degauque, a 38-year-old white European woman who converted to Islam and attacked the U.S. soldiers' checkpoint in Iraq, these cases cast further doubt on the practice of profiling.

As mentioned above, the suicide bombings typical of the past two decades began with the suicide bombing in Sri Lanka in July 1987 that was carried out by Hindu Tamil (both men and women) as an act of revenge and anger. The LTTE, also known as the Tamil Tigers or Black Tigers, use suicide bombing in their struggle for an independent Tamil state in northern Sri Lanka. Ironically, the Tamil Tigers follow Hinduism, the religion of Mahatma Gandhi. This group also bombed the World Trade Center in Colombo, Sri Lanka, in 1997, and assassinated two Sri Lankan heads of state. LTTE suicide missions are inspired by devotion to Velupillai Prabhakaran, who is the group's political leader rather than a religious leader. Tamil women have carried out suicide bombing missions out of a sheer sense of nationalism and the LTTE's aim to achieve independence. The 1997 attack brought to at least 115 the number of people killed in one month in the resurgence of violence linked to the conflict between the majority Sinhalese and minority Tamils that has claimed over 60,000 lives since 1972. On April 25, 2006, a female suicide bomber disguised to look pregnant blew herself up in front of a car carrying Sri Lanka's army chief, Lt. General Sarath Fonseka, killing eight and wounding two dozen, including Fonseka, on the heavily fortified grounds of the country's army headquarters. The attempted assassination by suicide bombing was attributed to the Tamil Tigers. Here it becomes apparent that Tamil Tigers have used, and continue to use, terrorism as a tactic in their struggle against the state's military power. Clearly the Tigers' terrorism indicates that suicide bombing need not be connected to any particular religion or culture.[9] A Marxist-Leninist philosophy, rather than Islam, influences the Kurdish PKK of Turkey, whose members used suicide bombers in their struggle for Kurdish autonomy, in a war against what the PKK saw as occupation of their land, and for the release of their imprisoned leader, Abdullah Ocalan.

The Palestinians adopted terrorism, with suicide attacks adopted as their primary technique and an act of desperation, seeing themselves as weak and helpless in the face of Israeli state power. The Popular Front for the Liberation of Palestine and certain Palestinian organizations, such as HAMAS, Palestinian Islamic Jihad, and the al-Aqsa Martyrs Brigade, regard suicide attacks as a way to counteract Israel's conventional military superiority and to maintain a sense of power and legitimacy among their own constituencies. Violence since the start of the Palestinian *Intifada* (Uprising) in 2000 is estimated to have claimed thousands of lives from both sides.

Militant Islamists have employed terrorism as a weapon of first choice, adopting it from Western terrorist groups as noted in this chapter. Today Militant Islamists carry out terrorist acts in a number of countries throughout the world, including Chechnya, where women are also perpetrators, and places such as Iraq after the invasion, Afghanistan, and Indonesia, where men are the exclusive perpetrators of the actions, although more women have also changed that perception in Iraq. It must be emphasized that suicide bombing is not connected to any particular religion or culture.[10] As Oliver Roy aptly points out,

The figure of the lonely metaphysical terrorist who blew himself up with his bomb appeared in Russia at the end of the nineteenth century and was treated as a literary topic by Andre Malraux in *La condition humaine* (1933). (Cheng, the terrorist, commits a suicide attack because he feels that his ideal of purity and justice will fail if he wins, to the benefit of an earthly and disappointing compromise with human mediocrity.)[11]

In no way can Militant Islamist terrorist attacks, suicidal acts of violence, be predicted at this point. Consequently, it would be very difficult, if not impossible, to protect soft targets against terrorism. The root causes of terrorism must be tackled directly, and the motivations that make people willing to turn themselves into human bombs must be addressed if the incidence of terrorism is to decline.

Sheikh Naim Qassem, deputy secretary general of *Hizbullah,* glorifies the fact that the militia had no field desertions in its two-decade war with Israel. Abandonment of jihad was a disgrace, inviting punishment from God. In Imam Ali's words, "Death shall defeat you in life, and you shall defeat life through death." Citing Ali's son Imam Husain as a role model, Qassem describes love for martyrdom as "part of the love for God." He presents "martyrdom operations" as part and parcel of Islamic Jihad. He adds that many operations resulted in the martyrdom of *Mujahideen,* but it was a feature in the calculations of the Resistance. Qassem, highlighting the asymmetrical character of the military balance, states, "The power imbalance could only be equalized through martyrdom," and further observes that "martyrdom renders the military power threatening death ineffective, for such a menace acts only upon those who fear it, and is powerless in front of those who seek it."[12] Thus, he credits "martyrdom" for the rapid vitalization of Islam in Lebanon, resulting in the forced Israeli withdrawal in 2000.

Violence, terrorism, and, in this case, Militant Islamist are like poverty: they are enduring problems that can be diminished but not be eradicated. One of the major characteristics of the phenomenon is that it cannot be defined as clearly as Communism, Nazism, or extreme nationalism because it is not an ideology or political philosophy, but rather a tactic to achieve a group's objectives. It is appropriate to this study to make reference to a saying attributed to T. E. Lawrence, who mobilized the Arab insurgents against the Ottoman Turkey in World War I:"Making war upon insurgents is messy and slow, like eating soup with a knife."[13] Intellectually grasping the concept that fighting insurgents is messy and slow is a different thing from knowing how to defeat them; knowing how to win, in turn, is a different thing from implementing the measures required to do it.

This book consists of 12 chapters, and each deals with a particular relevant topic and geographic areas where the Militant Islamists remain active. This introductory chapter presents a number of definitions in order to assist the reader to develop a certain comprehension of terrorism and the aim of such a tactic. Chapter 2 explores the development of Muslim Brothers (commonly known as Muslim Brotherhood) in Egypt as a response to domestic, regional, and international developments. The lifeline of any organization—and in this case a terrorist one—is its funding sources. Chapter 3 demonstrates the use of the "traditional transfer of funds" by those who view the system as being an easier, less costly channel and who want to keep the authorities out of the process. The invasion of Afghanistan and the overthrow of Taliban regime that dispersed *al-Qa'ida* in 2001 prompted many Militant Islamists to engage in terrorist activities. Chapters 4 through 8 discuss the consequences of the invasion of Afghanistan , in addition to the development of numerous Militant Islamist groups in such places as Indonesia, Philippines, Caucasus, and Central Asia. Adoption of Militant Islamists tactics in Lebanon and the Palestinian territories are presented in chapter 7 by studying the development of *Hizbullah* in Lebanon and HAMAS organizations. It presents the differences between these two organizations and other Militant Islamists under study in this book. Chapter 9 studies the impact of the U.S.-led invasion of Iraq on the Middle Eastern countries as well as Afghanistan and Pakistan, specifically its role in the spread of the Militant Islamist cells in those countries. Militant Islamist terrorist campaigns have not been limited to the Muslim countries, and chapter 10 discusses the Militant Islamists' terrorist actions and the emerging cells in Europe. The Madrid and London bombings are evaluated as well as their impact on the development of more Militant Islamist cells in European countries. The United States, as the world's most powerful country, possesses numerous resources at the service of its foreign policy objectives. Among them is "soft power," or "Weapons of Mass Solution," which can readily be used in many ways to achieve those objectives. Chapter 11 discusses and evaluates the use of such a power in the United States' war on terror.

CHAPTER 2

The Development of Modern Islamist Militancy

Egypt has played a major role in the development of Militant Islamism, which is rooted in the anti-British and anti-Western world view traced back to nineteenth-century Islamists scholars. One of the main crises was the revolt of al-Urabi, which precipitated the British occupation of Egypt in 1882 and strengthened the rise of anti-British and anti-Western sentiments, particularly among Islamic scholars. Jamal al-Afghani (1839–1897) was one of those scholars, and he was instrumental in the development of Pan-Islamism because of his politico-religious convictions. He viewed the Western threat as a "challenge of the intellectual, social and ethical dynamism underlying that power to an Islamic super-structure no longer suitable to the present age."[1] Later, Mohammad A'bduh (1849–1905), Qassim Amin (1849–1905), and others became known as the core of the Islamic Reformation movement.[2] However, the counterpart of the Islamic Reformation, the *Jamiat al-Ikhwan al-Muslimun* (literally, the Society of Muslim Brothers), demanded a return to the orthodoxy of Islam as well as dedication to practical programs of education and scientific, economic, and social development rather than limiting themselves to theological devotion and the intellectual discussion of the needs and wants of the public.

Thus, the Islamist militancy, the Muslim Brothers as a secret organization, came into existence in 1928 by such individuals as Hassan al-Banna, Mohammad al-Ghazzali, Sayyid Qutb, and Mustafa al-Siba'i. In 1929 the organization was officially announced. Al-Banna railed against colonialism, particularly the British occupation of his country, called for a revival of the Islamic *Umma*, (the Muslim community and way of life in its totality), and developed mass support by building schools, clinics, and hospitals. The organization soon spread throughout Egypt, Sudan, Syria, Lebanon, Jordan, and Palestine. Al-Banna became known as

Murshid al-A'mm (the Supreme Guide), and he defined the Muslim Brothers as an *al-Salafi* organization, thus advocating the establishment of a theocratic state. It becomes very clear that the current Militant Islamists's ideology is rooted in the Muslim Brothers's *al-Salafi* Islamic orientation. In 1949, al-Banna was assassinated by the Egyptian secret police, which subsequently dismantled most of his organization. It is widely believed that al-Banna's assassination was in retaliation for the attempt on the life of the Egyptian prime minister, allegedly by a member of the Muslim Brothers. It should be noted that HAMAS has followed much the same pattern as al-Banna in supplying Palestinians with a basic infrastructure and social services that the Palestinian authorities could not—and still cannot—offer.[3] Moreover, the widespread corrupt practices of the Palestinian authorities, dominated by the Palestine Liberation Organization, caused disappointment and anger among many Palestinians, which was a God-sent opportunity for the HAMAS leadership to promote their political, social, and economic programs.

Egyptian Islamist Sayyid Qutb (1906–1966), a literary critic in the 1930s and 1940s, was executed on August 29, 1966, by the Egyptian government for his active membership in the Muslim Brothers. He is increasingly cited as the thinker who has most influenced *al-Qa'ida* leaders and their world view. In the late 1940s, Qutb spent two years in the United States. He detested the experience, and it appears to have turned him against what the West would call modernity but which he saw as something much worse. Because of his experience in the United States, he began to demonize modernity, referring to it as *jahiliyya*, a term meaning, variously, ignorance, savagery, and pre-Islam paganism. He expressed his views in his book, *Ma'alim fi'l-tareeq* (literally "Sign-posts on the path," and translated as Milestones). In this book he denounced non-Muslim societies and their dominant political-social systems, which Qutb characterized as overwhelmingly *jahiliyya,* and presented measures that Muslim activists should take to establish a society based on divine guidance.

Qutb denounced *jahiliyya,* which he described as the domination of human over human, or subservience to fellow humans rather than to Allah. Such a state of affairs had existed in the past, he said, and would continue to threaten Muslim society in the future if allowed to remain. He believed that *jahiliyya* exists in direct opposition to Islam, and its existence presents a choice to each individual Muslim to either obey the decree of human society and fall into *jahiliyya* or to observe the decree of Allah. He contended that the modern incarnation of *jahiliyya* in the industrialized societies of Europe and America was analogous to the *jahiliyya* of pagans and pantheists and the idol worship of pre-Islam societies in Arabia. In both periods of *jahiliyya,* he argued, humans are ruled by themselves rather than by Allah.[4]

Qutb was not the first Muslim intellectual to look at the world in this way. In fact, he was influenced by a contemporary living in India, Abdul A'la Mawdudi (1903–1979), who was a follower of the *Deobandi* school of Islam and founder of *Jammat al-Islami*, (Islamic Community), a political and social activist group. Mawdudi was appalled by modernity and its social consequences in the West and by rapidly expanding ideologies such as Marxism and Leninism.[5] Qutb interpreted Islam to be the central frame of reference for all human activity. He did not believe that religion itself was simply a private choice, as it is viewed in secular societies, and he did not believe Islam was a private choice, as religion is viewed in secular societies. Both he and Mawdudi also drew on earlier events and ideas of Muslim thinkers. One such intellectual was Taqi al-Din ibn Taymiyya (1263–1328), who in reaction to the Crusaders and Mongol onslaught of the thirteenth century preached a return to the essentials of the Islam. He believed in strict adherence to the Qur'an and authentic *Sunna* (practices of the Prophet).[6] Ibn Taymiyya believed those two sources contained all the religious and spiritual guidance necessary for Muslim salvation in the hereafter. He preached a return to these essentials, which he believed the *Ulema* (Muslim scholars) had abandoned. Another eighteenth-century Muslim thinker, Muhammad ibn Abd al-Wahhab, advocated purging Islam of modern interpretations and relying strictly on the *Qur'an* and *Hadeeth* (the record of the Prophet's words and deeds). Abd al-Wahhab was also the founder of the *Wahhabi* Islamic school of thought.

Qutb also drew upon his immediate experiences and firsthand knowledge of twentieth-century colonialism in the Arab world as well as the oppressive nature of the Arab regimes. The Muslim Brothers, who had taken root in Egypt and surrounding Muslim countries, gave Qutb an avenue to spread his views. He also believed that there were forces in 1950s and 1960s—capitalism, individualism, promiscuity, and decadence — that undermined Islam. Qubt's views are still seen today as potent threats by the Militant Islamists, and even moreso with the advent and power of globalization.

Qutb rejected Arab nationalism, which was the prevailing political ideology during his time, as he strongly believed in the *Umma* and the totality of *Dar al-Islam,*or Abode of Islam rather than in separate independent nation-states because such a division hampered the practice of Islam and the application of *Shari'a* (literally meaning the Path), or Islamic law. He feared that the pan-Arab nationalism would place the Arab world and Muslim nations on the path of becoming part of *Dar al-Harb,* the Abode of War, rather than on the path toward *Dar al-Islam.* He advocated and encouraged Muslims to fight against it.

Therefore, there is a direct connection between Qutb's writing and the world views of Usama bin Ladin and Ayman al-Dhawahiri—the two symbols and icons of the Militant Islamists—and their followers in *al-Qa'ida*. Like Qutb, *al-Qa'ida*'s followers perceive Islam to be under a double attack: not just military attack from a hostile West, especially the United States (in Iraq, Palestine, Chechnya, and so forth), but also from within. They believe attack from within occurs because the weakness of individuals, which stems from a perceived disengagement from Islam, allows Western values to be spread by the corrupt and oppressive Muslim regimes that are seen as undermining Islam. The double-pronged attacks, according to the Militant Islamists, must be resisted by *jihad*. Each Muslim, individually, needs to struggle constantly to become a true believer by submitting faithfully to Allah and then committing to an armed struggle against Islam's enemies. These enemies include the international enemy—Western European governments, America, and Israel—and regional enemies, specifically the Arab regimes. For bin Ladin and other Saudi Militant Islamists, the Saudi regime is as much an enemy as the United States.

Militant Islamists, therefore, do find justification in Islam for their violent approach to bring about change. However, most of this justification is rooted in Islamic views that were developed in the twentieth century and are a departure from previous Islamic teachings. Contemporary militant interpretation of political and religious "theory" also claims connection with some of the principal ideals and practices of the Islamic religion itself. Therefore, zealous adherents of Islam, such the Militant Islamists, view Islam as a religion that not only is concerned with religious teaching but also as a religion that encompasses society as a whole—its politics, economics, law, the judiciary, and state behavior—as well as many other aspects of everyday life. The Militant Islamists cannot separate the complexities of modernity and the modern state from Islam as a religion. Although one may argue for separation of "state" and "mosque," for the Militant Islamists this not a possibility because to do so would violate Islam as they interpret it. Thus, it is clear that Militant Islamists have succeeded in de-secularizing all forms of social, political, and economic problems and grievances in addition to the regional and global conflicts. This particular characteristic makes it difficult if not impossible to challenge their world view and alleviate the ever-persistent root causes of terrorism.

The Muslim Brothers sought to defeat Western Colonialism, Marxism and Leninism, Maoism, and Arab nationalism, all of which the group viewed as anathema to Islam and the Islamic world view that encourages the universalism of the *Umma*. However, the Western secular ideologies were the exclusive domain of the intellectuals, the educated, some labor union leaders—who were emerging in some Islamic countries—and high-level bureaucrats. Additionally, the activities and world view of the Egyptian Muslim Brothers and secular ideologies were almost unknown in the Arabian Peninsula, or *al-Shebah al-Jazeera.* So, it is not difficult to notice that the Militant Islamists's orientation and world view is a recent development in Saudi Arabia and other Persian Gulf Arab traditional societies.

Al-Banna and Qutb believed strongly in the concept of jihad as a holy war against the foreign occupation of Muslim lands, even if the occupying forces were the people of the book, Old and New Testament and *Qur'an* (i.e., the Christians, Jews, and Muslims). Furthermore, they characterized the occupying forces as infidels, regardless of their religious beliefs. Both Qutb and Mawdudi thus introduced a new interpretation of jihad to the Muslim world.

But it is Qutb's writings and views that today offer more insight into the world view of Militant Islamists and those in Saudi Arabia.[7] ,As a Wahhabi conservative Muslim nation, Saudi Arabia was and remains a natural haven for radical Islamist scholars, including the Militant Islamist ideologue, Ayman al-Dhawahiri. In the 1950s Qutb took the arguments of al-Banna and Mawdudi a step further. For Qutb, all non-Muslims were infidels—even the people of the book—and he predicted an eventual clash of civilizations between Islam and the West. Azzam Tamimi, director of the Institute of Islamic Political Thought in London, points out that Qutb's writings in response to Nasser's persecution of the Muslim Brothers became popular throughout the Arab world, especially after his execution and the Israeli defeat of the Arab neighboring countries in the 1967 war. One of the most spectacular violent acts by the Militant Islamists—seen live on television— came in October 1981 when a Militant Islamist military cell led by Lieutenant Khaled al-Islambouli assassinated the Egyptian president, Anwar al-Sadat.

Qutb and Mawdudi inspired a whole generation of intellectual Islamists, including Ali Shariati, a "closet secular" Iranian whose anti-Western views became popular among some religious youth because of the political, social, and economic conditions of Iran under the absolute monarchy of Shah Mohammed Reza Pahlavi. French-educated Shariati contended that all Western views were monolithic and corrupting, and he often referred to the phrase "West-toxication," coined by Jalal Ale-Ahmad, to describe the effects of those who dominated Iranian society under the Shah. Both were critics of the state and the Iranian society of their time. Many others existed before them, but these two adopted an Islamic orientation to their approach. Also among those influenced by intellectual radical Islamist views, particularly the anti-Western aspects, was Ayatullah Khomeini, who later introduced an Iranian interpretation of Qutb's and Mawdudi's radical Islamism in the 1970s when he established himself as Iran's (whose people are mainly Shi'a) *Valayat-e-Faqih*,[8] or Absolute Jurist. Becoming the Shi'a Absolute Jurist gave Khomeini the means to justify authoritarianism and the perpetuation of a nonsecular dictatorship. He truly believed, as did most Muslim radicals before him, in the establishment of an Islamic dictatorship. Unlike previous radicals, he was able to establish such a dictatorship and continued to advocate Qubt's militant views and policies. However, the intellectual Islamists, who publicly became concerned about the injustices in the Muslims nations (injustices that persist today), began to raise questions regarding the interpretation of Islam with regard to these transgressions and widespread repression. Such religious interpretative conflict continues to haunt the Islamic world.

The Militant Islamists of the 1950s and 1960s also were familiar with Marxist concepts and jargon because modern radical Islamic literature was infused by these concepts, which often were juxtaposed with Islamic verses or formal titles of power, such as Pharaoh, especially in the context of anti-colonialism, anti-imperialism, and repression of the masses. However, this familiarity should not be interpreted as if Militant Islamists are Marxists and that therefore their anti-Americanism stems from Marxism. Rather, current Militant Islamists are fanatically dedicated Muslims who adhere to and exploit certain radical aspects of Islam by trying to apply it to present-day national, regional, and global ills as they see them. Although they are practicing Muslims, Militant Islamists should not be viewed as the followers of any particular radical Ulema (Muslim scholars). In fact, intellectual and Militant Islamists directly question and challenge the Ulema, who have become in many societies part of the social, political, and somewhat economic elite, as long as they do not question authority.

ROOTS OF THE NEW INTERPRETATION OF JIHAD

The Arabic word *jihad* is interpreted in several ways: perseverance, persuasion, and coercion.[9] Literally, jihad means struggle or effort, but it also means a call to arms in the case of direct or perceived threat. For the majority, if not all scholars, jihad refers to the struggle or effort to defend one's faith and its ideals against harmful inner emotional and mental threats as well as external social and physical threats. It can encompass goals such as striving to rid one's self, society, or nation of a harmful habit such as smoking, striving to achieve a better understanding of a problem and development of a solution, or striving to achieve a personal goal, such as improving one's education. Because they are a permanent and personal obligation, these goals are part of the individual's (*al-fardi*) religious consciousness and moral struggle rather than required religious acts, such as prayer or alms giving. Heads of state or organizations may use the concept of jihad to mean a campaign. In Afghanistan in December 2004, President Hamid Karzai declared a jihad, meaning a national campaign, against the cultivation of opium and drugs. To assist Karzai in his nation's jihad, the United States decided to make drug eradication a priority, pledging $780 million in 2005 to help Afghanistan combat drugs. In another such example, Prime Minister of Pakistan, Perviz Musharaf, in a televised address to the Pakistanis in connection with the London bombings of July 7, 2005, which reportedly involved three ethnic Pakistani British, denounced the bombings and said he did not consider those behind the bombings to be human. Additionally, he said, "I urge you, my nation, to stand up and wage a jihad against extremism and to stand up against those who spread hatred and chaos in the society."[10]

It is important to highlight that traditional Islam classifies jihad into two major categories: *al-Jihad al-Nafs,* also referred to as *al-Jihad al-Akbar,* or the greater striving, and *al-Jihad al-Asghar,* or the minor struggle. Al-Jihad al-Nafs is sometimes called the *Fard al-ayn,* which is an individual's personal duty or obligation and reflects the fact that al-Jihad al-Nafs involves one's own struggle for self-purification, or in secular terms, a struggle against ego. In contrast, al-Jihad al-Asghar is an individual's or community's struggle to protect Islam against injustice and oppressors in the earthly world. It is the latter definition that is interpreted as holy war because in the *Qur'an* the word *Qitaal* (war, warfare, or killing) is used in reference to this category of jihad. The following *Suras* (verses) from the Qur'an address the issue of Jihad:

- And whosoever strives, strives only for himself (29:6).
- As for those who strive hard in Us [Our Cause]. We will surely guide them to Our Paths [i.e. Allah's religion—Islamic Monotheism]. And verily, Allah is with the *Muhsinun* [doers of good] (29:69).
- And fight [*Qatalao*] in the Way of Allah those who fight you, but transgress not the limits. Truly, Allah likes not the transgressors (2:190).

For today's Militant Islamists, jihad is an individual, personal decision and endeavour. This is clearly evident in the violent and nonviolent actions of the individual Islamist, whose actions are disengaged from the family, community, ethnicity, and nation. Thus, the Militant Islamist is an isolated individual who finds connection with other militants, with the end result being attacks against perceived enemies of Islam.[11] Such individuals may receive logistical assistance from Muslims who sympathize with an attack against those who are believed to oppress Muslims. The suicide bombings in the Palestinian occupied territories, Chechnya, Afghanistan, Indonesia, and Iraq are clear examples of those who are committed to suicide bombing in order to achieve their objectives.

It is important to underscore that in the 1980s and 1990s the Militant Islamist movement in Egypt was principally dominated by the Egyptian Islamic Jihad (EIJ), led by al-Dhawahiri, with the principle objective to topple the Egyptian government and establish an Islamic state. For al-Dhawahiri, jihad, as part of the name of the movement, is intended to be holy war that is initiated to bring about change. That jihad also refers to ridding the Muslin world of Western influence in the form of corrupt and despotic leaders and any Western military presence has become widely accepted among the majority of Muslims. Indeed, Muslim support against those perceived as oppressing Muslims is ubiquitous, even among nonradical and moderate Muslims. What is not so universally accepted is that the Militant Islamist groups such as *al-Qa'ida* as well as other organizations (e.g., Hizbullah, HAMAS, and *Jammah Islamyya*, among others) have adopted violent methods to achieve such jihad.

In the 1960s and 1970s, the ruling Saudi royal family, which had been criticized for its pro-American stance, seized upon the Soviet invasion of Afghanistan as a cause, an action which could rally Islamist support and deflect internal criticism. Historically, the Saudi family has drawn its legitimacy from the blessing of Wahhabi clerics. The oil boom of the mid-twentieth century enabled the Saudi government to spend huge amounts of money to promote the Wahhabi school of Islam abroad by establishing mosques and schools in many regions outside the Middle East, including the Caucasus, Central Asia, and even Europe and North America. Some radical offshoots of the Wahhabi school vigorously oppose the economic or military influence of non-Muslim countries—notably the United States and Israel, whose influence is referred to as International Zionism—in the Middle East and have justified terrorism as a weapon against them.

The Saudi government began to use its political and financial power in support of Afghan jihad against the 1979 Soviet invasion, and this Saudi support was directly backed and supported by Pakistan and the United States. However, the jihad against the Soviet invaders consolidated the other interpretation of jihad: that of the holy war, not only in the minds of the fighters but also in the minds of many others in local Afghan communities. Therefore, the countries that backed the Afghan fighters nurtured the development of the present-day Militant Islamists, who adhere to the concept of jihad as violent holy war.

The chair of the Organization of Islamic Countries (OIC), Abdullah Ahmad Badawi, the prime minister of Malaysia, told participants in a 2005 OIC conference that Muslims were as much to blame as non-Muslims for misinterpretations of jihad, which is often distorted as a religious justification for violence. He said it was unfortunate that some people had narrowed the concept of jihad to mean armed war and "even more unfortunate that this is the only meaning commonly understood by the general public. Muslims must take effective measures to deconstruct the intellectual and ideological foundations of religious extremism and sectarianism, for they do great damage to the cause of Islam and the welfare of Muslims."

In his remarks, Badawi also remarked that "equally high in the Commission's agenda would be the questions of how poverty and illiteracy in the Muslim world can be eradicated."[12] Although illiteracy rates are generally falling in Arab countries, rising populations mean that the total number of people unable to either read or write continues to increase. A report released in 2005 by the Arab League Education, Science, and Culture Organization (ALESCO) notedthat 70 million people 15 years or older in Arab League member countries were illiterate. It stated that an estimated half of all women in the countries concerned, or 46.5 percent, were unable to read or write, as opposed to 25.1 percent of men. The report noted that as a percentage of total population, the number of illiterate individuals had fallen over the past 35 years. The overall rate stood at 73 percent in 1970, but it was now down to 35.6 percent. However, because of population increases, in absolute numbers there are 70 million illiterate people currently, whereas in 1970 the total was only 50 million.[13]

THE RISE AND BELIEFS OF *AL-QA'IDA*

The Muslim Brothers have followers in many Muslim nations; some advocate a nonviolent approach toward achieving their aims, whereas others employ violent means. Regardless, their goals are the same—to establish an Islamic *Umma,* which refers to the totality of the Muslim community as it existed during the time of the Prophet Mohammed and his immediate four successors. This period is termed the *Kholafa.* Establishing the *Umma* is one of *al-Qa'ida*'s primary goals, and therefore the origins of Usama bin Ladin's concept of jihad can be traced back to the Militant Islamist world view of the founder of the Brothers, Hassan al-Banna, and Sayyid Qutb. Bin Ladin and other *al-Qa'ida* leaders have been able to introduce politics into religious struggle by interpreting jihad as a holy war against those regimes that they perceive to be the enemies of Islam and thus seek to establish a theocratic system in which the head of state would also be the religious leader. However, it must be underscored that such a rule would be monolithic in the Islamic world, meaning the end of separate and independent Muslim nation-states.

The new groups such as *al-Qa'ida* (which stems from the word *Qa'id*) were established throughout the Islamic world, but each has different objectives. *Al-Qa'ida* means the base, as in a camp or foundation, but it also means rule, principle, maxim, formula, precept, or method.

Understanding the roots of the Muslim Brothers and the world views of both *al-Qa'ida* and EIJ provides more useful insight into the source of Usama bin Ladin's beliefs than examining his experiences fighting the Soviets and establishing an Islamic regime in Afghanistan or his experiences and socialization during the unbridled materialism of 1970s Saudi Arabia. Analysis of bin Ladin's world view clearly reveals that his ideas as well as those of *al-Qa'ida* are founded in the writings of Sayyid Qutb.

Like Qutb, Usama bin Ladin, Ayman al-Dhawahiri, and the *al-Qa'ida* followers perceive Islam to be under external and internal attacks: military attacks from hostile Western nations (in Palestine, Afghanistan, Chechnya, Iraq, and so forth) and attacks from within, where they believe Western values spread by immoral regimes in Islamic countries are undermining the Muslim way of life. *Al-Qa'ida* and other Militant Islamists believe these attacks must be resisted by jihad, through a call to arms and violence. At the same time, the individual Muslim must wage personal jihad to submit more completely to Allah by resisting Western values that are present in the Muslim nations.

In 2001 *al-Qa'ida* and the EIJ the extremist offshoot of the Muslim Brothers led by al-Dhawahiri formally merged to form a new organization known as Qa'ida al-Jihad (the Base of Jihad), meaning the foundation of holy struggle or war. The followers of the EIJ movement had argued that "Afghanistan should be a platform for the liberation of the entire Muslim world." The Persian Gulf War of 1991, which brought thousands of American military forces to Saudi Arabia, strengthened his views. Upon the defeat of the Soviets and the establishment of the Taliban regime, the continued presence of American forces in Islamic lands—perceived not just as occupiers but as infidels in the Militant Islamists's interpretation —was a blow to Usama bin Ladin, al-Dhawahiri, and the Militant Islamists in Saudi Arabia as well as other militants. This event led to *al-Qa'ida*'s 1998 "declaration of war" on the United States, which was followed by terrorist attacks against American targets.

On February 23, 1998, *al-Quds al-Arabi,* an Arabic language newspaper published in London, printed the full text of Usama bin Ladin's "Declaration of the World Islamic Front for Jihad Against the Jews and the Crusaders." *Al-Quds al-Arabi* said that the statement was "faxed to the newspaper and signed by Shaykh Usamah Bin-Muhammad Bin-Ladin (the prominent Saudi oppositionist); Ayman al-Zawahiri (sic.), *amir* of the Jihad Group in Egypt; Abu-Yasir Rifa'i Ahmad Taha, a leader of the [Egyptian] Islamic Group; Shaykh Mir Hamzah, secretary of the *Jamiat-ul-Ulema-e-Pakistan;* and Fazlul Rahman, *amir* of the Jihad Movement in Bangladesh."[14]

Al-Qa'ida subsequently expanded its operations and recruitment efforts throughout the Sunni Muslim nations. It is noteworthy that the Militant

Islamists and their followers are Sunni and often steadfastly anti-*Shi'a* in their Islamic world view and would do whatever possible to undermine the *Shi'a* sect. *Al-Qa'ida* refers derogatorily to the *Shi'a*s as "*al-Rafidha*," or those who reject the faith. The Islamic Republic of Iran, ruled by *Shi'a* clerics, was fiercely hostile to Afghanistan's extremist Sunni Muslim Taliban and *al-Qa'ida* and has vehemently denied allegations that it is supporting them. Militant Islamists, who are exclusively from the Sunni sect, consider the mourning rituals of *Ashoura* (meaning ten in Arabic; it occurs on the tenth day of the month of *Moharram*, when the Prophet's grandson, Hussein, was killed by the ruling Umayyad *Khalifa* in 680 AD near Karbala), to be against the teachings of Islam and demand that Shi'as be declared non-Muslims. Pakistani Militant Islamist groups such as *Lashkar Jangavi* also advocate a similar anti-Shi'a view. Fierce suicide bombings and other attacks against the *Shi'a* community in Iraq since the National Assembly Election in which the Iraqi *Shi'a*s received the majority vote and specifically during the *Ashoura* are clear evidence of the anti-Shi'a view of the Militant Islamists. However, these attacks also could have been encouraged and assisted by the former *Ba'thist*s, whose aim is to force Iraqi *Shi'a*s to respond to the killings and ignite a civil war.[15]

There is a need to highlight certain aspects of the Militant Islamist culture that enables them to justify in their own mind the separation of the "real" and "unreal" Muslims (see Table 3.2) . This culture is based on the concept of "*Takfir*," which is the predominant part of the Militant Islamists's world view. Such an orientation contends that contemporary Muslim societies have reverted to a state of unbelief, or *Kufr,*, and those who revert to a state unbelief are *Kufar* (*Kafir* in singular form). The Militant Islamists thus consider them legitimate targets for both rebellions against the state or government, and believe they are permitted to carry out violence against such a Muslim society. Militant Islamists justify such a view by the concept of *fitnah* (seduce, disgrace, mislead, discord, division, or civil war) among Muslims. They point to *Qur'an* verse 8:39 "So fight them until there is no more *fitnah* (discord, disbelief) and all submit to the religion of Allah alone," and *Qur'an* 8:40 "If people are obstinate, and refuse to surrender, know Allah is your Supporter."

As to whether Militant Islamists ought to be regarded as a monolithic or decentralized entity is an important issue because of a dramatic change in the characteristics of their terrorist attacks. Overall, terrorist attacks since the 1990s suggest the former view, but recently attacks suggest that, although the actions and goals remain the same, the Militant Islamists have become more decentralized. The invasion of Afghanistan and Iraq has changed the characteristics of bombing drastically. Most of the attacks have concentrated in Iraq, and the majority of those are suicide bombings involving the killing of civilians and Iraqi security forces. It appears the aim is to demoralize the public in the country's chaotic situation and at the same time present those who are working with the "government" as the supporters of the invasion by the U.S.-led forces. Additionally, Usama bin Ladin's videos and audio messages are attempts to show his continuing importance in the Militant Islamist movement despite the increasing number of attacks by groups that appear to be independent of *al-Qa'ida*. In his messages, he highlights the issues that energize and mobilize the Militant Islamists, and simply by doing so he is also maintaining his role as its leader. In his messages, bin Ladin has remained consistent: U.S. administrations have repeatedly humiliated Muslims with a foreign policy that has propped up corrupt governments in the Middle East and perpetuated conflict in the region. "Should a man be blamed for defending his sanctuary?" he asked, speaking in a composed manner and using formal Arabic. "Is defending oneself and punishing the aggressor in kind objectionable terrorism? If it is such, then it is unavoidable for us." Although bin Ladin has consistently charged that the United States oppresses Muslims, the examples he cites have changed over the years.

In 1996, when bin Ladin issued his declaration of war against American interests, the primary offense he mentioned was the presence of U.S. troops in Saudi Arabia. They had used military bases in the kingdom during the 1991 Persian Gulf War and remained there afterward at the request of the Saudi royal family. Having "Crusader warriors," which is the term he used for American forces, near the holy shrines of Mecca and Medina was a grave insult to all Muslims, bin Ladin and other Militant Islamists complained. U.S. troops largely withdrew from the kingdom by September 2003, but their departure did not end *al-Qa'ida* operations in the region. Instead, sympathizers of the group have since increased their attacks on the interests of the United States and others they consider to be enemies in the kingdom.

He has continued to list U.S. support of the Saudi royal family—that bin Ladin regards as corrupt and beholden to outside interests—as one of his principal grievances. But he has also tapped into two other issues that have inflamed public opinion in the Middle East: the war in Iraq and the Israeli-Palestinian conflict. A close evaluation of his messages indicates that he has been able to adapt his message to the time and the target audience. Close analysis of the *al-Qa'ida* posted audio and videotape messages clearly reveals that bin Ladin and al-Dhawahiri have demonstrated their ability to adapt their statements to changing circumstances while maintaining their commitment to the ideological objectives of Militant Islamism. Transnational terrorism, which presents an alarming danger to the world, came into being immediately after the

Second World War. The wave of terrorism that emerged changed the political, social, economic, and military relations among nations. Cooperation among different terrorist groups from various ethnicities and nationalities has created the perception of terrorism as a monolithic entity, and the international terrorism perpetrated by Militant Islamists differs from previous international terrorism. Its extent and seriousness is very important. The *The Economist* publishes a new Global Terrorism Index, which measures the risk of terrorist attacks in various countries. However, the invasion of Iraq and subsequent developments have altered the activities of the Militant Islamists, as Iraq has become a magnet for Muslims who tend toward the Militant Islamist world view and find the Iraqi situation to be ripe for campaigns against the American and coalition forces and for promoting cooperation with other anti-U.S. occupation forces.[16]

Moreover, the Cold War and the role of certain countries, particularly Pakistan, cannot be minimized in direct connection with the entry of *al-Qa'ida* into Afghanistan and its close cooperation with the Taliban rulers. In Pakistan, the Taliban [plural for *Talib,* meaning one who inspires to learn] were schooled according to the Deobandi Islamic teachings. Pakistan helped *al-Qa'ida* members launch their operations in Afghanistan in the 1990s and even secretly ran a major training camp used by Usama bin Ladin's terror network. Evidently the Afghan guerrilla commander Ahmad Shah Masood, who was killed by a suicide bomber just two days before the September 11, 2001 attacks, may have been assassinated because he had learned something about bin Ladin's plan and was viewed as an obstacle to the *al-Qa'ida* objectives in Afghanistan.[17]

In its secret dispatches, obtained under the Freedom of Information Act by the National Security Archive, a nonprofit research organization in Washington, D.C., the Defense Intelligence Agency (DIA) warns that the documents represent only raw intelligence. They nonetheless paint a complex picture of factional rivalry in which Pakistan had tried to use the Taliban and *al-Qa'ida* to promote its influence in war-torn Afghanistan, only to eventually lose control over both of them.

Taliban acceptance and approval of fundamentalist non-Afghans as part of its fighting force was merely an extension of Pakistani policy during the Soviet-Afghan war, when they performed well in their war against the Soviet troops. Pakistani security agents recruited and facilitated and often arranged for Arab youths from the Middle East to travel to Afghanistan to strengthen the Taliban and make it an even more viable fighting force. Importantly, the dispatches reveal the significance of U.S. support of the Taliban force against the Soviets via Pakistan: Throughout the war years against the Soviet troops, jihad was embraced, not rejected, among the U.S. decision-makers. The United States employed Pakistan as the conduit for billions of dollars in arms to the Afghan resistance.[18] Pakistan even built a training camp located outside the Afghan village of Zahawa, near the border between the two countries. Thus, Islam and, specifically, the conservative schools of Islam, Wahhabi and Deobandi, were akin to a "liberation theology" that the U.S. administration used to justify its fight against communism in Afghanistan.[19]

According to the DIA, the camp was built by Pakistani contractors funded by the Pakistan ISI Directorate and was protected by a local and influential Jadran tribal leader called Jalalludin. The DIA documents indicate that the ISI was the principal facilitator, which supports the early arguments of ties between bin Ladin and Pakistani intelligence. In retaliation for the terrorist bombings of the U.S. Embassies in Kenya and Tanzania that left 257 people dead, the U.S. military fired cruise missiles into the camp in August 1998.

With regard to the nature of terrorist organizations and, specifically, Militant Islamists, evidence clearly shows that they are fully dedicated to their cause and would easily adapt to operational requirements.

Militant Islamism has not developed solely in countries that have majority Muslim populations, as has been portrayed by the media. Many Western countries with large Muslim populations, such as France, Germany, the United Kingdom, Italy, Spain, and the Netherlands, also have produced such individuals. For example, two suicide car bombers killed at least 26 people and wounded hundreds in Istanbul on November 20, 2003, as a protest against the war in Iraq and U.S. and U.K. support for Israel. The bombings left in ruins the British consulate and the British Bank, HSBC, which is one of the world's largest banks and is headquartered in Istanbul. The attacks coincided with President Bush's visit to London and came less than a week after the simultaneous car bombings of two Jewish synagogues in Istanbul on November 15, 2003, a Saturday (the Jewish Sabbath), killing 23 and wounding 300 Jews and Muslims. Both Washington and London blamed "international terrorists," specifically *al-Qa'ida* for the attacks. On November 20, 2003, Reuters reported that, "A caller to the Anatolian news agency claimed responsibility on behalf of Usama bin Ladin's al Qaeda [sic] network and a Turkish group known as the Islamic Great Eastern Raiders Front (*Islami Buyuk Dogu Akincilar Cephes*) and linked to Saturday's bombings."

Shortly after the Istanbul bombings, a suicide car bomb killed a number of people in an attack near the offices of the Patriotic Union of Kurdistan (PUK), a leading Kurdish party in northern Iraq just hours after two others were killed in a car bombing west of Baghdad. The leaders of the PUK and Kurdish Democratic Party are members of the U.S.-appointed Iraq Governing Council.

Since the September 11, 2001, attacks in New York and Washington, D.C., attacks by Militant Islamists have spread throughout countries with majority Muslim populations as well as in countries where Muslims are not in the majority. For example, militant groups have become active in the Philippines and Indonesia, with the Indonesian group *Jammah Islam-yya* being responsible for a bombing in Bali that killed at least 188 and wounded hundreds of people, most of whom were Australian. Several bombings have also occurred in Turkey.

The new attacks are being committed throughout the world by Militant Islamists groups that are not direct branches of *al-Qa'ida* but that adhere to its world views. They form a loose network of Islamic militants who have same goals and targets as *al-Qa'ida*. Thus, since September 11 the militants apparently have become more decentralized, operating independently of *al-Qa'ida*, although they may look to bin-Ladin and *al-Qa'ida* for inspiration.

However, these new Militant Islamist cells that have emerged since the dispersal of *al-Qa'ida* do not maintain the views that developed and predominated during the war against the Soviet Union and during the Taliban regime. The bombing campaigns and direct terrorist actions perpetrated since the early 1990s indicate that these groups attract ideological adherents who adopt a cruel and cold-blooded Machiavellian approach toward achieving their objectives, suggesting that Muslim radicalism has become even more extreme. In what one may consider Militant Islamist movements (see Table 3.2), *Ulema* (religious scholars) play hardly any role, as was the case in past Islamic radicalism. They are more information-technology savvy and use the Internet and the World Wide Web toward that end. Information technology enables the Militant Islamists to transcend geography, with the purpose of widely disseminating their ideological, financial, and terrorist campaigns. The usefulness of violence to instigate change was learned by the Militant Islamists during the decades of Cold War, which was permeated with state-sponsored violence to win by any means at every level, national and international.[20]

The Militant Islamists pay very close attention to the policies and actions of the Western Europeans and the United States toward the Muslim world. Thus, it is vital to comprehend their world views—even those statements that one may easily ignore and discard as palaver. Understanding does not mean agreeing with those views of American and Western European foreign policy actions. Having such understanding would allow the Operation Enduring Freedom or "global war on terrorism" to develop the proper means to counter the transnational Militant Islamists.

In a 2005 audiotape al-Dhawahiri said, "Our freedom...and the reform that we are seeking depend on three concepts—the rule of *Shari'a* [literally meaning the Path, Islamic law], freeing Islam from any aggressor, and liberating the human being." He claimed that in the Islamic world, the people had the "right to choose its leader, hold him accountable and criticize him...I do not think that we can achieve reform while we are under American and Jewish occupation." A few days later al-Dhawahiri said in a videotape that the U.S. military prison in Guantanamo Bay, Cuba, "explains the truth about reforms and democracy that America is allegedly trying to impose in our countries...Reform is based on American detention camps like Bagram, Kandahar, Guantanamo and Abu Ghraib, it will be based on cluster bombs and imposition of people like (Afghanistan president Hamid) Karzai and (Iraq's interim prime minister Iyad) Allawi...Real security is based on mutual cooperation with the Islamic nation on the basis of mutual respect and the stopping of aggression.[21]

The development of the philosophical underpinnings of today's Militant Islamist perspectives can be traced to the beliefs of several Muslim thinkers in the 1940s and 1950s who were affected by international, regional, and national factors and were particularly disturbed by Western modernity. However, the emergence of the Militant Islamists as we know them today and as represented by *al-Qa'ida* is more complex, involving the 1980 Soviet invasion of Afghanistan, which became a battleground for those opposing the Soviet Union in the context of the Cold War. To counter this Soviet expansionism and possibly create a Vietnam for the Soviet Union, the U.S. administration and its regional allies, Pakistan and Saudi Arabia, promoted Islamic fundamentalism as a force to recruit and mobilize fighters from Muslim nations to fight alongside the Afghans as a way to achieve their Cold War aims. Thus, it is in the Soviet war in Afghanistan where *al-Qa'ida* and Militant Islamists become a unified and formidable force. It was also during this period that radical Islamists embraced and solidified their interpretation of jihad as a violent holy war rather than a nonviolent spiritual struggle. After the Soviet withdrawal, *al-Qa'ida*, with the aid of Pakistan, Saudi Arabia, the United Arab Emirates, and the United States, helped to establish rule in Afghanistan by a militant clerical group, the Taliban, which gave the Militant Islamists free reign to promulgate their ideas.

The September 11, 2001, terrorist attacks on New York and Pentagon resulted in the invasion of Afghanistan by U.S. forces, which led to the overthrow of the Taliban regime and ultimately the scattering of the *al-Qa'ida* fighters to various Muslim nations. The U.S.-led invasion of Iraq in 2003 and subsequent developments created a haven for the Militant

Islamists to recruit and train individuals for holy war against the new invaders of another Muslim country.

The disintegration and dispersal of *al-Qa'ida* as a centralized organization has fueled the establishment of local Militant Islamist movements throughout Muslim nations (see Chapter 9). The Militant Islamists follow the same world view as the *al-Qa'ida* founding fathers, but their terrorist campaigns revolve around local grievances as well as regional and international factors that are presented as anti-Islamic and expansionist in nature.

CHAPTER 3

Causes for the Spread of the *Al-Qa'ida* Doctrine

A number of factors contributed to the emergence and spread of the Islamist Militancy, including *al-Qa'ida.* The majority of Muslim countries, particularly Pakistan and those of the Middle East and North Africa, are nondemocratic, dictatorial, and in many ways corrupt. Each is ruled and dominated by a group of people who control and monopolize politico-military power in addition to the economic sectors of the country. This tight circle of people linked by shared background and common interests have monopolized power in the hands of a small group of *Nukhbah* (Elite) in these countries. The members of the Arab League's 22 nations constitute the most uniformly oligarchic region in the world. Not a single Arab leader (including those in Pakistan and Afghanistan) has ever been ousted peacefully at the ballot box. For decades, millions of Arabs throughout the Middle East have privately, and on rare occasions publicly, cried loudly, *"Kifayaa!"* (Enough) regarding the political, social, and economic conditions in their countries and the external supporters of the regimes who perpetuate the existing systems.

The Islamic world reached its intellectual zenith during the Middle Ages, declined in the subsequent centuries, and has not recovered. It is clear that the modern Arab nation states and other Muslim countries have created and continue to promote a culture of obedience and repression of women, minorities, and society generally through educational, social, and economic systems. Without exception, the Muslim countries—and the Arab countries in particular—are failing to respond to the demands and expectations of those portions of their populations that are highly urbanized, better educated, and politically aware. A study by the Arab League points out that in 10 years the Arab region could have 50 million jobless youths, up from 15 million in 2004. According to the United Nations's

2002 Arab Human Development Report (AHDR), more than 50 percent of Arab youths say they would like to emigrate, which alarms European countries.[1]

A United Nations International Children's Emergency Fund (UNICEF) report, produced in cooperation with the Arab League, indicates that many Arab countries have made progress on child rights and protection, but that more still needs to be done. Millions of children in the Arab world are out of school, and they then become the future illiterates, most of them living in Egypt, Iraq, Morocco, and Sudan, although it is difficult to access figures for the total number of school-age children in the Middle Eastern Arab countries. The report, released in Cairo, Egypt, on April 11, 2005, stated that although many countries had established a basis for a child's right to an education, they still fell short of the United Nations's millennium development goals for primary education, especially for girls. It reveals that more than half of the women in the Arab world are illiterate, thus making it impossible for them to obtain the necessary information on issues of pre- and post-natal health, the leading causes of high infant and child mortality rates in those countries.[2]

The United Nations's 2004 AHDR called for greater political freedom, warning that the Middle East region could face "chaotic upheavals" if Arab governments refused to curb corruption and relinquish some of their absolute power. The report, which focused on the period from October 2003 to October 2004, also notes that Arab governments suffer from a crisis of legitimacy. It presented a harsh assessment of Arab governments's efforts to stifle political freedom, saying political participation in the region has "often been little more than a ritual" and that elections typically preserve the status of "ruling (*nukhbah*) elites." The report stated that by the current standards, Arab countries have failed to meet the people's aspirations for development, security, and human rights.

The authors charged that many Arab governments have cited traditional interpretations of Islamic laws to challenge the legitimacy of international human rights norms. It further stated that Arab governments routinely use a variety of other means to restrict individual freedoms, including the imposition of emergency laws in Egypt, Syria, and Sudan that strip citizens of their constitutional rights. The authors challenged the notion that there is a cultural aversion in the Arab world to many of the fundamental political values that are associated with Western democracies—freedom of expression and association and human rights. "There is a rational and understandable thirst among Arabs to be rid of despots and to enjoy democratic governance," the report stated. It cited a survey of political attitudes in Algeria, Jordan, the Palestinian territories, Lebanon, and Morocco that revealed mounting concern over government corruption, poverty, and the absence of independent courts capable of delivering justice to all.[3]

A brief look at the history of Muslim nations, and Arab nations in particular, identifies a number of causes for the upsurge in Islamic militancy, which can be divided into four categories. It is worth noting that no single one of the causes alone would fuel Islamic militancy. Rather, these multiple causes are interconnected and together become the contributing factors in the present-day rise in Militant Islam.

ISLAMIC WORLD VIEW

Muslims today would argue that slavery is not a valid practice in Islam. This belief must be interpreted as a change in Islamic thought because historically slavery was accepted in Islam, as it was in other religions. From a historical perspective, then, Islam has evolved ideologically to become intolerant of slavery. Therefore, it is plausible to expect that Muslim societies could begin to repudiate the rigid patriarchal structure that defines their social, political, and religious communities, thereby becoming less circumscribed in their world view. However, Muslim communities so far have failed critically to examine the anachronistic, patriarchal nature of their social and religious systems—which are major obstacles to change in the Muslim societies—in the same way that they once examined the practice of slavery.

Almost all Muslim countries use a banking and financial system that gives its customers interest (known in Islam as *"reba,"* or usury). This system does not comply with *Shari'a* law and, in fact, is strictly prohibited, or *haram* (meaning forbidden or unclean).[4] Islam and Shari'a forbid the trading of money to make money, and thus interest-based loans are not permitted. The argument made by the Militant Islamists for the return of the *Khalafat* system would apply not only to the current modern financial system used by Muslims but in fact would also present justification for dictatorship and curtail any political development and modernization. The general view that Islam as a religion is incompatible with democracy is a simplistic and intellectually lazy way to criticize Islam and its cultural dictates. It is not Islam itself or Muslim culture that is incompatible with democratic principles, but rather it is the stifling institutions, distorted politics, and misguided policies embedded in Muslim society that block change and present hurdles to the development of institutions that would challenge the current political system. At same time, these obstacles perpetuate dictatorship, authoritarianism, and dynastic rule.

Domestic political conditions in the Islamic countries

Internal conditions in Islamic countries are contributing causes to the upsurge in militancy. The following three characteristics are common to domestic politics in these nations and are spurring unrest:

1. Leaders of the Muslim nations have failed to respond to the ever-growing demands of the public for change.
2. The lack of open, unhindered, and legitimate political participation as well as the absence of legitimate, well-established political avenues to express political concerns and grievances are creating a distraught and desperate population.
3. The persistent repression by the ruling governments, widespread corruption, and a great gap between the rich minority and the poor majority contribute to an unstable domestic environment.

In a videotape message addressed to the American public and aired on Al Jazeera TV on October 29, 2004, Usama bin Ladin said, "We had no difficulty in dealing with Bush and his administration because they resemble the regimes in our countries, half of which are ruled by the military and other half by the sons of kings...They have a lot of pride, arrogance, greed, and thievery."

On November 29, 2004, Al Jazeera aired a videotape of *al-Qa'ida*'s second-in-command, Ayman al-Dhawahiri, who said *al-Qa'ida* would continue to attack the United States until it changes its policies in the Middle East. His messages contained information that indicated the videotape was made before November 2, 2004, the date of the U.S. presidential election. He said, "The two U.S. presidential candidates are challenging each other to satisfy Israel, to continue a crime against the Islamic nation in Palestine that began 87 years ago...I say to Americans, vote for whomever you want: Bush or Kerry or even the devil—it is not of any importance...What concerns us is to purify our nation from the aggressors and to resist whoever (is) attacking us, profaning our sanctities and stealing our wealth." Al-Dhawahiri warned various Middle Eastern governments that "the fall of Baghdad was just the beginning...The fall of Baghdad was in fact a fall to all regimes which have ceded the holy struggle [Jihad] and backed invaders." He went on to pose the question as to which Arab country "has not been occupied by crusader forces...Baghdad did not fall on April 9, 2003. It fell when al-Khudawi Tawfiq called on the British army for help, it fell when al-Sharif Hussain agreed with the British to fight the *khaliphat*...It fell when Abd al-Aziz al-Saud agreed to go under the protection' of the British and then the Americans...it fell when Arabs recognized the 1949 truce agreement [in Palestine]."[5]

In connection with the above historical reference and the recent development in Iraq and other Muslims countries, al-Dhawahiri also ridiculed the recent call for democracy by the Bush Administration, specifically "electoral democracy." He reiterated the belief that Iraq and other Muslim countries have been occupied by outside forces, and he criticized the governments in a number of Muslim countries for acting on behalf of the United States. He stated, "Driving out the invading crusader forces and Jews from our Muslim homes cannot be realized solely through demonstrations and speaking out in the streets...We cannot imagine any reform while our countries are occupied by crusader forces which are spreading throughout our land...We cannot imagine any reform while our governments are being ruled from the American embassies in our countries." He called on the Palestinians "not to forsake their jihad, not to lay down their arms...and not to be dragged into the game of secular elections under a secular constitution." The *al-Qa'ida* announcements and declarations indicate that occupation of Muslim countries—which includes the presence of foreign military bases— appears to play a major role in their grievances.

It should be noted that in his February 2005 tape (which Al Jazeera aired on February 20, 2005), al-Dhawahiri warned the West that it faced defeat in what he termed the West's new crusade against the Islamic world. In that message, which he said was to mark the third anniversary of the internment of Muslims at the U.S. military base at the Guantanamo prison camp, al-Dhawahiri attacked U.S. plans for reform in the Arab and Islamic world.[6]

In a Zogby poll published in November 2004, most of the 2,600 respondents in five Arab countries said they were more interested in expanding employment opportunities than in political change. Their second most serious concern was resolving the Israeli-Palestinian conflict. The poll results indicated that true political change, like expanding democracy and promoting open political debate, ranked "at the list's bottom," the Zogby organization said. Some views of Western intentions were darker.[7]

On April 23, 2006, Al Jazeera aired an audiotape of Usama bin Ladin, in which he said:

> Their [the West's] rejection of HAMAS after it had won election...confirms that there is a crusader-Zionist war against Islam...The war is a responsibility shared between the people and the governments. The war goes on and the people are renewing their allegiance to its rulers and masters...They send their sons to armies to fight us, and they continue their financial and moral support while our countries are burned and our houses are bombed and our people are killed." He said the situation in Sudan was part of the "crusade against Islam" and called "...on *mujahedeen* [holy warriors] and their supporters, especially in Sudan and the Arab peninsula, to prepare for long war against the crusader plunderers in Western Sudan. Our goal is not defending the Khartoum government but to defend Islam, its land and its people...I urge holy warriors to be acquainted with the land and the tribes

in Darfur." The Al Jazeera news reader said bin Laden, in a portion of the tape not aired by the network, scoffed at Saudi King Abdullah for his calls for a "dialogue among civilizations" and blasted liberal-minded Arab writers for taking part in the Western cultural invasion of Muslim lands. The European Union, Canada, and the United States cut off funding and boycotted the HAMAS-led government, which took office in March 2006 after its election victory in January 2006.[8]

It is appropriate to note that HAMAS's ideological objectives for the Palestinian territories and in connection with Israel are clear, and they are vastly different from those of *al-Qa'ida*.

However, each Muslim nation and region has its own particular and specific problems, which makes the population vulnerable and the target of Militant Islamist recruiters, who tailor their message according to each region's particular grievances and problems. They focus on widespread poverty and repression in the Caucasus republics (and Chechnya's war against the Russian forces) Central Asia, Bangladesh, and Mauritania. In Algeria it is driven by the military coup against the nation's Islamist electoral victory in the early 1990s, and in Pakistan they target poverty and the Pakistani government's strong support of the United States. In Saudi Arabia the recruiters take advantage of the widespread opposition to the ruling royal family and the government's strong support of the United States, and in Yemen the target is poverty and tribalism. In Indonesia the concern is with the country's local issues regarding the the Islamic movement, and in Somalia the focus is on lawlessness in the failed state.

Tension and clashes increased in the lawless Somali capital of Mogadishu between the warlords and the powerful Islamic courts. The latter declared a jihad [holy war] against the militia, which was backed by the United States. Since the establishment of the U.S.-backed Alliance for the Restoration of Peace and Counter-Terrorism (ARPCT) in February 2006, armed clashes between the two sides have soared. At least 52 people were killed and hundreds displaced in Mogadishu in March 2006 when the two sides squared off in the bloodiest clashes since the country collapsed into anarchy with the 1991 ousting of strongman Mohamed Siad Barre.

At a demonstration attended by hundreds in southern Mogadishu after Friday prayers on April 21, 2006, Sheikh Nur Ollow, an imam and senior Islamic court figure, told the crowd it was time to fight the warlords, whose militias cooperate with the United States and are funded by the "enemy of Islam [United States]." The crowd denounced the warlords and chanted "Down with the agents of America and down with agents promoting Satanic teaching." The ARPCT is seen by many in Somalia as a Washington-backed, anti-Muslim instrument of the U.S. war on terrorism, and fears among Somalis of new battles between the ARPCT and gunmen loyal to the Islamic courts have surged since February 2006.[9]

On June 4, 2006, heavily armed Militant Islamists in alliance with the fighters belonging to the *Shari'a* Islamic courts (known as Union of Islamic Courts) after weeks of heavy gun battles seized control of the Mogadishu and the surrounding areas and defeated the armed secularists, the so-called ARPCT backed by the warlords, who controlled Mogadishu for the past 15 years. The ARPCT never provided security because of tribal rivalry among the warlords and the self-serving business objectives. The United States never publicly confirmed or denied its support for the ARPCT, but U.S. officials told Agence France Presse they had given the warlords financial and intelligence assistance to help rein in "creeping Talibanization" in Somalia. The ARPCT was established with the support of the United States in February 2006, when the armed clashes began to counter the spread of the Islamists in Somalia. Shortly afterwards the ARPCT forces disintegrated, and since then at least 330 people were killed and 1,500 were injured. The recent fighting was the bloodiest in the country in the past 15 years. The Union of Islamic Courts fighters took complete control of Mogadishu, and the ARPCT warlords either fled the country or switched sides. The Union of Islamic Courts has become the power in Somalia's political struggle, and as of this writing the Supreme Islamic Council of Somalia was able to control most of the country, including Mogadishu.

The Bush administration is concern about the developments in Somalia,[10] which should not be viewed as bringing about an end to chaos, lawlessness, and poverty because Somalia is not a single,unified country, which contributes further to the existing problems. However, it clearly indicates that the past 15 years of lawlessness and devolution of the country into a failed state presented opportune conditions for the spread of Militant Islamism in Somalia. On June 7, 2006, President Bush expressed concern about the fall of most of Mogadishu to Islamist forces and said he would ensure Somalia did not become a haven for terrorists. The chairman of Mogadishu's Union of the Islamic Courts, Sheikh Sharif Sheikh Ahmed, warned that U.S. intervention would result a disaster similar to the botched 1993 operation that left 18 U.S. soldiers and 300 Somalis dead.[11]

A four-day conference on terrorism hosted by the Saudi Arabian Interior Ministry is the lone instance of a deliberate and visible effort by a Muslim country to formally address the issue of Militant Islam. The Counterterrorism International Conference was particularly notable because it was held on February 5, 2005, when the country was in the midst of armed attacks on government targets. It is also either a clear example of a lack of understanding by the Saudi government on what causes Islamist extremism to emerge or it was an intentional diversion of international attention from the actual root causes of militancy.

Regardless, the conference appears to have been a public relations effort designed to improve the image of Saudi Arabia rather than a serious meeting to discuss and evaluate the real issues faced and perpetrated by Arab and Muslim governments that lead to Muslim militancy.

Saud al-Faisal, the Saudi foreign minister, told reporters the conference was a serious effort to improve international antiterrorist collaboration. "Our efforts are aimed at ending this scourge from the region, not to improve our image in any society," he said. "No one can blame Saudi Arabia, saying it didn't do its due diligence when it comes to terrorism." He also added that the conference would deal with four major issues, including the ideology of terrorism, terrorism and drugs, past experiences, and terrorist groups and organizations.[12]

Prince Abdullah, then the de facto head of the state who became king in August 2005, said in his opening remarks at the same conference, "I know that terrorism will not go away overnight and our war against terrorism will be long and bitter." The Saudi Interior Minister, Prince Nayef, said, "Terrorism is not only an act but is essentially the result of deviant [a reference to *al-Qa'ida*] thought which it is our duty to confront." The theme of the conference was "The Link Between Terrorism and Money Laundering, Arms and Drug Trafficking," but none of these themes are considered by the *al-Qa'ida* to be the root causes of the Muslim militancy in any of the Muslim countries. This is especially true in Saudi Arabia, where the public at large supports or sympathizes with the views of Militant Islamists. The official goal of the event was to share information about better ways to catch terrorists, but the Saudis were also using the event to try to convince the world that they are serious about addressing the problem of Militant Islamism, both at home and abroad.[13]

Speakers at the opening session all condemned terrorism, but none directly referred to the *al-Qa'ida* network that carried out the September 11, 2001, attacks on U.S. cities and was blamed for a wave of attacks in Africa, Europe, and Asia. Moreover, the conference took place less than six weeks after an *al-Qa'ida* suicide bombing occurred outside the Saudi Interior Ministry, but no mention of *al-Qa'ida* was made. However, Saudi Interior Minister Prince Nayef did say there had been 22 attacks in the kingdom in the last two years, which killed 90 civilians and 39 members of the security forces and resulted in one billion riyals ($266.7 million) in material damage. He said police had killed 92 militants during that period.

The only call for an exploration of the causes of Islamic terrorism came from a United Nations official, not a representative of an Arab or Muslim government. Speaking on behalf of U.N. Secretary General Kofi Anan, the official called on countries not only to look at and address counterterrorism but also to look at the causes of terrorism, such as public grievances.[14]

Overall, the conference is a mark of change compared to a few years previously, when Saudi officials complained that they were unfairly maligned for the existence of Militant Islamists in their country. For months after the September 11, 2001, attacks on the World Trade Center and the Pentagon, Saudi officials refused to even acknowledge that most of the hijackers were Saudi citizens. Some senior members of the ruling Saudi family went so far as to say that Arabs were incapable of carrying out such a well-organized plot and suggested that "Zionists"—a reference to Israelis—were responsible. These same officials refused to acknowledge or turned a blind eye to Militant Islamist threat in their own country. In November 2002, Prince Nayef, the interior minister, declared in an interview with a Kuwaiti newspaper that there were no *al-Qa'ida* cells inside the kingdom and repeated the allegation that Israel was behind the September 11 terrorist attacks on the United States.

A major turning point in Saudi attitudes came six months later, on May 12, 2003, when Militant Islamist cells that had been present in the kingdom for more than a year carried out bombings against three residential compounds for foreign workers in Riyadh that killed more than 20 people and wounded more than 200 others. Ironically, the Saudi Arabian government was one of the states that sponsored religious opposition to the Soviet invasion of Afghanistan and to the development of *al-Qa'ida*.

Regional conditions within the Middle East

Regional dynamics and situations within Middle East nations also contribute to the increase in Islamist militancy. The main regional factors include the following:

1. The repeated humiliation of Arab governments in their wars and conflict with Israel.

2. The persistent and unresolved Israeli-Palestinian conflict. The Palestinian issue has become an emotional touchstone for Muslims because of the mistreatment of Palestinians by Israelis and the international community —Western countries in particular—related to Israeli control of the Palestinian territories through sheer force. The Muslim emotional fervor is similar to that of the Zionist movement in Europe, which was a consequence of constant persecution of Jews by the Europeans. This particular issue has been used by the Militant Islamists as a "call to arms" against Western Europe, the United States, and their allies. During his speech to the U.N. General Assembly in New York on September 20, 2006, Kofi Annan reflected on his 10-year service as the Secretary General and highlighted the Israeli-Palestinian conflict as the key challenge for the future leader of the United Nations. Terrorism helped to feed a false idea of

a "clash of civilizations," Annan said, adding that "this climate of fear and suspicion is constantly refueled by violence in the Middle East…We might like to think of the Arab-Israeli conflict as just one regional conflict amongst many, but it is not. No other conflict carries such powerful symbolic and emotional charge among people far removed from the battlefield."[15]

3. The invasion of Iraq, which Muslims refer to as neocolonialism, and its aftermath has become an additional obsession for Muslims. The invasion continues to suffer from a lack of legitimacy, as the White House argued for the invasion on the premise that Iraq harbored weapons of mass destruction, which have yet to be found. The greater the suffering, death, and destruction in the country, the easier it is for the Militant Islamists to justify the use of extreme violence and the easier it is to recruit new members to the cause throughout the Muslim world. The destruction of the city of Fallujah and its mosques by U.S. troops in an effort to fight opposition presented the Militant Islamists with another effective tool as well. Fallujah was a city of 250,000 and was known throughout the Middle East as the city of mosques. The battle for the city left it uninhabitable.

International conditions and the superpowers

Many Muslims perceive that they have been maligned by the international community and believe they are not welcome in international policy circles. This belief has the following five primary causes at its core:

1. The Crusades, Western colonialism, and Western ideological hegemony have created and contributed to Islamic militancy and the emergence of Militant Islamists. The Militant Islamists engage in an exaggerated victimization, holding other nations responsible for the ills of all Muslims. Specifically, the rhetoric of Militant Islamists suggests that there is a monolithic center in the West that is the primary cause for the poverty among Muslims in Islamic nations, and consequently the West is perceived as being directly responsible for the resulting ills that afflict poor Muslims worldwide. The specific grievances against the West—high unemployment, poverty, and repression in Muslim nations—are not problems in all Muslim countries, however. For example, there is a low rate of unemployment in Bangladesh and Malaysia, and conversely high rates in Algeria, Iran, Jordan, and Turkey (see Table 3.1). Further, these problems are not comparable to those perceived and experienced by Muslims living in Western countries, albeit in some Western European countries Muslims are disproportionately unemployed. Thus, because rates of poverty and unemployment vary widely between Muslim countries and because Muslims in the Western European countries suffer unemployment for vastly different reasons, the West cannot be held responsible for these ills.

2. The collapse of Communism in the Soviet Union and Eastern Europe and the subsequent thaw in the Cold War, in particular the change in U.S. strategy from direct intervention in the fight against global communism to one of

Table 3.1
Poverty and Unemployment Rates in Nations that are Members of the Organization of Islamic States

Country	Population	PBPL% (year)	Unemployment % (year)
Afghanistan	29,928,987	53 (2003)	40 (07)
Algeria	32,531,853	23 (1999)	14.5 (05
Bahrain	688,345	N/A	15 (98)
Bangladesh	144,319,628	45 (2004)	2.5 (05)
Brunei	372,361	N/A	3.2 (02)
Chad	9,826,419	80 (2001)	N/A
Djibouti	476,703	50 (2001)	50 (04)
Eritrea	4,561,599	50 (2004)	N/A
Gambia	1,593,256	N/A	N/A
Indonesia	241,973,879	15 (2004)	10 (05)
Iran	68,688,860	40 (2002)	11.2 (02)
Iraq	26,074,906	N/A	N/A
Jordan	5.759,732	30 (2001)	30 (04)
Kazakhstan	15,185,844	19 (2004)	7.6 (05)
Kuwait	1,044,294	N/A	2.2 (04)
Kyrgyzstan	5,146,281	40 (2004)	18 (04)
Lebanon	3,826,018	28 (1999)	20 (06)
Libya	5,765,563	N/A	30 (04)
Malaysia	23,593,136	8 (1998)	3.6 (05)
Mali	12,291,529	64 (2001)	14.6 (01)
Mauritania	3,086,859	40 (2004)	20 (04)
Morocco	32,.725,847	19 (1999)	15 (07)
Niger	11,665,937	N/A	63 (93)
Nigeria*	128,771,988	60 (2000)	5.8 (06)
Pakistan	162,419,946	32 (2001)	7.5 (07)
Palestinian Territories	2,385,615	46 (2004)	26.7 (0)
Qatar	863,051	N/A	2.7 (01)
Saudi Arabia	20,841,523	N/A	25 (04)
Senegal	11,126,832	54 (2001)	48 (01)
Somalia	8,591,629	N/A	N/A
Sudan	40,187,486	40 (2004)	18.7 (02)

Country	Population	PBPL% (year)	Unemployment % (year)
Syria	18,448,752	20 (2004)	10 (07)
Tajikistan	7,163,506	60 (2004)	12 (04)
Turkey	69,660,559	20 (2002)	9 (07)
Turkmenistan	4,952,081	58 (2003)	60 (04)
U.A.E.	957,133	N/A	2.4 (01)
Uzbekistan	26,851,195	28 (2004)	20 (05)
Yemen	20,727,063	45 (2003)	35 (03)

Sources: C.I.A.; U.S. State Department, 2005; N/A (Not Available); PBPL=population below poverty line $2.75 and $1.75 per day. *40% Christians.

supporting low-level insurgencies with the collaboration of third world regimes, including those in control of Islamic countries, has also fueled Islamist militancy.

3. Also a contributor to the emergence of Militant Islamists is U.S. and Western European involvement in the Palestinian-Israeli conflict, which mostly favors the Israeli cause over that of the Palestinians by providing unconditional support to the Israeli government while isolating the Palestinian leadership, or paying lip service to the Palestinians while failing to support their efforts. European support for the Israeli cause rather than the Palestinians is exceedingly troubling to Muslims, who perceive Europeans as culpable for the Holocaust of the Second World War (that killed more than 6 million Jews).

4. The unilateral policies of the United States—neocolonialism—toward the Middle East and Muslim world through the use of force to bring about favorable resolution to conflicts is another key cause of Miltant Islamism.

5. The overall slant of Western European foreign policy is considered to be overtly hostile to Muslim nations. For example, under U.S. and Israeli pressure, HAMAS was declared a terrorist organization, and the European Parliament declared in a nonbinding resolution that Lebanon's *Hizbullah* is a terrorist organization.

Practicing Muslims have almost no relevant models for effecting political change because most existing models are secular. The ideology of Marxism-Leninism, for example, is unappealing because of its outright rejection of religion and advocacy of atheism or secularist views.

Moreover the Militant Islamists and practicing young Muslims view the invasion of Afghanistan and Iraq and the Israeli-Palestinian problem as part and parcel of the United States and its coalition allies to declare war on Islam rather than as a "war on terrorism." The-war-against-

Islam view has been expressed clearly in messages left on a number of electronic Web sites.

During 2005 and 2006, Ayman al-Dhawahiri, while in hiding, was able to inspire and persuade young Militant Islamists, who operated independently, to deliver suicide or conventional bombs throughout Iraq, Saudi Arabia, Qatar, Madrid, Amsterdam, and London.

It is important to note that *al-Qa'ida* has become an ideology, or an inspirational world view, and no longer can be considered a structured organization. The Militant Islamists have become tightly knit small cells —they may not even pledge allegiance to the *al-Qa'ida* leadership—and are far harder to battle than a more organized group. Thus, the Muslim nations must work to address these root causes of Militant Islamists if terrorist activity is to decline. The United States and Western Europe must also work to eliminate these causes because they are directly involved in perpetuating regimes that stifle political development and progress.

Thus, the development and spread of the Militant Islamist world view has not occurred because it is imbedded in Islam and the *Qur'an* as some contend, nor does it stem solely from encroachment and direct intervention in the Muslim nations by the United States and Western Europe. Rather, the reasons are numerous.

Ayman al-Dhawahiri, in a video aired on Al Jazeera on August 4, 2005, warned that U.K. Prime Minister Tony Blair's policies would bring more destruction to London. He also warned the United States that Militant Islamists will continue to launch deadly attacks until U.S. troops leave all Muslim countries. He said in the tape, "Blair's policies brought you destruction in central London and will bring you more destruction..." Al-Dhawahiri did not take credit for the attacks, and neither did his statement indicate that *al-Qa'ida* had any knowledge of the London bombings, which suggests that *al-Qa'ida* has evolved into an ideological guide rather than an operational organization for terrorist attacks. He also did not make any references to the bombing of Sharm el-Sheikh, Egypt, on July 23, 2005.[16]

The numerous messages from various Militant Islamist groups on Web sites and in audiotapes and videotapes clearly state similar grievances as the causes for their terrorist actions: Western anti-Muslim policies and actions, the invasion of Afghanistan and Iraq, the Palestinian-Israeli conflict, and Western support for existing oppressive and corrupt political systems in the Muslim nations. These grievances can also have a local basis; for example, in Chechnya, Philippines, Thailand, and Indian-administered Kashmir, and play a role in the spread of Militant Islam.

Table 3.2
A Transnational Phenomenon: Militant Islamist Terrorist Groups

- **The Supreme Council of Islamic Revolution in Iraq (SCIRI),** founded in 1982, was headed by Ayatollah Mohammad Baqir Al-Hakim and his brother Abd al-Aziz Hakim, who lived in Iran under the protection of the Islamic Republic for 23 years and returned to Iraq after the invasion in 2003. One of the aims of this group has been to establish an Islamic government in Iraq. He was assassinated in the Shi'ite holy city of Najaf on August 29, 2003, three months after his return from Iran, which was attributed to the pro-Ba'thist Iraqis. SCIRI was an umbrella organization for al-Dawa and its armed-wing al-Badr Organization. These organizations remain very active in the Shi'a communities and regions of Iraq. Iraqi Sunni leaders believe that al-Badr fought alongside Iranian forces in Iraq-Iran war of 1980–88. On May 12, 2007, Abd al-Aziz Hakim announced that the party changed its name to **Surpreme Council of Islamic Iraq,** as an indication that Saddam has been overthrown and revolution had occurred. Thus, Sunni leaders view the Shi'ite majority government in Baghdad as an Iranian implant.

- **Abdullah Azzam Brigades,** *al-Qa'ida,* **in Levant and Egypt:** claimed via a Web site that it was responsible for the bombings in Sharm el-Sheikh, Egypt, of July 23, 2005. This is of one of the two groups that claimed the responsibility for the bombings of the Taba resort area in Sharm el-Sheikh, Egypt, in October 2004. The Abdullah Azzam Brigades are apparently named after Abdullah Azzam, a Palestinian scholar of Islamic law who led Islamic fighters against the Soviet troops in Afghanistan and was killed in 1989 by a roadside bomb. He was regarded as the one-time spiritual mentor of *al-Qa'ida* leader Usama bin Laden. During the Soviet invasion of Afghanistan, Azzam was financed by Saudi Arabia to establish camps for the anti-Soviet Muslim fighters.

- **Abu Sayyaf:** A Militant Islamist in the Philippines founded in the early 1990s has been waging a violent bombing and kidnapping campaign against the central government in Manila. The United States has included the group in its list of "terrorist" organizations, saying it has links with the *al-Qa'ida* network. Khadafy Janjalani, the group's leader (who carried a $5 million bounty on his head by the U.S. authorities), was killed on September 4, 2006, in a military campaign that involved 100 members of the U.S. special forces. Khadafy's brother and cofounder of the group, Abubakar Abdurajak Janjalani, was killed in 1998.

- **Al-Gama'a al-Islamyiah (Al-Jama'a al-Islamyiah) "Islamic Society":** The primary goal of this Egyptian Militant Islamists organizationis to overthrow the government of Egypt and replaced it with an Islamic system.

- **Al-Itahaad al-Islamyiah (Islamic Unity):** A Militant Islamist group in Somaliland, the group's aim is to establish an Emirate of Somalia or an Islamic rule in Somalia along the Wahhbi sect of Islam. It is an anti-Ethiopian group because of the direct cooperation between Ethiopian's secret police and the American counterterrorism forces in Somaliland.

- **Al-Jihad:** Also known as Egyptian Islamic Jihad, or Jihad Group, "**Islamic Jihad**", the group's aim is to overthrow the government of Egypt and establish an Islamic system. This organization under Ayman al-Dhawahri joined the *al-Qa'ida* organization in the 1990s.

- **Al-Jihad ul-Islamyiah fi Falisteen "The Palestine Islamic Jihad" (PIJ):** This Palestinian Militant Islamist organization is committed to the establishment of an Islamic Palestinian state in all of the Palestinian land. Along with its military wing, al-Quds, this organization continues to carry out suicide and other armed attacks in the Israeli-occupied territories as well as in Israel proper. It was founded in Egypt by Palestinian students and has been active in the Palestinian territories, especially Gaza, for the past three decades.

- **Al-Mahakim al-Islamyiah "Union of Islamic Courts":** They were founded as a judicial system—consisting of 11 independent courts—by the warlords to bring about law and order in Somalia in 2004. However, within a year they emerged as the strongest armed group in the capital city. In June 2006, it overtook the Mogadishu and expelled the warlords who were in charge of the capital city since the early 1990s.

- **Tandhim Al-Qa'ida (The Base):** This Sunni umbrella for the Militant Islamist group is committed to the establishment of Umma, or the transnational Muslim community. Openly anti-United States and Israeli, it is known as an extreme terrorist group. However, since the overthrow of the Taliban regime and the forced expulsion, it has become a "state of mind" rather than a commanding organization for transnational Militant Islamists.

- **Al-Qa'ida in South Asia:** This neo-Militant Islamist group announced its existence two days before two suicide bombings in Bangladesh on November 29, 2005. In early December of that year Militant Islamists issued death threats to judges, lawyers, officials, and journalists.

- **Al-Qa'ida Organization for Holy War in Iraq:** This group began in Iraq and has made numerous claims for the suicide bombings in Iraq. Also known as *al-Qa'ida* in Mesopotamia (Bain al-Nahrain), it joined a newly announced group known as Mujahideen al-Shura (Council of Holy Warriors).

- **"Al-Mujahidoon fi al-Kuwait Holly Warriors of Kuwait":** This group announced in an Internet message its role in the January 10 and January 15, 2005, armed shootout with Kuwaiti security forces that resulted in death.

- **Al-Tawheed wa al-Jihad, "Oneness or Unity and Struggle":** This group was set up in the northern Sinai by a young dentist, Khalid Mosaed, in 2002. Apparently he was able to recruit a number of residents of Sinai Peninsula, but the number of followers cannot be estimated due to the nature of the organization. It appears the invasion of Iraq presented it with an opportunity for recruitment. As noted throughout this book, the newly developed Militant Islamists have organized themselves into small cells rather than into a single organization. Thus, the arrest of one cell does not result in the elimination of the whole organization. It has claimed responsibility for numerous suicide bomb attacks in Iraq since the invasion of Iraq. The group's name, particularly the use of al-Tawheed, reveals its strong Sunni belief and, in fact, may even have a strong "Wahhabi" adherence, which would reject Shi'-ites whom they call (al-Rafidah or Rejectionist), in addition to other non-Sunni Islamic sects. Suicide bombings, kidnapping, and gruesome killing (beheading) of its kidnap victims make it the most dangerous of Militant Islamists in Iraq. However, they remained active in Egypt and particularly in Siana resort areas.

- **Ansar al-Islam fi Kurdistan "Supporters of Islam of Kurdistan":** This group emerged in 2001 in Kurdish-controlled provinces of northern Iraq, and it was responsible for several suicide bombings before and after invasion of Iraq. Commonly known as Ansar ul-Islami, it became a formidable violent organization in Iraq. .

- **Armed Islamic Group (GIA):** This Algerian Islamists and Terrorist group aims to overthrow the government of Algeria. GIA carried out terrorist attacks against Muslims in Algeria because of their adherence to the concept of *Takfir* [those who accuse others of committing (Kufr) and not adhering to the literal interpretation and tradition of Islam]. A faction of this Al-Salafi group is known as (Al-jamaa'atu l-salafiyyatu li l-da'wati wa l-qitaal) Group for Call and Combat (Groupe Salafiste Pour la Predication et le Combat), or GSPC. The GSPC has expanded it armed violent activities into the surrounding countries and into some non-Arab countries in Africa, and it has also focused its recruitment efforts in Europe (e.g., France). In Sepember 2007 the GSPC announced that it had joined the *al-Qa'ida* and became known as the al-Qa'ida in the Islamic Land of Maghreb (AQLIM).

- **Eastern Turkistan Islamic Movement:** This Militant Islamists movement in based in the northwestern province of Xinjiang.

- **Fatah al-Islam:** This Palestinian Militant Islamist group is located in the Palestinian refuge camp of Nahr al-Bared, with at least 40,000 Palestinians in the city of Tripoli. It was established in November 2006—at same time Lebanese security forces arrested two of its members—as a splinter group of the Palestinian Fatah armed militia group that was established and led by Shaker Youssef al-Absi. [He was killed by the Lebanese military on September 3, 2007, ending the takeover.] The group's alleged aim is to protect 12 scattered Palestinian refugee camps, home to estimated 400,000 Palestinians who fled after the establishment of Israel in 1948. However, their stated public goals appear to have larger objectives, such as imposing Shari'a in the refugee camps, waging war against Israel, and to driving the United States out of the Muslim nations. This group seems not to be a member of *al-Qa'ida*. The conditions in the refugee camps and the Palestinian-Israeli conflict had direct influence on the development of this group.

- **HAMAS, which is an acronym of the first letters of the Arabic words for Harakat al-Muqawamah al-Islamyiah (The Islamic Resistance Movement):** The acronym HAMAS, meaning "Zeal" in Arabic, was founded by a Palestinian Muslim activist group in 1979 and 1980. It consists of several different wings with different agendas and programs. It provides social, health, and educational services to needy Palestinians. Its armed wing carries out terrorist actions, including suicide bombings against Israeli civilians.

- **Al-Harkat ul-Islamyiah fi Kurdistan "Islamic Movement of Kurdistan":** Established in 1987, this group brought together various groups and individuals who had fought in the Afghan war against the Soviets. In an armed confrontation with the PUK in 1993, IMK ultimately ended up in the north of Halabjah and broke up into several factions. Ansar ul-Islam fi Kurdistan emerged as one of the splinter groups in 2001.

- **Holy Jihad Brigades (A New Palestinian Militant Islamists):** The new Palestinian Militant Islamists announced their existence with the kidnapping of a Fox News television correspondent and cameraman. The two hostages were freed on August 27, 2006.

- **Al-Moqawamat al-Islamyiah fi al-Araq—Jaiysh al-Abbas (The Islamic Resistance in Iraq—Abbas Brigades):** A self-styled Shi'ite armed group calling itself Al-Moqawama al-Islami fi al-Araqh—Jaiysh al-Abbas (The Islamic Resistance in Iraq—Abbas Brigade)—made a public announcement of its existence on July 2, 2006, with a videotape that was broadcast on a Lebanese New TV station, "We have (been) patient enough and we have given the political process (a) chance." The group pledged to fight Americans, the British, and other coalition forces, but not Iraqi civilians and Iraqi soldiers. The statement, read by a Lebanese TV announcer, said U.S. troops came to Iraq under the pretext of overthrowing Saddam Hussein's government but are now "building bases, looting our resources, interfering in everything, sowing sectarian sedition between Sunnis and Shiites, Arabs and Kurds...We assure them [Iraqis] that operations against civilians are great transgressions. Members of the Iraqi army, police and Iraqi security agencies are our sons, brothers and beloved. They are our hope for the future to preserve the land of Iraq and its security. So are state employees." The station, New TV, said it received the tape along with the statement exclusively. The three-minute video showed five separate attacks in which military vehicles and tanks similar to ones used by coalition forces were blown up by roadside bombs. The statement said the footage came from recent operations by the group. Appearing in the corner of the videotape is a palm of a hand, a Shi'ite symbol, and a picture of what appeared to be one of Iraq's Shi'ite shrines, a golden-domed mosque with a red flag.

- **Harakat ul-Jihad al-Islami (Huji) "Movement of Islamic Jihad":** This Bangaladeshi Islamic organization was declared a "global terrorist" by the United States on March 6, 2008. The government of Bangaladesh banned the group in October 2005 after police arrested its alleged chief, Mufti Abdul Hannan, who once fought against Soviet troops in Afghanistan.

- **Harakat ul-Mujahideen "Movement of Holly Warriors":** This group is a Pakistani Militant Islamist organization.

- **Harakat al-Mujahideen al-A'lami "Movement of Global Warriors":** This Pakistani Militant Islamist group is based in the Kashmir region.

- **Hizb ut-Tahrir "Liberation Party":** This group was formed in Jordan in 1953 by Taqi Eddin al-Nabahani, a Palestinian Qadhi (Islamic Jurist) in Haifa durig the British Mandate (1922–1948). He broke away from Muslim Brothers in 1950 and died in unclear circumstances in the Palestinian territories in 1978. The organization has long been underground and was led by Palestinian Abdul-Kadhim Zalloum, a religious scholar educated at Al-Azhar University in Cairo, until his death in April 2003. Sheikh Ata Abu Rhta, a Palestinian-Jordanian Islamic scholar, replaced him. Some may think of this group to be the same as Hizb ut-Tahrir al-Islami (Islamic Liberation Party). This party has expanded its operation throughout Muslim nations, including Palestinian occupied territories and Europe.

- **Harkat al-Islamyiah fi Uzbekistan (Islamic Movement of Uzbekistan [IMU]):** This group's aim is to overthrow the government of Uzbekistan and replace it with an Islamic system.

- **Jaiysh-e Mohammed (J-eM) "Army of Mohammed":** This Militant Islamist group operates from Pakistan. It has carried out numerous actions against India, particularly in the Indian-administered Kashmir, in addition to the terrorist acts in Pakistan against foreigners and Pakistani government targets.

- **Jemat ud-Dawat Pakistan:** This socio-political organization emerged after Lashkar e-Tayyba (l-eT) was declared illegal. The United Statesdeclared Jemat ud-Dawa a terrorist organization, but not the government of Pakistan.

- **Jamaah Islamyiah (Islamic Community):**A This Militant Islamist organization is dedicated to the establishment of an Islamic state in the Islamic countries in those regions that have a significant Muslim population, such as Indonesia, Singapore, Brunei, Malaysia, and the southern region of Thailand and the Philippines. It was founded by a small number of Indonesians in Malaysia in the 1980s. It emphasizes the victimization of Muslims by the United States and Western European countries in the region and in other Muslim nations.

- **Jund al-Sham (Army of Greater Syria referring to Syria, Lebanon, Jordan, and Palestine):** This group was established by Palestinians living in the refugee camps in Lebanon. Thus, while it adheres to the *al-Qa'ida*'s global ideology—rejection of national borders and promoting anti-U.S., anti-Israeli, and anti-European sentiments—the group maintains primary concern for the Palestinian plight, the war in Iraq, and vehemently opposing Arab regimes. Clearly, similar to Fatah al-Islam, it sees itself as part of larger Militant Islamist movements.

- **Lashkar-e Tayyba (L-eT) "Army of the Righteous":** This Pakistan-based Militant Islamist and terrorist armed group carries out armed actions against India in the Indian-administered Kashmir. It operated for years with the blessing of Pakistan's Inter-Services Intelligence Agency, which provided the group with arms and training and helped launch its fighters across the cease-fire line separating Pakistani and Indian forces in Kashmir. It is an anti-U.S. group. It is highly probable, because of its Militant Islamist world view, that it gives support to other Militant Islamists and is the remnant of *al-Qa'ida* in the region. Under intense U.S. pressure, Musharraf banned the organization in 2002. Its parent organization, Jama'at ul-Dawa, founded in 1989 under a different name, is an active charity organization. Jama'at ul-Dawa is one of several hard-line Islamic groups that have assumed a prominent role in relief operations following the devastating October 8, 2005, earthquake in Pakistani-controlled Kashmir and adjacent areas.

- **Lashkar -e-Jhangvi (L-e J) "Army of Fighters":** This Pakistani-based Sunni Militant Islamists and Terrorist armed group, formed in 1996, is regarded as the fiercest of Pakistan's Sunni extremist organizations that carries armed actions against Pakistan Shi'a. Police authorities have accused it of killing thousands of Shi'a Muslims in recent years. They are strong and very active in Quetta, the capital of Baluchistan. Since 1980 more than 4,000 Pakistanis have died in Shi'a-Sunni clashes. Twenty percent of Pakistan's population is Shi'as. It is blamed for most of the sectarian bloodletting by the police and has also targeted top government officials, Western concerns, and religious minorities since Pakistan joined the U.S.-led war on terror following the September 11, 2001 attacks on the United States.

- **Lebanese Hizb-Allah (Hizbullah)"Party of Allah or God":** This Militant Shi'a Islamist organization consists of several wings, whichprovide the social, educational, and health needs of its constituents. Its armed wing carries military actions, including terrorist ones. Its main goalcontinues to be protecting and serving the Shi'a minority population of Lebanon. Its major armed activities have occurred in Lebanon, but some have also been targeting at Israeli occupation forces.

- **Moroccan Islamic Combatant Group (GICM):** This fast-growing network known by its French initials, GICM, was founded in 1997 by the veterans of the Afghan war, who returned to Morocco and Europe with the aim of spreading their Militant Islamists world view in Morocco by overthrowing the Moroccan government and establishing an Islamic republic. However, there are a large number of Moroccans in Europe, so it would not be difficult to move its agenda into those communities.

- **Mujahideen al-Shura (Council of Holy Warriors):** This group announced its formation in January 2006. It has been a result of *al-Qa'ida* in Mesopotamia, joining five other Militant Islamists and Iraqi opposition forces.

- **Sazeman-e Mujahideen-e Khalq or Mujahideen-e Khalq "Organization of Peoples' Fighters, or Peoples' Fighters" (also known as National Council of Resistance):** The primary goal of this Iranian Islamist armed organization is to overthrow the Islamic Republic of Iran. It was allowed to operate and maintain a camp in Iraq since the Iraq-Iran war in 1980s, but since the invasion they are under the control of the U.S. military forces. It has become an insignificant movement and will soon disintegrate. SMKO was and still is a cult of personality (Masood Rajavi), and most of its members have not been inside Iran for more than 24 years. The average age of its following in the Ashraf camp in Diyala, Iraq—underU.S. control—is over 40, with some even older than 50.

- **Sepah-e Sahba Pakistan"Corp 'Army' of Prophet's Companion":** Earlier known as Anjumaneh-e Sabah-e Sahbah Pakistan (SSP), which was established in 1985 in Punjab, this is an Islamist—exclusively Sunni—Militant organization. The SSP is believed to have been established at the behest of General Zia ul-Haq's regime. Pervez Musharraf outlawed this group on January 12, 2002, for its alleged involvement in terrorist-related activities. After the government's action it was renamed Milat-e Islami-e Pakistan. This organization is extremely anti-Shi'ite and targets the sect's followers and mosques.
- **Mujahideen of Egypt and Abdullah Azzam Brigades:** Two unknown groups claimed responsibilities for bombings in Egypt during April 2005.
- **Tehreek-e-Nifaz-e-Shari'at-e-Mohammadi (Movement for the Implementation of Mohammad's Shari'a Law):** This pro-Taliban and Militant Islamist movement has sent thousands of fighters into Afghanistan to battle the U.S.-led invasion after the ouster of the Taliban regime in 2001. The banned armed group has been fighting against the Pakistani troops in the tribal semi-autonomous region.
- **The Secret Organization of** *Al-Qa'ida* **in Europe:** This organization claimed responsibility for the London bombings of July 11, 2005.
- **Tanzdhim al-Qa'idat al-Jihad Fi Bilad al-Rafidayn (***Al-Qa'ida* **Organization of Jihad in the Land of theTwo Rivers):** This Militant Islamist group headed by Abu Musab al-Zarqawi is a notorious terrorist organization in Iraq. It claimed responsibility for numerous killings of kidnapped individuals, bombings, suicide bombings, attacks in the Jordanian port of Aqaba, and suicide bombing attacks in three U.S.-based hotels in Amman, Jordan.
- **Tandhim Qaedat [sic] al-Jihad "Organization for the Basis of Jihad":** This splinter group from Jammah Islamiyah, founded by Noordin M. Top, is said to be responsible for the restaurant bombings on the resort island of Bali that killed 20 people in October 2005. It claims to be active in Indonesia, Malaysia, Philippines, and Brunei. Its aim is to overthrow the government of Uzbekistan and replace it with an Islamic system.

  A number of newly formed extreme Militant Islamist groups—e.g., al-Qa'ida Organization of Jihad in the Land Between Two Rivers (Tanzim Qaedat al-Jihad Fi Bilad al-Rafidayn); Jaiysh Ansar al-Sunnah; Al-Mujahidoon fi-al-Kuwait; and Al-Jaiysh al-Islami (The Islamic Army) group in Iraq—have emerged in Iraq since the invasion. Ansar al-Tawheed wa al-Sunna claimed responsibility for the kidnapping of two German engineers in Iraq. Lions Brigade of Peninsula announced its existence with an armed clash with the Kuwaiti police and security forces in January 2005. In 2006, seven Militant Islamist groups in Iraq established an umbrella organization known as Mujahideen al-Shura [Council of Holy Warriors] for several Militant Islamists in Iraq.

Sources: Compiled from news service, networks, printed media; AP; BBC; Reuters, and http://www.state.gov/s/ct/rls/pgtrpt/2000/2450.htm.

CHAPTER 4

Hawalla: Traditional Funds Transfer System (TFTS)

The viability of Militant Islamist and other terrorist organizations and their ability to carry out terrorist actions depend largely on their access to funding. Thus, this particular issue demands close scrutiny and evaluation

An important concern for global community in connection with international and local Militant Islamist terrorism is determining how fund their activities. Prior to the September 11 attacks, funding for the Militant Islamists was carried out in open through a regular banking system or in a traditional way, which is known in Asian and African societies as *Hawalla,,* or bill of exchange "transfer" or promissory note in Arabic.

This section provides linguistic background on some Arabic, Hindi, Urdu, and Farsi (Persian) words associated with *Hawalla*. The words *Hawalla* and *hundi* are both used to describe the alternative remittance system discussed in this book. The word *Hawalla* comes from the Arabic root Howl, which means 'change' and 'transform.' The word '*Hawalla*' is defined as a bill of exchange or a promissory note. It is also used in the expression *Hawalla Safar*, traveler's check. When the word came into Hindi and Urdu languages it retained these meanings, but it also gained the additional meanings of 'trust' and 'reference,' which reflect the manner in which the system operates. Furthermore, in popular usage '*Hawalla*' is often used to refer to any sort of financial crime, particularly money laundering or fraud. *Hawalla,* Traditional Funds Transfer System (TFTS) is used in many different cultures and nations. Different terms are used, but the meaning and the operation is the same, such as *Fei-Ch'ien* (China), *Padala* (Philippines), *Hui Kuan* (Hong Kong), and *Phei Kwan* (Thailand). The term *Hawalla* is widely used in Southwest Asia, the Middle East, Africa, Europe and North America.

A *Hawalladar,* meaning a *Hawalla* operator, is made up of two words: "*Hawalla,*" meaning bill of exchange or transfer, and "dar" (singular and *dars* for plural), meaning the bill holder or the person who would make the transfer. The word *Hundi* comes from the Sanskrit root meaning 'tcollect.' In India, *Hundi* refers to collection boxes found in Hindu temples. A *Hundi* operator, or *Hundiwala,* means banker or foreign exchange dealer. *Hundi* is a preferred term in northern Pakistan, while *Hawalla* is exclusive to Indian journalism. In Iran, the term *Havalla,* also spelled the same in Urdu, carries the same meaning except for the difference in the pronunciation of the letter: *w* in Urdu, *v* in Farsi. The Arabic root *Sirf,* meaning 'pay,' 'spend,' and 'disburse,' is the root of Masrif in Arabic and of Sarraaf, meaning moneychanger or remitter, in Farsi, thus creating the term, Saraafi.[1]

TFTS is a mechanism and process used to transfer money from one place to another, within or between nations, that existed throughout Asia and Africa for centuries predating the Western banking system. This system was developed to protect the transport of precious goods, such as gold and silver, and trade investments through an insecure environment dominated by organized bandits and thieves. Even with the advent of international banking systems, the TFTS continued to be the means of transferring money within a country and between nations. It was used widely among the population of immigrant workers in Europe and other parts of the world, which caused TFTS to become a global feature of the post-Second World War. This system is referred to as "underground banking" or "black market" in industrialized, developed countries, but it is practiced openly by legitimate *Saraafs,* or currency-changers or any other business enterprises in east and south Asia, Russia, China, the Middle East, Africa, Europe, and North America.

The TFTS or *Hawalla* system has numerous features that make it very attractive to its customers. It is faster than formal banking or other financial forms of fund transfer systems partly because of the lack of intermediaries and the simplicity of its operating mechanisms and processes. The message is sent to a counterpart by phone, facsimile, or e-mail, and funds are often delivered door to door within 24 hours by an individual courier who has quick access to the destination, even in remote areas. The minimal documentation and record keeping removes all the obstacles that would slow down the transfer of funds. Moreover, the fees charged by *Hawalladars* on the transfer of funds are much lower than those charged by banks and other financial institutions, due mainly to minimal overhead expenses and the absence of regulatory costs to the Hawalladars, who often operate other small businesses. To encourage foreign exchange transfers through their TFTS, Hawalladars sometimes exempt expatriates from paying fees. In the latter situation, *Hawalladar*s would make money from the exchange rate spread. While the system is used for the legitimate transfer of funds, its anonymity and minimal documentation, if any, have added to its attractiveness and made it vulnerable to abuse by individuals and groups transferring funds to finance illegal activities.

In addition to economic factors, the kinship, ethnic ties, and personal relations between *Hawalladar*s and their customers (e.g., expatriate worker or any other person in need of transferring money) make this system convenient and easy to use. The primary foundation of this traditional form of transfer of funds is absolute trust. This particular feature is what has made *Hawalla* a functioning system for thousands of years. The flexibility of hours and the proximity of the *Hawalladar* is appreciated by the customer in need. To accommodate their clients, *Hawalladars* may instruct their counterparts to deliver funds, based on absolute trust, to beneficiaries or recipients in emergency situations before the customer or expatriate worker makes payments.

Moreover, cultural considerations and trust encourage expatriate workers to remit funds through a particular *Hawalladar,* and such considerations also apply to family members in the home country. A customer in need may walk to the Hawalladar's home after hours and request a transfer of funds. Many expatriate communities are exclusively male because wives and other members of the household remain in the home country, where family traditions prevail. These traditions may require family members, especially women, to maintain minimal contact with the outside world. A trusted *Hawalladar,* known in the village, town, or neighborhood of major cities, is aware of the social codes and would act as an acceptable intermediary, protecting women from having direct dealings with bank employees (strangers) and other agents. Thus, a system based on national, ethnic, and village solidarity depends more on absolute trust between the participants than on legal documents.

On the receiving side, repressive financial policies and inefficient banking institutions, which have often lacked interest in the remittance business, have contributed to the ever growing TFTS. In addition to overly restrictive economic policies, unstable political situations have offered fertile ground for the development of the *Hawalla* and other informal systems. Most TFTSs have prospered in areas characterized by unsophisticated official systems and during times of instability and also in areas where individuals wish to maintain a sense of privacy and anonymity involving individual or family financial affairs. They continue to develop in regions where financial systems are either underdeveloped or where development has been slow or repressed. Overall, financial development tends to check the spread of TFTS, even though they exist in financially mature countries as well. Economic and cultural factors explain the attractiveness of the TFTS, as it is less expensive, swifter, more reliable, more convenient, and less bureaucratic than the formal financial sector.[2]

In their campaign against terrorism, the United States and its allies have placed many obstacles for the transfer of funds to terrorist organizations, but such restrictions have only forced the international supporters of Militant Islamists and Muslims to return to the use of *Hawallah*, which is based on trust, anonymity of transaction, and the reputation of the *Hawalladars* or *Sarraaf*, or for that matter the local jeweler or merchant who has counterparts in other locations in the country or overseas.

This system does not involve any written or recorded documents, and it is a simple way of transferring funds from the sender in country A to the recipient in country B in a relatively short period of time. American officials believe that mosques and charitable organizations, particularly in Saudi Arabia, are the main sources of financing for the *al-Qa'ida*. However, Operation Enduring Freedom, the U.S. "war on terrorism," requires war on terrorist financing, and effortsduring the past two years have concentrated on Islamic charity organizations, as they are believed to have been the major avenues of funds transfer. U.S. law enforcement officials acknowledge that gaining a clear understanding of how terrorists move their funds has proven far more difficult than many anticipated. The bombings and attacks of 2003 in Indonesia, Chechnya, Morocco, Saudi Arabia, and Turkey point out that the terrorist groups still have access to significant resources.[3]

Since the September 11, 2001, attacks, American security authorities, in cooperation with international agencies, have been able to either close down charity organizations or curtail their activities, thus depriving terrorist groups of their inflow of money even though the TFTS continues to flourish in many countries.

A United Nations study of late August 2004 concludes that international measures aimed at restricting access to funds to *al-Qa'ida*'s sympathizers have been less successful than hoped, as the terrorists have managed to evade certain sanction mechanisms. It worth noting that their need for funds decreased as well. The report states that the Madrid train bombing in which 191 people died cost only $10,000, while the suicide truck bombings in Istanbul in November 2004 that killed 62 people cost less than $40,000. These comparatively small figures contrast with the September 11, 2001 attacks, which cost $400,000 to $500,000 (excluding the hijackers' training in Afghanistan), according to the September 11 Commission. The U.N. monitoring panel report in January 2004 states, "al-Qaeda has shown great flexibility and adaptability in stay(ing) ahead of them." It concludes, ". . .a recent mutation of al-Qaeda into a looser network of affiliated underground groups has made sanctions more difficult."[4] The Militant Islamists and those from Eastern cultures and societies are using alternative methods of transferring funds outside the formal banking system. Rather, those who are in need of funds would continue to resort to traditional financial systems where money brokers in the Middle East, Pakistan, India, South Asia, Africa, and South America can move cash from one *Hawalladar* or *Sarraaf* to another based on trust.

The Netherlands government has realized this to be a problem and possible contributor to terrorism, so it intends to tackle the problem of TFTS (*Hawalla'*) by making it illegal in the country. The authorities believe, as do other Western industrialized countries with large immigrant populations, that TFTS plays a significant role in financing terrorist activities.

The TFTS in the Netherlands—as in other industrialized countries—are not visible, but they do exist. They're usually found in small shops, travel agencies, or international phone centers in urban areas with significant ethnic minority populations. They provide the service to people from Africa, the former Dutch South American colony of Surinam, and immigrants from Latin America who are in need of transferring funds to family members at home.

Dutch authorities believe the simplistic, inexpensive service and the lack of any paper trail have also made the Hawalla attractive to criminals. Money obtained from the trade in drugs can also be moved from country to country without attracting much, if any, attention. A good deal of this money is believed to end up in countries such as Pakistan and India, but also in the Caribbean.

The international campaign to find and stop the sources of funding for terrorist organizations has prompted terrorist groups to seek less noticeable ways of getting their hands on money, such as the *Hawalla* system of fund transfer. Dutch authorities believe that "investigations have revealed that the perpetrators of the September 11 attacks in the United States made use of transfers through Hawalla banks."

Dutch authorities believe a considerable amount of money passes through TTFTS each year. The International Monetary Fund estimates that, worldwide, around 82 billion euros ($100 billion dollars) are "transferred" through this system. The figure for Hawalla transactions in the Netherlands is believed to be about 600 million euros, and the market continues to grow along with the increase in the immigrant communities.

In 2002, the Dutch government tightened the rules for official institutions—such as Western Union, the market leader in the Netherlands—so that people wanting to send money abroad must now identify themselves first. Furthermore, these organizations are now required to report any "unusual transactions" involving amounts in excess of 15,000 euros.

Approximately 27 money-transfer offices are currently registered with the Bank of the Netherlands, although the actual number operating in the country is much higher. What remains the most difficult—in some ways impossible—aspect of monitoring the *Hawalla* system is the absence of any form of evidence of such transactions.[5]

Southeast Asian states, facing threats from terrorist groups, must crack down on international funding of such groups, said Danish diplomat Ellen Margaretthe Loj, the head of the U.N. Security Council counterterrorism panel on April 20, 2006. In a U.N.-sponsored meeting on terrorism in the Philippines, experts from 60 countries gathered to devise new methods to counter terrorist threats. "One of the key challenges in this area will be responding to the ways in which terrorist organizations find new, unregulated ways of channeling funds," said Margaretthe Loj, adding that regional Militant Islamists such as *Jemma'ah Islamiyah* and Abu Sayyf continue to receive funding through informal TFTSs. The transfer channels include religious, charitable, and relief organizations.

The U.N. Security Council is troubled over the slow pace of progress in criminalizing the financing of terrorism in Southeast Asia, as more than half the countries in the region have yet to enact such laws. Not even half of the 10-member Association of South East Asian Nations (ASEAN) have yet to ratify the international convention concerning the financing of terrorism.

Jose Ramos-Horta, East Timor's foreign minister, underlined the dilemmas in the fight against terrorism by saying, "We must not become monsters ourselves in order to defeat the monster, states must not sanction state terror to allegedly fight terror...The superior morality of the rule of law, democratic and transparent government and respect for diversity are the most powerful weapons against extremism and intolerance."[6]

Currently the practice of *Hawalla* in Iraq is the way of life, and without it business, whatever is left of it, will seize to function. The unofficial banking system is common throughout much of the Middle East, similar to all underdeveloped countries, where it helps smooth business dealings and sidestep red tape.

Agence France Presse reports that, in a grimy *Hawalla* storefront in Harthiya, western Baghdad's unofficial financial district, two men at a high wooden table do business using just four phones, a ledger, and stacks of hard cash—dollars, euros or Jordanian *dinars*. They handle $2 million to $3 million a day, according to the manager Haydar, who declined to give his full name.

Iraq's two state-run banks are barred by the American officials from doing business with the outside world because of "attachment risks" on an estimated $30 billion in commercial debt, referring to fears that creditors would try to seize money owed by Iraq. In addition, commercial banks are so expensive and slow that businessmen often find it more convenient to deal with Hawalla dealers, said Baghdad Chamber of Commerce Chairman Mohammad Hassan al-Kazzaz.

There are 17 commercial banks in Baghdad, according to the report, and they take at least 10 days and charge up to 3 percent per transaction to transfer money. In contrast, a Hawalla operator in Baghdad typically charges a flat 0.05 percent, and the money is available almost instantly. "It is vital for the private sector in Iraq to have such a flexible financial system as *Hawallas*," Kazzaz told AFP. "If the government or anyone tries to impose restrictions on this 'TFTS,' the impact would be heavy on Iraqi businessmen." Most businessmen keep deposits in banks outside the country, he added, because of Iraq's current instability.

To transfer foreign currency to Iraq, a businessman can, for example, deposit money via a *Hawalla* merchant in Amman. With a simple phone call to a partner in Iraq, the money can be cashed out in a matter of hours, minus a small fee. Iraq remains very much a cash economy, with businessmen often carrying briefcases crammed full of hundred-dollar bills, the U.S. Treasury official said.

U.S. and Iraqi troops often find car trunks full of greenbacks during routine traffic stops. "People carrying large amounts of money around will have to register in the future," the U.S. official said. "We want to develop a list of names and find out who they deal with to ferret out the networks."

A senior U.S. diplomat acknowledged that the funding issue had been neglected in the U.S.-led crackdown on the insurgency and said future efforts would increasingly focus on cutting the seemingly limitless cash supply of the rebels.

Kazzaz himself admitted that the *Hawalla* system is likely being used by some of Iraq's neighbors to provide financial backing for the insurgency. "Huge amounts of money are being transferred to Iraq from Syria and Iran," Kazzaz said. "The ruling regimes in those two countries are afraid that a stable Iraq might threaten their survival."[7]

However, information technology has been adopted to serve the purpose of modern *Hawalla* or TFTS. Imam Samudra, the Indonesian who was charged with the Bali nightclub bombings that killed 200 people, mostly Australians, is a good example of a Militant Islamist. In the fall of 2004 he published a jailhouse autobiography in which he gave his justification for the bombing, but the most surprising part of the book was titled "Hacking, Why Not?" In this part Samudra urges his fellow Muslim radicals to take the jihad into cyberspace by attacking U.S. computers, with the particular aim of committing credit fraud, called "carding." In the same part he provides an outline on how to start "carding."

Even though its instruction for "carding" is rudimentary, "the chapter provides a rare glimpse into the mounting threat posed by terrorists using Internet fraud to finance their operations...The worry is that an army of people doing cybercrime could raise a great deal of money for other activities that terrorists are carrying out," said Alan Paller, research director of the Sans Institute, an American Internet security training company. Also noted is "Phishing," which comes in the form of messages that pretend to be from banks but are actually attempts to steal passwords and other personal information. Phishing, relies on deception by tricking people into giving their information to a fake Web site. Phishing is an older form of cybercrime, while "keyloggers" record a person's typing whenever he or she visits their banks online. The tiny programs then send the stolen user names and passwords to the "keyloggers" and the "keylogging" programs exploit security flaws and monitor the path that carries data from the keyboard to other parts of the computer. This is a more invasive approach. In most cases, a "keylogger" or similar program, once installed, will simply wait for certain Web sites to be visited (e.g., a banking site or a credit card account) wait for certain keywords to be entered (e.g., Social Security Number), and then starts up.[8]

Funding of terrorism campaigns remains a major issue for government authorities throughout the world. Of course, most of the focus is on official transactions via banking or other legitimate financial institutions and business. On December 9, 2005, Spanish security agents arrested seven people suspected of funding Algerian Militant Islamists. Interior Minister Jose Antonio Alonso said police who made the arrests had turned up no evidence that the detainees were planning an imminent attack in Spain. Alonso said the detainees were suspected of aiding an Algeria-based *al-Salafi* Militant Islamist organization, the Group for Call and Combat (GSPC). On November 23, 2005, Spanish police arrested 11 Algerians suspected of providing financing and logistical support to the same Algerian group. Police found links between the seven arrested and those individuals elsewhere in Europe and had notified police in several other European countries.[9] However, the TTFS remains vital and active throughout the third world as well as industrialized countries. It is highly probable that this system is used to fund terrorist activities, as without funding it would be difficult if not impossible to carry out international campaigns. Instead, terrorism would be limited to localized actions, which would not require the transnational transfer of funds.

The low cost of terrorist operations also reduces the relevance of antimoney-laundering efforts in the fight against terrorism. As mentioned earlier, the September 11, 2001, terrorist attacks was estimated to have cost approximately $500,000, but the cost for the subsequent Madrid bombings was estimated to have been less than $10,000.[10] Due to the localization of Militant Islamist terrorist actions, funding costs are much lower and could be raised easily either within the country of operations by the traditional transfer of funds or by couriers within the immediate region.

CHAPTER 5

Terrorist Attacks Since the 1990s

The defeat of the Soviet Union in Afghanistan and the subsequent developments that brought the Taliban Militant Islamists—the Sunni theocrats—to power, emboldened Militant Islamists throughout the Islamic and non-Islamic countries. The victory of the Taliban came not too long after an Islamic Republic was established in Iran by *Shi'a* theocrats in 1979. Pleased with their victory in Afghanistan, thanks to support from Pakistan, Saudi Arabia, the United Arab Emirates (UAE), and the tacit support from the United States (see Chapter 2), the Militant Islamists began to return to their countries and regional homes with the aim of spreading the *al-Qa'ida* world view via terrorist attacks.

The twin bombings of the U.S. embassies in Kenya and Tanzania, located 450 miles from each other, occurred only minutes apart on August 7, 1998 and killed 224 people and injured more than 1,700 others. These attacks appeared to be well coordinated and were the first major terror attacks against the United States since the June 25, 1996, bombing outside the Khobar Towers housing complex near Dhahran, Saudi Arabia. The latter attack killed 19 Americans and injured more than 500 Americans and Saudis. In November 1995, seven people were killed in a smaller bomb blast near a U.S. facility in Riyadh. These attacks are illustrative of terrorist attacks perpetrated by Militant Islamists since the 1990s: they are well coordinated, not limited to a specific geographic region, and use the latest information technology and other media to spread Militant Islamist ideas and further its cause. This chapter reviews Militant Islamist attacks that have occurred since 1990 in regions in which the majority of the population is Muslim. In these regions, domestic problems exist that fuel discontent and rebellion and thus create opportunities for Militant Islamists to promulgate their ideas and carry out terrorist activity in an effort to establish Islamic governments.

ATTACKS IN THE ARABIAN PENINSULA AND AFRICA

Yemen is home to many radical Muslim groups, and there is strong public support of Militant Islamist views. The country is believed to be a staging ground for *al-Qa'ida* fighters to be sent to Iraq and Afghanistan to battle U.S. forces.[1] In 2000, the USS Cole, a Navy destroyer, was attacked in the Yemeni harbor of Aden. The terrorist attack killed 17 Americans, wounded 39, and damaged the destroyer severely. Evidence showed that extremist Muslim groups directly linked to the *al-Qa'ida* network were responsible. Two years later, in October 2002, 15 Yemeni Militant Islamists were involved in a bomb attack on the French tanker Limburg as it prepared to enter a Yemeni port. The extremists were arrested shortly afterward and were sentenced in August 2004 for the Limburg bombing and a series of other attacks. The Limburg attack killed one crew member and injured 12 others. The terrorists had used an explosive-laden boat, which was rammed into the tanker. The 15 admitted to being members of *al-Qa'ida*. Yemen, a poor, tribal country with a dictatorial regime, has been an important country for the Militant Islamists, as the chaos and corruption in the country has contributed to arbitrary arrests by the government in order to provide a sense of security. The absence of the clear and consistent rule of law, along with the fact that smuggling is deeply rooted in the culture of the coastal areas of the Persian Gulf, the Gulf of Oman, and the predominantly Muslim eastern coast of Africa, has turned Yemen into an arms trafficking source for the Horn of Africa, fueling civil wars and creating further opportunities for Militant Islamists.[2] The following cases illustrate the disorder that exists in the Yemeni government and its legal system.

In February 2005, the Yemeni appeals court upheld the death sentence for Hauzam Saleh Mejalli, the ringleader in the Limburg attacks, while Fawaz al-Rabei, another key figure who initially had been given a 10-year prison term, was condemned to death. Both were also convicted of killing a policeman in one of the other attacks. In March 2005, a Yemeni court sentenced six Yemeni *al-Qa'ida* suspects to two years in jail for forging travel documents in an attempt to join those fighting the U.S. forces in Iraq and Afghanistan.

A group of 14 *al-Qa'ida* suspects were detained for alleged links to attacks in Yemen. Lawyers said six of the defendants had been handed over to Yemen by the Saudi government, which has been and still is fighting the *al-Qa'ida* Militant Islamists in its own country. Eleven of the 14 were acquitted of another charge of setting up an armed group to carry out attacks in Yemen. The men shouted *"Allahu Akbar"* (God is greatest) after the verdict was read in court.[3]

The U.S. government sent military advisers to Yemen in 2002 to train government forces in antiterrorism and to hunt for remnants of al-Qa'ida. A missile fired by a C.I.A. unmanned "Predator" drone aircraft killed six suspected al-Qa'ida operatives in Yemen in November 2002, including a suspect in the bombing of the USS Cole. Despite the assistance of military forces and nonmilitary personnel, Yemen, a poor country of an estimated 20 million with high unemployment and low literacy rates, has not been able to shake its image as a country that is home to Militant Islamists.

The nation's domestic concerns and problems are more important issues for the government than the U.S. "War on Terrorism." The proximity of Yemen to Saudi Arabia, UAE, and other Arab Sunni Muslim nations makes it much easier for Militant Islamists to transfer funds, especially in traditional form, than if they attempted to do the same from Europe, North America, and North Africa. This should be assessed within the context of the prevailing poverty in Yemen. It is important to underline the recent developments, particularly emotional responses from Muslim communities in connection with the Prophet Mohammad cartoons published by a Danish newspaper and picked up by other media outlets in Europe, New Zealand, Australia, and the United States.The responses by the governments of those nations would exacerbate and in many occasions fuel the willingness to further support the Militant Islamists, the most clandestine manner to express emotional reactions.

On November 28, 2002, suicide bombers attacked an Israeli-owned hotel in Mombassa, Kenya, killing 13 people, and at the same time two missiles narrowly missed an Israeli passenger plane carrying more than 200 Israeli tourists shortly after it had taken off from Mombassa airport. For the first time after a long lull, Israelis became the target of terrorists outside Israel. Reports indicated close connections between a Somali Muslim group, Al-Ittihad al-Islamiyah (Islamic Unity), and al-Qa'ida. This Somali group is on the U.S. State Department's list of terror organizations and is seen as a possible perpetrator of the Mombassa hotel bombing.[4]

The U.S. investigators concluded that the missiles fired at the Israeli plane carried the same serial number as a missile that was fired in an unsuccessful attack on a U.S. military plane taking off from Prince Sultan Air Base, about 70 miles southeast of Riyadh, Saudi Arabia. The missiles were identified as Soviet-made SA-7 shoulder-fired missiles and reinforced the connection of al-Qa'ida to the Mombassa terrorist attack, indicating that the al-Qa'ida network was again active in Kenya. According to the U.N. report, the missiles and the explosives used in the twin attacks on Israeli targets in Kenya were smuggled by sea into Mombassa from Somalia.[5]

Shortly after the November 28 bombings, a vehicle loaded with explosives plowed into the Paradise Hotel, 20 kilometers north of Mombassa. Ten Kenyans, three Israelis, and at least two bombers were killed by the blast at the hotel, which was frequented by Israelis. On an Islamic Web site several days later, the *al-Qa'ida* network claimed responsibility for the attacks. The group also warned the United States and Israel of future strikes. Further information on the Web site indicated that the Militant Islamists had become decentralized and established local organizations and cells that aimed to carry out actions that would be more localized but still directed at the same targets. The Web site added, "The Jewish Crusader Coalition will not be safe anywhere from the fighters' attacks." ("Jewish Crusader Coalition" is commonly used by Militant Islamists for what they see as a U.S.-Israeli alliance). The Web site continues, "We will hit the most vital centers and we will strike against its strategic operations with all possible means."[6] The statement was attributed to *al-Qa'ida* spokesman Sulaiman Abu Ghaith.[7]

TERRORISTS ATTACKS IN SOUTHEAST ASIA

Militant Islamist activity in Indonesia

On October 13, 2002, terrorist bombings of nightclubs on the island of Bali, Indonesia, killed 222 and injured more than 200 people, most of them Australian tourists. The blasts and ensuing fire destroyed an entire city block. Another explosion occurred about the same time near the U.S. consular office on the island but did not cause any casualties. Evidence at the sites indicated that the Malaysian and Indonesian Militant Islamist group, *Jammah Islamiyah* (JI), which is linked to the *al-Qa'ida* network, was directly involved in the attacks. Ustad (cleric) Abdullah Sungkar who lived in exile and fought against the Soviets in Afghanistan was the founder of JI, along with Abu Bakr Ba'asyr (Bashir). They were founders of country's *Peasantren* (Islmic boarding schools, or what is called *Madressah* in Pakistan). These schools in Indonesia are similar to those in Pakistan, Saudi Arabia, and other Muslim countries that are accused of breeding Militant Islamists.[8] The bombing was deliberately aimed at foreigners and tourists. This region of Asia is home to one-third of the world's Muslims and is often viewed as a moderate Muslim society. However, such a terrorist act cannot be carried out without a well-organized network and support from the community.

The population of the Aceh province is mainly Muslim, and *Shari'a* (Islamic) law was instituted in the province in 2002. A pro-independence conflict began in 1976, with the *Gerakan Aceh Meredeka* (Aceh Independence Movement, known as GAM) staging armed insurrections against the Indonesian government. Many in the region had rejected incorporation into Indonesia following independence from the Netherlands in 1949, arguing that the territory had never been formally part of the former Dutch East Indies. Aceh was given a certain degree of autonomy in 1959, but this did not placate local resentment at developments such as Jakarta's policy of using the province to relocate people from other, more crowded parts of the country. In 1998 the conflict seemed as if it might be nearing an end following the fall of the country's dictator General Suharto, and in 2002 a truce agreement between the government and GAM-armed rebels was signed. However, both sides failed to implement the deal fully, and in May 2003, the Indonesian military launched a tough, new campaign in an attempt to crush the GAM. Between 1976 and 2003, over 10,000 people lost their lives in the Aceh conflicts. The Indonesian army claims that, since the start of its current offensive in May 2003, it has killed an estimated 1,000 rebels.[9]

The tsunami disaster on December 26, 2004, which devastated Aceh, provided an opportunity for Indonesian Muslim radicals to participate actively in the reconstruction and publicize a role beyond radicalism at domestic, regional, and even international levels. The Islamic Defender Front (IDF), another Indonesian militant group, flew volunteers into Aceh from Jakarta to help in the relief effort. The IDF immediately decided to clear bodies and debris from the gleaming white Baiturahman Mosque, the main symbol of Islam in Aceh. The radical IDF should not be confused or associated with JI, because the latter has been responsible for bombings in the country, whereas the IDF has not perpetrated terrorist attacks.

The IDF also has made a name for itself in Jakarta by trashing bars during the Muslim holy month of *Ramadhan*. It has no known links to Indonesia's JI or any other underground Muslim terrorist or supporting movements. The IDF criticizes the Western countries, and particularly the U.S. influences in the country. Such criticism is mostly connected to U.S. foreign policy and military actions in Muslim countries, such as Iraq and Afghanistan, and includes the Palestinian-Israeli conflict. Ansufri Sabow, a 34-year-old IDF member and college lecturer on mathematics and Islamic studies in Aceh, specified that he welcomed the U.S. Navy helicopters working out of Banda Aceh to deliver food and relief supplies to isolated refugees, but Indonesians do not want those Westerners who come to their country mainly to take part in sex tours.[10]

In Indonesia certain Militant Islamist groups, such as the *LashkarJihad* (Army of Jihad) and GAM, were directly involved in armed confrontation with the Indonesian government. Indonesia's GAM rebels formally disbanded their armed wing on December 27, 2005, effectively ending their 30-year separatist insurgency.[11]

Jamaah Islamiyah (Islamic society)

Since its formation, JI has been active in numerous social, economic, political, and educational aspects of Indonesian society. The Indonesian police arrested the radical cleric and presumed spiritual leader of JI,

Abu Bakr Ba'asyir, shortly after the Bali tragedy. Ba'asyir was tried on charges that he leads JI. He was also accused of subversion by using his "religious position" or status to incite attacks, including the suicide bombing of Jakarta's JW Marriott Hotel in 2003 that killed 12 people and the nightclub bombings in Bali in 2002, both of which were blamed on JI.[12] In September 2003 a panel of five judges found him guilty of supporting the terrorist attacks and sentenced him to a four-year prison term. However, the court failed to convict him on the subversion charges. Conservative and radical Indonesian Muslims characterized the ruling as an appeasement of the United States and Australia.

In a subsequent trial, Ba'asyir was convicted of conspiracy in connection with the nightclub and Marriott hotel bombings but was cleared of more serious terrorism charges. The verdict represented the second major setback for Indonesian prosecutors, as they had failed in the previous trial to convict him of subversion for his alleged role as the spiritual head of JI. The judges noted that Ba'asyir was in jail at the time of the Marriott attack, awaiting his earlier trial. Ba'asyir's statement in the court after the verdict was announced and his supporters reacted is noteworthy: "I refuse this sentence," he told the judges. "It's unjust and an act of repression. With God's permission, I will appeal." Then, as dozens of his supporters rose to their feet in the courtroom and spread their arms in supplication, Ba'asyir began to beseech God: "We are your followers who are under repression. We are now going down in deepest humiliation. Make us more faithful and strong. Make us fighters to uphold Islamic law. To all holy warriors, you must be united."[13] Ba'asyir's statement reveals that his position and clerical authority among Muslim radicals and those who are anti-Western is much deeper than previously believed and carries tremendous credence because of the country's many problems and its government's pro-U.S. foreign policy. The statement and the reaction of his supporters clearly suggest that Ba'asyir is not only the spiritual leader of JI but is, in fact, the ideological and spiritual leader of JI.[14]

It seems that the Indonesian government, despite the pressures from the United States and Australia, is cognizant of Ba'asyir's status among Indonesian Militant Islamists, and thus the authorities are reluctant to prosecute him vigorously because of reaction from the politically active Muslim community. Also, the widespread distrust of the United States and the West by Indonesian Muslims—as is the case throughout the Muslim world—is another factor in the soft treatment of Ba'asyir. Before entering the courtroom, Ba'asyir told reporters that the United States was behind the trial. Detaining him repeatedly is much easier than sentencing him to a long prison term or death.

The fact that he has been sentenced to any jail time provides him an opportunity to enhance his status among his followers and exploit anti-

American and anti-Australian feelings. Ba'asyir's statements as he arrived in court and after sentencing clearly indicate that he is a master of publicity. He and his hard-core followers will use the sentence as proof that the charges against him were not based on hard facts but prompted by the United States and Australia, both of which have exerted considerable pressure on Indonesia to apprehend and prosecute terrorists. Thus, Ba'asyir's appeal against the verdict will garner more publicity and strengthen the Militant Islamist belief that this is all the work of a foreign anti-Muslim conspiracy. Overall, this particular case will most likely strengthen support for the Militant Islamists in the region. Ba'asyir was freed from prison on June 14, 2006.[15]

On October 1, 2005, suicide bombers attacked restaurants, killing at least 25 people and injuring more than 120 others in the resort area of Bali, Indonesia. The attacks, in which the authorities immediately blamed JI, came less than two weeks before the third anniversary of the Bali nightclub bombing in October 2002. . The suicide bombings were a clear indication that Militant Islamists are still active in the country. Less than a month after these attacks, the United States issued a new warning to Americans to avoid nonessential travel to Indonesia.[16]

In order to tackle the problems of terrorism and Militant Islamists, which have been detrimental to the tourist industries and the country's reputation, Indonesian authorities stated on November 26, 2005, that the government would take action in the newly declared war on militants and that such measures could include closing Islamic *Madressaha*. All major bomb attacks in Indonesia in recent years have been blamed on the JI network, which is seen as the regional advocate of the *al-Qa'ida* world view. Antiterrorism campaigns and government-adopted rules in Indonesia have often been viewed as advocated by the United States, which is part and parcel of America's war on Islam.[17]

Militant Islamist activity in the Philippines

Among Southeast Asian Militant Islamists are those who have been in armed conflict with the Philippine government and involved in a number of terrorist actions. Their aim is to achieve independence for the Muslim population in the country. The majority of Philippine Muslims live on the Mindanao islands in the southern part of the country. Militant Islamists maintain military camps on the island of Mindanao and other places in the south. In Mindanao, Militant Islamists train in the use of explosives and have conducted bombing campaigns in the country. Since the mid-1990s, the Militant Islamists have maintained their focus on terrorist activities in the south, giving sanctuary and training facilities to JI as well as to the Mindanao-based Abu Sayyaf group.[18]

Three bombs jolted Manila, the capital, and two southern cities on February 14, 2005, killing at least nine people and wounding more than 100 others. The Muslim extremist group Abu Sayyaf claimed responsibility. The group said the bombings were retribution for a major military offensive against Islamic Militants in the southern Philippines, in which more than 60 people were killed. "You can attribute this to us," an Abu Sayyaf leader, Abu Solaiman, told the DZBB Philippine radio station 20 minutes after the first two blasts. "There is one more to come," he added, before the Manila bombing. Thus, this group is dedicated to its objective through the use of terrorist campaigns.[19]

In February 2005, the Philippine government began a major military campaign against Abu Sayyaf and the Moro Islamic Liberation Front (MILF)—a breakaway from Moro National Liberation Front—and this campaign is the one Solaiman gave as the reason for the bombings. Abu Sayyaf is best known for a series of kidnappings of Western nationals and has also been blamed for the bombing of a passenger ferry in Manila Bay in February 2004, which resulted in the deaths of more than 100 people. In addition to Abu Sayyaf and the MILF, JI is also active in the Philippines. On June 29, 2004, the Philippine police arrested four members of the JI in Manila. In the house where the suspects were staying, police found ammonium nitrate, clocks, electrical wires, other bomb-making materials, and a manual with instructions for making bombs. This and other evidence point to JI activity throughout the region, and it is likely that JI had directly participated in bombings.[20]

A bomb went off on a ferry in Manila Bay in 2004, killing 116 people in the country's worst terror attack. Abu Sayyaf was thought to be responsible. Abu Sayyaf, which is on the U.S. and European lists of terrorist organizations, has been accused of a number of other bombings in the Philippines. Philippine security officials say the group also has ties to JI. In the summer of 2004 the Philippine military, along with U.S. counterterrorism units, began a military offensive in the Maguindanao province of Mindanao with the aim to capture members of Abu Sayyaf and its leader Khaddafy Janjalani.[21] However, despite this action and a second campaign begun in February 2005, Abu Sayyaf and the MILF are still active: On August 28, 2005, a bomb exploded on a ferry in the port city of Lamitan in the southern Philippines, injuring more than 30, including at least nine children. The region had been on alert for terror attacks. This bombing came after the Abu Sayyaf carried out a bomb attack that wounded 26 people on August 10, 2005, in Zamboanga.

Militant Islamist activity in Thailand

JI is the most active Militant Islamist organization in Southeast Asia and the Asia-Pacific, and this movement is present in the southern part of Thailand. Southern Thailand was once a Muslim kingdom, and the majority of the population is Muslim. Islamist separatist groups have existed in the southern Thai provinces for some time because southern Thais are Muslim and a minority in a Buddhist nation. Moreover, the region's poverty and underdevelopment relative to the rest of country, Bangkok's policies of forced assimilation of the Muslims, and the constant intimidation by security forces and local governments have exacerbated the existing discontent and sporadic violence. The situation thus has created an environment in which support for JI and other regional Militant Islamists can grow and spread throughout southern Thailand.

On October 25, 2004, Thai Muslims demonstrated at a police station in Tak Bai in the southern province of Narathiwat. Thai police killed at least seven demonstrators, and afterwards 78 others died, mostly from suffocation while being transported in overcrowded trucks to detention centers. Seven other protesters were missing. What made the event even more shocking to local Muslims was that it occurred during the holiest month in the Islamic calendar, Ramadhan, when the Muslims observe daily fasting from dawn to sundown for a month. The killings at Tak Bai significantly increased grassroot support for Militant Islamists.

Since then, assassins riding motorcycles, a hallmark of Thai Militant Islamists, have killed a number of non-Muslim Thais. Thai officials have said that Militant Islamists seeking to create a separate state in the Muslim-dominated south are behind the violence. Thai Muslim leaders, however, say heavy-handed tactics by security forces have alienated Muslims in the provinces. Regardless, tensions between Muslims, who make up 4 percent of the Thai population, and Buddhists in southern Thailand have been simmering for decades and appear to have worsened in 2004, as more than 600 people have died since violence erupted in the province in January 2004. Most of Thailand's 6 million Muslims live in the four southern provinces (Pattani, Yala, Song Kha, and Narathiwat) where separatists, Militant Islamists, and other disaffected individuals are fighting the Thai authorities. Many Muslims feel alienated by the Buddhist administration in Bangkok. Thailand's prime minister, Thaksin Shinawatra, said the unrest in the country's Muslim-majority south is the greatest concern for his second term. His statement came on February 12, 2005, when another four people were killed in attacks by suspected Militant Islamists. The attackers have targeted government forces, officials, teachers, and Buddhist monks and villagers in a campaign that has seen almost daily shootings, stabbings, bombings, and arson.[22] The worsening violence in the southern provinces forced Thai Buddhists to flee.

On February 15, 2005, after his reelection, the prime minister traveled to Narathiwat. On the day he arrived, Militant Islamists set off a bomb near a Buddhist temple in the province, injuring four villagers, and another on a road in the province's Ra-Ngae district, wounding a soldier. The government deployed 21,000 troops to quell the violence as part of Thaksin's policy of the use of stick and possibly carrots. The new military forces were to be educated about Islamic culture before deployment. Moreover, the prime minister stated that he would use military muscle and economic sanctions to punish villages that failed to cooperate. Local leaders warned that the plan could backfire in the largely Muslim region, which is in serious need of economic support rather than military forces. In an interview to Radio Singapore International, Somchai Homalaor, chairman of the Human Rights Committee at the Law Society of Thailand, echoed this idea: "What the people really demand is that they should reduce the military operation in the south, and try to win the hearts of the people, and build confidence of the people in the government." He added, "I don't think the prime minister really understands the situation in the south, especially what I call the difference between the people in the south and the majority of the Thais."[23]

While in the southern provinces, Thaksin also announced that the government would be distributing $500 million among southern villages that had been identified as not supporting terrorism. In 2005, the government had surveyed 1,500 regional villages to evaluate their potential for cooperation and categorized them as red, yellow, or green, depending on the level of violence found in each. Of the 1,500 villages, 358 were designated as red zones and were not to receive any funding: "We don't give money to those red villages because we don't want them to spend the money on explosives, road spikes or assassins," Thaksin told villagers in Narathiwat on February 16, 2005. He added, "If the money sanctions do not work, I will send soldiers to lay siege to the red zone villages and put more pressure on them."[24]

Hours after Thaksin left the region on February 18, an explosive-laden car was detonated outside a hotel in the southern border town of Sungai Kolok, killing several and injuring more than 40 people. It was the deadliest single bombing in the Muslim-dominated four southern provinces since early 2004, in which attacks had claimed several hundred lives. The bomb was placed in a pickup truck outside the Marina Hotel in the evening in an area crowded with open-air beer bars. The size and the manner of its deployment indicate that the bombing was designed to have a maximum effect and to convey a direct response to the prime minister's declaration during his visit. Most of the previous bombings had been small by comparison. The location of the bombing, in a border town, suggests that outsiders, such as members of JI, may have either infiltrated the area or directly assisted the local Militant Islamists.[25]

Amid criticism over the heavy-handed policies to eliminate the insurgency and further terrorist killings, the government—within a week of Thaksin's policy announcements— stepped back from the contentious scheme to categorize Muslim villages based on their perceived support for the insurgents. Human Rights Watch (HRW) slammed Thaksin's overall tactics, saying it threatened to attract more Islamic militants. "The policies that the government seems to be pursuing almost seem aimed at attracting *jihadis*," said Brad Adams, HRW's executive director for Asia, noting discomfort in Malaysia and Indonesia over the heavy-handed approach. He also said the policy of blocking funding to some Muslim villages "will inflame tensions rather than resolve them." The government's concern over Militant Islamist activities was so great that in March 2005 it called the first emergency session of parliament in more than 12 years to address the southern issue, which is the most intractable problem the Thai government has faced.[26]

On July 15, 2005, the government issued a decree giving the prime minister sweeping emergency powers—to tap phones, order curfews, and censor the press, among other measures. The emergency powers replaced the existing martial law. On July 14, 2005, at least 60 Militant Islamists had plunged Yala City, the capital of Yala province, into darkness by destroying electrical transformers and then roamed the streets with firebombs, explosives, and guns, targeting a hotel, two convenience stores, a restaurant, the railway, and a power station. Six bombs and exchanges of gunfire killed two policemen and injured 22 other people in the first coordinated attacks in a large city since the current wave of violence began in 2004. Officials said the attacks were highly coordinated, with gunmen lining the roads with spikes to prevent security forces from moving around the city.

The attack and government response were just the latest indications of the worsening tensions. The violence continued despite the fact that the Thai government has trained and armed 10,000 Buddhists to counter the Muslim separatists and Militant Islamists. However, the government's arming of the Buddhists will simply foment the religious and ethnic strife, worsening the conditions that have led to the violence and growth in Militant Islamist activity.[27]

Militant Islamists in the southern provinces of Thailand have caused the loss of lives of as many as 2,000 since 2004, with almost daily bombings, drive-by shootings, arson, and beheadings. As of this writing, the Thai government has not been able to stop the militants, even with the imposition of harsh martial law.

Their strategy has turned the Buddhists against Muslims in the region by attacking Buddhist religious symbols with gaudy brutality. The Militant Islamists operate like typical terrorists, picking and choosing the time and place of the action, which is very difficult if not impossible to control or stop unless the government turns the region into a military camp.

Militants have been able to create in remote areas "liberated zones" for themselves, without any intervention from the security forces, though the government flooded the region with nearly 20,000 new troops. Some Buddhist and Muslim villages have begun sealing themselves off from one another. People say that old friendships and patterns of cooperation are being undermined by mistrust. A number of Buddhist communities have fled, which is one of the major goals of the Militant Islamists.

Since 2006 Militant Islamists have not hesitated to use violence in any way possible to minimize the control of the Thai government and to weaken any form of resistance to the movement, even among the Muslim population. These include not only village chiefs and suspected collaborators, but those who work in government offices, government-funded schools, or even critical economic sectors like rubber tapping.

The level of violence in Thailand's four southern provinces has never been so high, and there had been more than 24 beheadings in the past three years and as many as 60 attempted beheadings. Human Rights Watch counted more than 6,000 violent incidents over the past three years. It said that more than 60 teachers and 10 students had been killed and 110 schools—the most visible signs of central government authority in many places—had been set ablaze.

Unlike other militant or terrorist movements around the world, Thai Militant Islamists have not set out their demands or published a manifesto. It is a collection of violent groups without an identifiable central leadership. "We are fighting a ghost," said Chidchanok Rahimmula, a lecturer in security at Prince of Songkhla University. These ghosts, however, exist in both urban and rural areas, and thus it makes it very difficult to combat the Militant Islamists in the predominantly Muslim southern provinces of Thailand.[28]

As long as serious local issues and tensions exist in the Muslim communities, whether separatist or religious or ethnic, they can become a source of instability, especially if Muslims are or are perceived to be the target of mistreatment, deprivation, and repression by Muslims in neighboring countries. Thus, problems can potentially affect an entire region.

In the Southeast Asian countries of Indonesia, Malaysia, the Philippines, and Thailand, which have either majority or significant minority Muslim populations, Militant Islamists are creating serious problems. To understand the sources of such Islamic militancy, similar to the Middle Eastern Muslim countries, one needs to look at the national and regional problems that are compounded by American foreign policy toward Muslim societies.

Since the Bali nightclub bombing, Roger Hardy points out "...the moderates are being weakened, and the radicals strengthened, by a tide of anti-Americanism that is sweeping the Muslim world...I watched students chanting angry slogans outside the U.S. embassy in the Indonesian capital, Jakarta. They were protesting at U.S. policy on an issue thousands of miles away in the Middle East—the Palestine problem, and of course, there's Iraq." He quotes one of Indonesia's known and most moderate Muslim leaders, Amien Rais, as saying, "George Bush has been successful in alienating the Muslim world by occupying Iraq."

However, in connection with the same issues, Anwar Ibrahim, the former Malaysian deputy prime minister, says, "The assumption of many Muslims is that all of the evils are because of the crimes and oppression and imperialism—all associated with the United States." While the people in the Muslim countries, "...overlook the corruption, the authoritarian rule, the oppression by Muslim tyrants and dictators in [their own] communities." Thus, it is clear that the three problems —national, regional, and international—are the feeding grounds for Militant Islamists.[29]

CHAPTER 6

The September 11, 2001, Terrorist Attacks: Invasion of Afghanistan and the Aftermath

The United States, with support from the United Kingdom, Australia, and the Afghan Northern Alliance, invaded Afghanistan on October 7, 2001, as part of America's "war on terrorism" campaign. The purpose was to capture or kill Usama bin Ladin and disrupt *al-Qa'ida,* which was suspected to be behind the September 11 terrorist attacks on the United States. A second objective was to overthrow the Taliban regime in Afghanistan, which provided support and an operational base for bin Ladin and *al-Qa'ida.* In December 2001, Afghani opposition forces met at a United Nations-sponsored conference in Bonn, Germany, and agreed, in the "Bonn Agreement," to establish an interim government in the country and to develop a process to establish a more permanent government system. Under the agreement an Interim Authority was formed in Kabul on December 22, 2001, with Hamid Karzai appointed as chairman. The Interim Authority stayed in power for about six months while preparing for a national "Loya Jirga" (Grand Council that represents various Afghan constituencies), which in mid-June 2002 decided on the structure of a new system, called the Transitional Authority. Hamid Karzai was named president of The Transitional Authority and the new Transitional Islamic State of Afghanistan (TISA). One of the TISA's primary goals was to draft a constitution, which was ratified by a Constitutional Loya Jirga on January 4, 2004.

Afghanistan held its first national presidential election on October 9, 2004, and Hamid Karzai was declared the office winner on November 3 and inaugurated on December 7, 2004, for a five-year term. Despite the fact that Karzai was elected with 50 percent of the vote, the country still remains a land of warlords and a place in which travel at night is quite dangerous. The United States, NATO, and Afghan government forces continue to fight an insurgency led by Taliban militants and *al-Qa'ida*, while poverty is increasing and opium production is booming again. Insecurity, lawlessness, and the absence of almost any law enforcement remain the paramount features of the country.

Soviet Union forces entered Afghanistan on December 23, 1979, under the pretext of upholding the Soviet-Afghan Friendship Treaty of 1978, and within four days they changed the leadership of the Afghani government. The Kremlin also wanted to secure its interests in Afghanistan from Iran, which was engulfed in the Islamic Revolution, and also from the West. Ten years later, in 1989, Soviet troops withdrew in defeat, leaving behind a devastated country and hundreds of thousands of Afghani dead.

To understand the problems that Afghanistan faces, one must consider the country's recent history. In February 1989, Soviet troops withdrew from the country, ending a bitter decade of war and occupation. However, the civil war continued, and the government of Najibullah was able to remain in power until 1992. His regime collapsed when General Abdul Rashid Dustum and his Uzbek armed men defected in March 1992. In the midst of the power vacuum many other armed groups entered Kabul with the aim of assuming power, and the rivalry among these groups led to civil war. According to the Red Cross, from 1992 to 1996 more than 50,000 civilians lost their lives in Kabul alone, and the city was destroyed. The Pakistani government organized and armed a group of Pashtun Muslim clerics, known as the Taliban, and, along with Pakistani military advisors, sent them into Afghanistan during the civil war. These armed Afghani groups were based in Pakistan and backed by Saudi Arabia, the United Arab Emirates (UAE), and the United States. The Taliban gained power in the mid-1990s, and by 1994 it was able to take over the city of Kandahar (which became the Taliban's stronghold) and went on to expand its control and capture Kabul in September 1996. By the end of 1998, the Taliban occupied most of the country, except for a small, mostly Tajik region of the Panjshir Valley—the heart of opposition to Soviet occupation in the 1980s and Taliban rule in the 1990s.

The Taliban imposed strict Islamic rules while the country and the people continued to suffer from severe economic problems. They were also the recipient of financial and military support from Pakistan, the UAE., Saudi Arabia, and the United States. However, the Taliban also provided sanctuary to Usama bin Ladin and the *al-Qa'ida* fighters who had been actively involved in the war against the Soviet forces. *Al-Qa'ida* and local

Militant Islamists were accused of direct involvement in the bombings of the U.S. embassies in Nairobi, Kenya, and Dar el-Salam, Tanzania in August 1998. Despite the repeated demands by the United States, the Taliban refused to expel Usama bin Ladin and the *al-Qa'ida* fighters from Afghanistan. After the World Trade Center attacks on September 11, 2001, the United States and its allies commenced a military attack against the Taliban regime beginning on October 7, 2001.

Afghanistan was and still is a very poor country. Historically, poverty has played a major role in making it a major center of opium poppy farming.[1] In the 1990s after the Soviet defeat, Afghanistan became the world's largest producer of the opium poppy, which is the source of opium, heroin, and morphine. Currently, it produces almost three-quarters of the global opium supply.[2] In a poor country such as Afghanistan opium is a lucrative cash crop. It is also a main source of credit, which is very difficult, if not impossible, to secure. It is a rich source of cash for Militant Islamist groups in the country, as well as for wealthy Afghanis living in Pakistan, and thus it has become a significant factor in the war on terrorism. In 2004 the U.S. State Department reported that opium is a multimillion-dollar business and a major source of income for criminal groups and a major contributor to corruption in the country. It must be controlled because opium production and smuggling is dangerous to the establishment of a stable democracy and the success of war on terrorism.[3]

In 2001, the ruling Taliban banned opium poppy cultivation and reduced production to 185 metric tons that year, compared to 3,276 metric tons in 2000. The reduction increased the price from an average of $30 per kilo in 2000 to $700 per kilo in 2001, prompting massive resumption of cultivation in 2002. According to the United Nations Office on Drugs and Crime (UNODC), poppy farming continued to grow in 2003, with the area under cultivation increasing by 8 percent from 74,000 hectares to 80,000 hectares and opium production increasing from 3,400 tons to 3,600 tons.[4] According to *The Economist*, poppy production amounted to 36,000 tons in 2003. Opium production was valued at $2.8 billion—equal to 60 percent of Afghanistan's gross domestic product (GDP) for the fiscal year, which ended March 21, 2004. The cultivation of opium poppies is concentrated mainly in the southwest, particularly in the Helmand Province, although it is also fairly common in the Nangahar and Badakhshan provinces. Trends in 2004 indicated that poppy cultivation is spreading further into remote areas. About 1.7 million people, or 7 percent of the population, are directly involved in poppy production.[5]

In 2003, poppy cultivation generated a gross income of approximately $1 billion, or about $3,900 per opium-growing family. This compares to an average national wage of $2 per day. In 2004 the price dropped to $92 per kilogram. Although this figure is much less than in 2001, it still provides substantial wealth in a country that has a GDP per capita of $200. However, for some rural farmers this figure would be much lower.[6] With the average price for raw opium in 2004 at $283 per kilogram and expected yields of up to 40 kilograms per hectare, poppy cultivation remains much more profitable for farmers than the production of other commodities.

The high value of the crop allows farmers, particularly returning refugees, to raise capital to buy livestock and other supplies for farming. Poppies also have become a source of credit to offset losses caused by weather and to get farms back into production. Poppies are estimated to earn approximately eight times more income per hectare than wheat, with less water, less labor, and fewer supplies needed for production. "Rural poverty and the lack of income are the main reasons why farmers produce opium...It will take a long-term commitment and probably more than a decade to create alternative income opportunities. The project aims to rehabilitate the agricultural infrastructure in some of the main poppy-producing areas and to boost horticulture, livestock, and cash crop production in order to create alternative livelihoods for small farmers, landless workers, and vulnerable groups," the UNODC report added.

The UNODC in Afghanistan points out that many farmers have little option in a poor country such as Afghanistan, and the war in particular has depleted the rural areas of their meager livelihood. Thus, a cash crop such as opium is a very attractive option. People need cash for very simple goods, such as school books for children, clothing, and tea. Also, growing opium poppies rarely involves any risk, and the sale of opium is not even punished by the authorities.[7]

The executive director of the UNODC, Antonio Maria Costa, said that opium production in Afghanistan dropped by just 2 percent in 2005. The land under opium poppy cultivation had been reduced by 21 percent, but heavy rains helped produce a bumper crop of 4,100 tons of opium. A report by the U.N. agency said the total amount of land being used to grow poppies dropped from 323,570 acres in 2004 to 256,880 acres in 2008. However, this reduction did not offset a jump of 22 percent in crop yield.

The UNDOC predicted it would take 20 years to eradicate the cultivation of opium poppies, despite government warnings and the destruction of some crops. It forecasts a significant improvement in the size of land cultivated in Afghanistan, but heavy rainfall and snowfall and the absence of crop infestation resulted in a very significant increase in production in 2005.[8]

In his later report, however, Costa said that opium cultivation in Afghanistan rose by 59 percent in 2006. The production forecast placed the 2006 harvest at around 6,100 tons of opium—approximately 92 percent of the total world supply. It exceeds global consumption by 30 percent. Opium is the raw material of heroin, and Costa accused corrupt administrators of pocketing aid money. Officers warned that the south of Afghanistan was "displaying the ominous hallmarks of incipient collapse, with large-scale drug cultivation and trafficking, insurgency and terrorism, crime and corruption." The bulk of the increase was recorded in the lawless Helmand province, where cultivation rose 162 percent and accounted for 42 percent of the Afghan crop. The province is facing an upsurge in attacks by Taliban-led militants fighting NATO forces. The survey conducted by the UNODC showed the area under poppy cultivation in Afghanistan reached a record 407,700 acres in 2006, up from 257,000 acres in 2005 and 331,360 acres in 2004.[9]

One of the major problems of Afghanistan, which cannot easily be solved either by the NATO-led forces or Western assistance is the weakness of the government, which is partially rooted in the widespread corruption from the top to the lowest governmental jobs under the existing political system. U.S. and Western European governments do not dare address the issue in public because they do not have any options to the existing U.S.-Western-client Karzai's presidency. The interdependent corruption makes it almost impossible to confront the warlords and opium production in the country.

Since the overthrow of the Taliban regime and the establishment of a parliamentary government in Kabul, many Afghan refugees returned from Pakistan and Iran. These refugees, especially the poor who lack housing, are becoming a source of major political and social problems in the country. Widespread corruption also is adding to the discontent. Given the present instability in Afghanistan and the continuing threat of the ousted Taliban and other Militant Islamist groups, the growing poverty could easily lead to agitation and civil disorder, creating opportune circumstances once again for Afghanistan to again become a training ground for Militant Islamists terrorists. Such an environment could even lead to the disintegration and breakup of the country into ethnic regions.

The World Bank expressed concerns about the way aid money is being used in Afghanistan. It said President Hamid Karzai's government needs to have clearer priorities for reducing poverty, tackling corruption, raising taxes, and improving public administration. Karzai needs to request at least $50 billion to finance its reconstruction program over the next five years. His government is, for example, looking for significant new funding to develop agriculture, which is crucial to the efforts to improve food security.

After a meeting of the World Bank's board, its director for fragile and conflict-affected countries, Alastair McKechnie, said there was a "huge issue" of the effectiveness of aid in Afghanistan. The Bank said the Afghan government has made "little headway" in the fight against corruption. It accepts that this is not easy when government authority is challenged by powerful figures—warlords, the Taliban, and Militant Islamists. It said that progress in the reform of public administration has been modest, and there needs to be clear priorities for achieving results in delivering services on the ground. It added that the collectionof more taxes is essential, which is very blunt language from the World Bank to everyone in the country.[10]

Poverty and corruption continue to exacerbate the problems in the country, which would make it a breeding land for Militant Islamists. Thousands of children, some as young as four years old, are being forced to work in brick factories in Afghanistan to pay their parents' debt. In the Sokhrod district in the east of the country, which is well known for producing bricks, there are about 38 factories, and about 2,200 children are believed to be working in them. "I don't want to do this with my life. I want to go to school, but I cannot because I am poor," 10-year-old Shafiq Ola told Al Jazeera. "My family is in debt for $800 and I have to work." Mohamed Gul, the owner of one factory in the area near Jalalabad, said, "Many of the children were forced into the brick factories after their parents became indebted to the owners. They are bonded labor, I am holding them...They don't have any other option; they have to, like a slave, work for me. Each family owes me thousands of Aghanis [the Afghan currency]. They have to pay me with their work." Each child earns as little as $6 a day, which makes it very difficult if not impossible to pay the debt and survive.

The United Nations Children's Fund (UNICEF) estimates that about 30 percent of 5- to 14-year olds in Afghanistan are involved in some form of labor. Almost half of the country's youth (15- to 24-year olds) are illiterate, according to UNICEF. An estimated 50 percent of the population of 24 million Afghanis are under the age of 18, and up to 71 percent of the adult population and 86 percent of women are illiterate. Poverty is one of the major reasons for such a high rate of illiteracy.[11]

The population of Kabul has swelled rapidly to 3.4 million from 700,000 in just a few years, creating a dire need for housing, according to the United Nations Habitat Human Settlements Program, which is advising the Afghan Ministry of Urban Development. An estimated 10,000 homeless people are in Kabul, about 4,000 of them in two squatter camps. In addition, groups of displaced people are living in public buildings and abandoned ruins throughout the city. Most of them are refugees who have returned from camps in Pakistan since the fall of the Taliban. Some families have been living the entire time in tents, with the men working at menial jobs such as being porters in the bazaar.[12] At the same time, a number of expensive private villas are going up around Kabul, some of them built by military commanders and government officials on former government land, a sign of increasing inequities.

Widespread crime, particularly kidnappings and atrocities against individual families, have created a growing sense of lawlessness in the midst of the increasing poverty. The complaints of the residents of Kandahar echo those of Afghanis across the country. On March 14, 2005, demonstrators in the northern city of Mazar-i Sharif called for the resignation of General Attah Mohammad, the governor of their province, complaining that he had stolen people's land. Human Rights Watch, a U.S.-based advocacy group, charged a week before that numerous former warlords, who hold many provincial governorships and top police jobs, "have been implicated in widespread rape of women and children, murder, illegal detention, forced displacement, human trafficking and forced marriage." There are also allegations that some militia leaders and civilian officials are involved in drug trafficking. Members of the Afghan Independent Human Rights Commission noted that many kidnappings may not be reported to police. The logbooks at Kandahar's independent radio station indicated that it had received 10 to 15 requests per month to broadcast reports of missing people, most of them children. However, the station does not keep track of the circumstances of each child's disappearance or whether they are found.[13]

Hamid Karzai, who was appointed interim president by the *Loya Jirga* and with the approval of the United States after the 2001 overthrow of the Taliban, was elected in a general election to a five-year term on October 9, 2004, in Afghanistan's first free election. He was sworn in at a ceremony in the former royal palace in Kabul on December 7, 2004, that the U.S. Vice President Dick Cheney and Secretary of Defense Donald Rumsfeld attended as an outward indication of success in the war against Militant Islamists and terrorism in Afghanistan. However, neither of the U.S. officials thought it wise to stay overnight in Kabul, which reveals quite a bit about the ability of the Afghan government and the coalition forces to maintain security. It also indicated that Taliban and *al-Qa'ida* were believed to still be capable of significant attacks. Karzai's new cabinet was sworn in on December 23, 2004.

Hamid Karzai still faces immense difficulties, particularly in the south and east of the country. The Taliban and *al-Qa'ida* are still active in Afghanistan, which has prolonged the insecurity and instability and limited the effectiveness of the Karzai government and security forces to the capital. During the 2004 election campaign, Karzai managed to hold one election rally outside Kabul on December 21, 2004. The U.S. ambassador to Afghanistan, Zalmay Khalilzad (who is an Afghan-American), said foreign troops would remain in Afghanistan indefinitely even as Afghan forces increasingly take on security responsibilities. He likened this scenario to the continued presence of U.S. troops in Europe and East Asia. He suggested Afghans, still bitter at their abandonment by Washington when the decade-long Soviet occupation ended in 1989, might welcome such a presence. A U.S.-led force of over 18,000 troops in Afghanistan is still hunting for *al-Qa'ida* leader Usama bin Ladin and for remnants of the Taliban regime. In addition, some 9,000 NATO-led military troops provide security, mainly in Kabul. However, the issue for the Afghanis would remain the future status of the U.S. forces in the country. U.S. and NATO forces undoubtedly will be in the country for sometime to come, and the U.S. official would welcome such a development.[14]

On January 20, 2005, a suicide bomber detonated explosives in the northern town of Sheberghan, where the Uzbek warlord, Abdul Rashid Dustum, had been praying, injuring more than 20 people. Dustum was a key player in the civil war that destroyed much of Kabul in the mid-1980s, and later he helped the United States defeat the Taliban. He was not among the injured, although his brother was.

A spokesman for the hard-line Taliban militia said it carried out the attack on Dustum—a former Afghan army general in addition to being a warlord—to avenge the killing of Taliban prisoners during the U.S. invasion in 2001. However, police said the attack was the work of *al-Qa'ida*. Dustum was an unsuccessful candidate in the October 2004 presidential election, but he did win votes, largely among the Uzbek and Turkmen minorities.

Despite his election defeat, Dustum continues to be an important political figure. Since 1980 he has displayed an uncanny ability to switch sides and stay on the right side of those in power during his career. One of Afghanistan's most feared regional military commanders, Dustum recently began disarming his local militia as part of the U.N.-backed plan to disarm armed groups in the country. However,he was allowed to retain a personal retinue of 200 bodyguards.

Dustum gained a reputation as a cruel maverick during the years of violence that shattered Afghanistan. He started out in the 1980s fighting for the Soviet Union against Afghan Mujahedeen commanders and then backed Communist president Najibullah after the Soviet withdrawal. During the civil war that followed the fall of Najibullah, he switched sides twice, first backing the North Alliance resistance leader, Ahmad Shah Masood, and then going over to a rival commander, Gulbuddin Hekmatyar.

Dustum retreated to northern Afghanistan and built a fiefdom in the city of Mazar-i-Sharif, after battling with the Taliban for control of the city in 1997 in a brutal campaign marked by the massacre of retreating troops. Since the fall of the Taliban regime, Dustum has backed the government in Kabul, but he keeps control of substantial oil and gas reserves in the north.

The Taliban's assassination attempt and statement, among other incidents, clearly indicate that Afghani militant groups are far from defeated, and the reformed Afghan security forces are still weak, ill-trained, and prone to desertions and infiltration. President Karzai's government will remain vulnerable for some time to Militant Islamists who are adamant on attacking it and the idea of democracy that has been introduced through the U.S.-led military invasion and occupation.

The first U.N. Afghan Human Development Report warned that the country could fall back into chaos if popular grievances were not met. The report was released on February 21, 2005, and indicated that some progress has occurred since 2001. However, it also emphasized that serious security problems remained and the country had some of the world's lowest life expectancy and literacy rates as well as some of the worst conditions for women and children. The chief editor of the report said "...but human security cannot take a back seat to national and international security interests of other nations." Decades of conflict have taken a devastating toll, leaving Afghanistan near the bottom of the 177 countries covered in the United Nations Development Program's Human Development Index (UNDPHDI), just above Burundi, Mali, Burkina Faso, Niger, and Sierra Leone.[15]

It appears that new Militant Islamist leadership emerges whenever the so-called known key figures are removed from the scene. The central government and the allied military forces together have not yet been able to establish stability in the country, and it is extremely difficulty, if not impossible, to travel in the country at large, and specifically in the southern provinces. Many of the Afghani lawmakers are rights abusers or involved in the drug trade, which is the source of money, power, and independence from the dictates of the central government. Opium and other drugs are a greater security threat in Afghanistan than the Taliban and the Militant Islamists. Opium production has boomed since the fall of the Taliban, stoking fears that Afghanistan is becoming a state financed by the illegal drug trade. Instability persists despite the presidential and parliamentary elections, which are presented as achievements against terrorism and toward democracy in the country. A sharp rise in suicide bombings in Afghanistan underlines the security challenge for the Kabul government, the United Nations said on March 8, 2006. Attacks by the former Taliban followers and Militant Islamists have created serious problems. There were 17 suicide bombings in 2005 and 11 in the first two months of 2006, U.N. Secretary-General Kofi Annan said in a progress report to the Security Council. Attacks on Afghanistan have soared since mid-2005 and have continued unabated throughout late 2005 and during the first three months of 2006.

The report provides new evidence that Taliban guerrillas and non-Afghan Militant Islamists are waging an increasingly vicious insurgency. Kofi Annan blamed the rising violence on a variety of factors, like weak state institutions, a thriving illicit economy based on opium, factional violence, and disputes over resources as well as the insurgency and terrorism. To succeed as a democratic state, the Afghan government must be able to demonstrate that it can deliver on its promises by providing basic services and by rebuilding the shattered country, Annan said. The U.N. report came out shortly before the March 24, 2006, expiration of the mandate of the U.N. Assistance Mission in Afghanistan. He called on the Security Council to renew the mission for another 12 months, even as he expressed concern over the safety of U.N. staff as they seek to provide the Afghan authorities with political and strategic guidance.[16]

More than three years after American-led forces ousted the Taliban government from Kabul, the United Nations has painted a gloomy picture of conditions in Afghanistan. Unless grievances such as poverty and the lack of jobs, health care, education, and political participation are addressed, it will collapse into an insecure state, which will then become a threat to the international community. The potential consequences of such a collapse are clear—the number of terrorist attacks has risen despite claims by the Untied States and its allies that more than two-thirds of the key *al-Qa'ida* figures have been neutralized or eliminated since the "war on terrorism" began. It appears that new leadership emerges when key leaders are removed. If the Afghanistan government and allied military forces are not able to establish stability, the country could very well become the training and operations base for the Militant Islamists once again .

Since the invasion of Afghanistan in October 2001, at least 284 American soldiers have died, including 99 in 2005, which was the deadliest year since the arrival of the International Security Assistance Force (ISAF) in December 2001. A total of 1,600 Afghans were killed by terror attacks in 2005. The situation in the country's south and southeast is alarming. Despite the almost five-year, U.S.-led campaign against the Taliban, the Militant Islamists once again control large portions of the southern provinces of Nimruz, Uruzgan, Helmand, Kandahar, and Paktika. There is virtually no sign of reconstruction in these provinces, which still lack electricity and running water, paved roads, schools, and hospitals. Aid organizations hardly ever venture into the region anymore. The government in Kabul is incapable of meeting the basic needs and wants of the population. Thus, anti-U.S. and anti-West feelings are high among the Afghans, particularly in the south and southeastern provinces, the heartland of the Taliban and the Militant Islamists.

Six years after the U.S.-led invasion of Afghanistan violence persists in much of southern Afghanistan, where the government of Hamid Karzai has no presence. Civilian deaths by the U.S. and the NATO-led forces even rattled the government in Afghanistan, where there were more than 140 suicide bombings, which became more sophisticated. In February 2007 a suicide bomber killed 23 people outside the main U.S. base at Bagram during Vice President Dick Cheney's visit. A suicide bomber in June killed 35 people on a police bus, and in November a suicide bombing that killed six lawmakers also left a total of 77 people dead, including 61 children, after security guards opened fire on a crowd of onlookers. The 14 deadliest suicide bombings between January 4, 2006, and December 6, 2007, killed an estimated 341 people.

A surge in violence in the border areas of Pakistan and Afghanistan is clear evidence of the increasing presence of pro-Taliban and other Militant Islamist fighters in the area, particularly in the southern provinces of Afghanistan. In 2007 Afghanistan saw record violence, which resulted in the death of 6,500 people, including 110 U.S. soldiers—the highest ever—and an estimated 4,500 Taliban and Militant Islamists. Britain lost 41 soldiers, while Canada and other nations lost a total of 30 troops. During the same year Afghanistan had record opium production, a clear evidence of failure in the control and eradication of opium production.[17] The government in Kabul on its own does not have the capability to either defeat or even diminish the violent attacks by the Taliban and the Militant Islamist fighters in the country.

Afghanistan and the southern provinces have remained safe havens for the Militant Islamists—non-Afghan fighters and would-be fighters. This presents clear evidence that the Militant Islamists, and in this case the Taliban, are not only waning in power and public support but, in fact, are gaining in both areas and will be around for some years to come even with the U.S. and NATO-led fighting forces. However, the extent of the willingness by the United States and NATO member countries to remain involved in the conflict remains the principal factor.

CHAPTER 7

Militant Islamists in the Northern Caucasus and Central Asian Regions

The political and economic conditions in the northern Caucasus and Central Asia are similar to those in the countries discussed in Chapter 5: governments are extraordinarily unstable, poverty is widespread, and security forces are weak. In addition, these areas are characterized by major ethnic conflicts. For example, in the northern Caucasus enmity exists between the Ingush, Chechens, and Ossetians, while in Central Asia ethnic rivalries occur between the Uzbeks, Kyrgyz, and Tajiks. Deteriorating economic conditions and the absence of a direct plan for an economic future as well as other political and social developments have created a sense of helplessness and frustration among the people, which has given rise to demonstrations in Kyrgyzstan, especially in the cities of Jalalabad, Osh, and Batkent. Uneasiness persists in Uzbek towns such as Tashkent, Namangan, and Andijan, where many people were killed in 2005.

In addition to ethnic problems that fuel radicalism and violence in the Caucasus, Russian control has resulted in tremendous bloodshed, particularly in the Russian republic of Chechnya, which seeks independence. Chechen resistance has been dominated by Militant Islamist groups. Similarly, influence by China and discrimination against Muslims by the Chinese government in the Xinjiang province is serving to attract Militant Islamists.

MILITANT ISLAMIST ACTIVITIES IN THE NORTHERN CAUCASUS: CHECHNYA

Anti-Russian (and anti-Soviet) sentiment has always existed among Muslims in the North Caucasus,[1] and thus it is not a new phenomenon;

however, the orientation of the current anti-Russian feeling is new. Sufi is a mystic form of Islam that has been the dominant practice among Muslims in the Caucasus, Central Asia, and other areas, including those in the Tartar region. In fact, throughout history Sufis in these regions were viewed as a symbol of opposition to Russian and Soviet domination. After the collapse of Communism and the breakup of the Soviet Union, however, this anti-Russian sentiment began to be exploited by Islamic radicals, especially the Militant Islamists. This development has been important in the spread of Militant Islamist terrorism throughout the Caucasus since the collapse of the Soviet Union in 1990. Islam is the dominant religious practice in the Caucasus.

Historically, the relationship between Russia and the Caucasus has been difficult. The region was strategically important to Russia in the nineteenth century as a base for military operations. After the collapse of the Soviet Union, four republics remained part of Russia while South Ossetia became part of Georgia—but did not want to be—when Georgia became independent of Russia. As a result of the conflict between South Ossetians and Georgia, Russia maintains peacekeeping forces in the breakaway republic of South Osseita. However, in 1994 Chechnya mounted a violent campaign for independence. Of the ethnic groups in the Caucasus, the Chechens have had the most adversarial and violent relationship with Russia:

- In 1830, the Russian military invaded Chechnya to establish a military base against the Ottomans.
- In 1859, Chechnya was incorporated fully into Russia.
- In 1917 through 1925, the Soviet Union quelled an uprising and Chechens opted for the Soviet government.
- In 1944, a Chechen revolt against Moscow led to mass deportation of Chechens to Kazakhstan, a central Asian republic.
- In 1956, Soviet Premier Nikita Khrushchev condemned the deportations and restored Chechnya as an Autonomous Soviet Republic.
- In 1994, Russian President Boris Yeltsin ordered Russian troops to invade Chechnya to suppress a Chechen attempt for independence, and as a result civil war erupted.
- In 1995, Chechen separatist terrorists seized a Russian hospital, an action which ended in a botched rescue attempt by Russian security forces and more than 100 deaths.
- In 1997, Moscow formally signed a peace treaty with the Chechens.
- In August 1999, Chechen militants invaded Dagestan, a neighboring republic, and Russian troops entered Chechnya.

Chechnya's quest for independence has continued, and Militant Islamists have taken advantage of the situation, conducting major terrorist actions against Russian targets. In Paris on December 20, 2002, the French Interior Minister arrested four Militant Islamists who had been planning terrorist attacks against Russian interests in Chechnya and France, including the Russian Embassy in Paris. The Ministry later revealed that two of the suspects had received training in the Pankisi Gorge, a remote region in Georgia that borders Chechnya, where they also had met with Chechen rebel leaders.[2] On December 27, 2002, suicide bombers drove two trucks packed with explosives into the front of Chechnya's pro-Moscow government building, killing at least 80 people and wounding many others. Officials claimed that three suicide bombers wearing Russian military uniforms and identification drove the explosives-laden trucks bearing Russian license plates through security checkpoints in Grozny. However, these events pale in comparison to the attacks on a school in Beslan, North Ossetia and a Moscow theater, which are discussed in detail later in this chapter.

The attacks against Russian targets have received worldwide attention, with the result being that on October 8, 2004, the U.N. Security Council voted unanimously on a resolution to step up its campaign against terrorism. The resolution states that hostage-taking and other acts against civilians aimed at provoking "a state of terror" can never be justified on political, philosophical, ideological, racial, religious, or ethnic grounds. It calls on all nations to prosecute or extradite anyone supporting, financing, or participating in these terrorist acts. The 15-to-0 vote ended several weeks of negotiations by Russia, which had introduced the resolution after sustaining attacks by militant Chechens in September 2004 that included the suicide hijacking of two planes and the taking of an entire school hostage in Beslan, North Ossetia. These attacks killed nearly 360, including 172 schoolchildren and 30 of the terrorists.

Many residents of Beslan and North Ossetia in general harbor a seething hatred for the Ingush in the neighboring republic. The Ingush and Chechens are predominantly Muslim, and the Ossetians are mostly Christian. These groups have a history of ethnic rivalry that culminated in a brief but bloody territorial war between the North Ossetians and the Ingush in 1992. The Beslan tragedy exacerbated the existing animosity among the three Caucasian republics. Shamil Basayev, the Chechen warlord who claimed responsibility for planning the seizure of the school, said in a statement posted on the Internet, that nine of the 32 terrorist hostage-takers were ethnic Ingush who cooperated with Chechen separatists in the war against Russian rule.[3]

In connection with the Chechen terrorist takeover of the school, a Chechen Web site posted the following:

> ...However many children in that school were held hostage, however many
> of them will die (and have already died)...it is incomparably less than the

42,000 Chechen children of school age who have been killed by Russian attackers...Dead children, dead adults—brutal murder of more than 250,000 Chechens peaceful civilians by the invaders [sic]—all of it cries to heaven and demands retribution. And whoever these 'terrorists' in Beslan might be, their actions are the result of Putin's policies in the Caucasus in response to terrorism and crimes committed by the Kremlin's camarilla, which is still continuing to kill children, flood the Caucasus with blood and poison the world with its deadly bacilli of Russism.

The Web site also quotes Bible verses in which Jesus says, "What measure ye mete, it shall be measured to you (Matthew 7:2, Mark 4:24, Luke 6:36").[4]

Newly discovered video footage of the Beslan school massacre broadcast by the CBS program *48 Hours* showed hostage-takers negotiating with local authorities before the crisis ended in tragedy. According to the television program, the videotape was shot by the terrorists and found in the rubble of the school in the days following the massacre. In the video, the former president of Ingushetia, Ruslan Aushev, is seen negotiating with the leader of the hostage-takers, Ruslan "The Colonel" Kuchbarov. Lydia Tsalieva, principal of the school, is also seen telling Kuchbarov: "For Christ's sake, don't hurt a single child of mine." Subsequent images show 11 mothers leaving the school with 14 children, apparently as a result of the encounter between Aushev and Kuchbarov. On the CBS television program, Aushev said that the hostage-takers presented a series of demands in return for the release of the hostages, including the withdrawal of all Russian forces from Chechnya. Although Aushev thought the conditions unrealistic, he hoped Moscow would agree in order to end the crisis and reverse its decision later.[5]

Immediately after the school tragedy, Moscow began to urge the international community, particularly the United Nations, to come up with a resolution regarding international terrorism. The U.N. Security Council eventually came up the resolution, which condemned in the strongest terms all acts of terrorism irrespective of their motivation, whenever and by whomever committed, as one of the most serious threats to peace and security. Algeria and Pakistan opposed some language in the resolution, which they said would make it a crime to fight in a liberation war. Negotiators later settled that issue on January 20, 2005, so that the resolution now calls on all countries to prevent or punish specific "criminal acts" against civilians carried out "to provoke a state of terror" that also are offenses in international conventions relating to terrorism.[6]

Women have regularly participated in Chechen terrorist attacks. In October 2002, 41 armed Chechen men and women attacked the Dubrovka Theater in Moscow. They declared their dedication to Islam and willingness to die for their cause, an act that was aired by the Al Jazeera television network. The theater attack is the first time that Chechen women participated in a suicide terrorist campaign. The takeover ended with an attack by Russian special security forces, which resulted in the death of 129 hostages and all of the terrorists. These women became known in the press as the "Black Widows," a name that has come to be applied to female Chechen suicide bombers. The Black Widows are believed to have lost brothers, sons, husbands, and other family members either in operations against the Russian security forces or in kidnappings by Russian security forces that tortured or murdered the victims. It is not so much ideology or religious motivation that drives these women, but rather desperation and desire for revenge.

Chechen Black Widow terrorist actions against the Russians have continued since the takeover of the theater. In 2003, women killed themselves at a Russian rock concert in a suicide mission in order to avenge the deaths of their immediate family members, as claimed by Militant Islamist Chechens. On May 12, 2003, a group that included women drove a truck packed with explosives into government offices in Znamenskoye, in northern Chechnya, killing 59 people. On June 5, 2003, a woman suicide bomber attacked a bus carrying Russian air force pilots near Chechnya, blowing it up and killing herself along with 18 others. This third attack in three weeks by women suicide guerrillas fighting for Chechen independence came on the eve of a Russian parliament vote on partial amnesty for rebel fighters that was designed to improve prospects for a Kremlin peace plan.[7] The Black Widows also are credited for explosions in late August 2004 that caused two Russian commercial airplanes to simultaneously crash, killing 89 people. A few days later, a suspected Chechen suicide bomber blew herself up outside a Moscow metro station, killing 10 and injuring 51 people.[8]

Moscow believes that Turkish sympathizers—as many Turks trace their ancestry to Chechnya or elsewhere in the Caucasus—give financial and other forms of support to the Chechen militants in their armed opposition to Russia. Therefore, Moscow has called on Ankara to crack down on Turkish charities that it claims channel funds and weapons to Chechen rebels. Very early in December 2004, Russian officials said their forces in Chechnya killed two Turkish militants who were fighting alongside Chechen separatists. On December 3, 2004, Turkish authorities apprehended 10 suspected Chechen militants and two pro-Chechen Turks apparently in a gesture to recognize Russian President Vladimir Putin's official visit to Turkey on December 5, 2004. Turkey has previously accused Russia of supporting the Kurdish Workers Party (PKK) which has waged a war for autonomy in Turkey's southeast since 1984, a battle in which about 37,000 people have lost their lives.[9] As in other areas that struggle with political or ideological conflict, the situation in Chechnya is persistently problematic.

On January 15, 2005, Russian security forces foiled a mass hostage-taking attempt by pro-Chechen rebels in southern Russia that would have been on the scale of the Beslan school hostage tragedy. A law enforcement source in Daghestan, which neighbors war-torn Chechnya, told the ITAR-TASS news agency that the five militants involved had planned to seize a large number of hostages. The security forces were able to block the terrorist while preparing for an attack.[10] One of the slain gunmen was Rasul Makasharipov, leader of the extremist religious underground network, Jannah (Arabic word meaning paradise), that has killed more than 30 policemen and security officials over the last two years. The group has vowed revenge on the police for torturing suspected Daghestani extremists. Jannah's main goal is to eliminate senior police and government officers in Daghestan and thus diminish the capacity of the security forces and local government. Its campaigns have become increasingly effective.

MILITANT ISLAMIST ACTIVITIES IN OTHER CAUCASUS REPUBLICS

Since Russia sent troops back into Chechnya in 1999, Militant Islamism has increasingly spread from Chechnya to the nearby Caucasus republics of Ingushetia, Daghestan, North Ossetia, and Kabardino-Balkariya. The authorities in these republics continue to have confrontations with the Militant Islamists. In January 2005, a police assault on an apartment in the town of Nalchik, the capital of the north Caucasian republic of Kabardino-Balkaria, appears to have wiped out a Militant Islamist cell with links to Chechen terrorists. Such elimination, however, does not resolve the underlying problem of young people being recruited into regional or local Militant Islamist groups. Reports indicate that youths are motivated to involve themselves with militants as "a way of expressing frustration at social, political and economic deprivations that permeate the region."[11]

The attack was the third of such assaults within a month on suspected Militant Islamists in Ingushetia, Kabardina-Balkaria, and North Osetia. In these armed conflicts, eight police officers were killed and seven others wounded, along with a number of militants. The attacks erupted first in Nalchik, in December 2004; four policemen died and militants fled with at least 200 firearms. The report notes that a few years ago these Militant Islamists "would have been dubbed 'Wahhabis,' a reference to the conservative Muslims, often used as a pejorative term for anyone deemed to hold radical and even militant views. These radicals, mostly young, are disenchanted with political authority, economic conditions, and society.

Ultimately they become attracted to views of several Jamaat [sic] movements, such as Yarmuk. Leaders of these groups have commonly studied Islam in an Arab country or fought in Chechnya. The core members of any Jamaat are young men from the Balkar ethnic group, who mostly live in the harsh mountains of the Caucasus whereas the Kabardin, ethnic Russians, and others in the ethnically mixed Kabardina-Balkaria live in the lowlands to the north.[12]

The nature of the attacks in the republics suggests the strength of the militants and illustrates their instability and lack of security. In June 2004 Militant Islamists and Chechen separatists attacked police buildings in the city of Nazran in Ingushetia and effectively seized control of Nazran for several hours. About 60 people, many of them police, were killed. In December 2004, armed men raided the regional branch of the federal Drug Control Agency in Nalchik, killing four employees, looting an arsenal, and setting the office ablaze. A gun battle between the government forces and the Militant Islamists erupted in Nalchik on February 19, 2005. Police said the raid was the culmination of a three-day operation to overcome Militant Islamist groups who had intensified attacks on Russian forces in the region of Kabardino-Balkariya over the last year. "They all belonged to a reactionary branch of Islam...and were in the general structure of bandit groups headed by (Aslan) Maskhadov and (Shamil) Basayev."[13]

On March 8, 2005, Russian officials announced that Russian forces killed Maskhadov, the former Chechen president and rebel leader. Security forces reported that "...in the republic of Chechnya in the village of Tolstoi-Yurt (Doikur-Aul, as called by the Chechens) an operation was carried out by special Federal Security Services, forces during which the international terrorist and leader of armed bands Maskhadov was killed and his closest collaborators arrested."[14] Akhmed Zakayev, a longtime ally of and spokesman for Aslan Maskhadov, confirmed to *Agence France Presse* that it was "definitely Maskhadov" that had been killed by Russian troops.

Maskhadov's death passed the leadership of the militants to the Chechen rebel warlord, Shamil Basayev, a Wahhabi Militant Islamist who claimed responsibility for the hostage taking at the Beslan School, and his aide, Doku Umarov. Although in general any Militant Islamist often is referred to as a Wahhabi, some of these individuals in the Caucasus region are in fact Salafi, who are scripture literalists of Qura'n. Its adherents contend that it is the most "pure" or "original" form of Islam, which had existed during the first 40 years of the Islamic Umma. "This will increase the power of the Islamists and it will be a free-for-all. I expect terrorist attacks in Russia and the North Caucasus."[15]

Maskhadov, a 53-year-old former Red Army officer, had been viewed as a moderate before aligning himself more closely with radical Islamists. He was elected Chechen president in 1997 in a vote recognized by the Kremlin and described as free and fair by international observers. Nevertheless, Chechnya remained chaotic, and Vladimir Putin sent troops back into the republic in 1999. Previously, Moscow had sent an estimated 10,000 troops into Chechnya in 1994. In 1997 Moscow agreed to withdraw its troops after 70,000 casualties resulted on both sides. Maskhadov has been blamed by the Russian government for numerous attacks on both military targets and civilians in recent years, including the Beslan school massacre, which he denied, and the October 2002 mass hostage-taking at the Dubrovka Theater in Moscow. The Kremlin had linked him and Shamil Basayev to Militant Islamists in the region, *al-Qa'ida* in particular. His death destroyed any chance of peace in the region. He had repeatedly invited Moscow to hold talks with him, but the Russian leadership refused by saying it did not negotiate with terrorists. Human rights groups who had called on the Kremlin to engage with Maskhadov voiced disappointment at his death.[16]

Chechen separatists announced a little-known religious leader as the successor to Aslan Maskhadov: Abdul-Khalim Saidullayev, a Militant Islamist separatist, whom Maskhadov had chosen as his successor. In 2003 he told AFP by telephone. "He [Abdul-Khalim Saidullayev] was one of the closest people to Aslan Maskhadov on the territory of Chechnya." Saidullayev is not widely known among the Chechens. He is thought to be in his mid 30s and is known to have served on Chechnya's Islamic *Shari'a* court in Maskhadov's government during the Caucasus republic's three years of de facto independence in between the two wars with Moscow. Pro-Moscow authorities in Chechnya labeled him a proponent of the Wahhabi sect of radical Islam. Saidulayev has tried to set up what he calls a "Caucasus Front." Since he took over the leadership of the movement in March 2005, Saidullayev has established a group called the "Caucasus Front" with the purpose of coordinating armed campaigns with other Caucasus Militant Islamists.[17]

In August 1999, Militant Islamist Chechens aided the neighboring republic of Daghestan when they sent fighters to support the Dagestani Militant Islamists against the Russian security forces. A Militant Islamist group of Daghestani and Chechen fighters led by warlord Shamil Basayev occupied several mountain villages in two regions of Daghestan. They later withdrew after heavy fighting with Russian troops. Militant Islamic Chechens have continued to be active in Daghestan. Most recently, during late June and the first two weeks of July 2005, a blast killed two policemen, a gunman shot dead a local politician, and an explosion killed 10 soldiers outside a bathhouse in the town of

Mkhachkala, on July 2, 2005. On the same day, a bomb exploded in a train near the town of Khasavyurt, killing a young woman and injuring several people. In late June a bombing injured nine police officers, a bomb derailed a train, a minister was blown up in his car, and a police chief was shot on a mountain road. Police authorities characterized all the violence as routine events and attributed them directly to the Militant Islamists, or *"al-Qa'ida*-linked *Shari'a Jammat."*

Russian authorities also insist the violent attacks in the mainly Muslim Caucasus republics are the work of *"Jihadi* groups" and international terrorists who bombed the London underground and the Sharm el-Sheikh resort area in Egypt. However, the developments in Chechnya—a consequences of the war, which began in 1994—and the widespread political, social, and economic problems, continue to have a direct impact on its neighboring republics, which face the same overwhelming problems. In addition to widespread poverty, corruption, particularly among the security forces, exists at all levels of government. Thus, the crisis and lawlessness in the Caucasus region offers a ripe environment for Militant Islamism to spread.[18]

On October 13, 2005, groups of armed Chechen Militant Islamists, ranging in numbers between 60 and 200, killed more than 100 and injured at least 116 people in a series of coordinated attacks in Nalchik, Kabardina-Balkaria..[19] The pro-rebel Kavkaz Center Web site said that a detachment of the Chechen-linked Kabardino-Balkaria Jama'at, called the Yarmuk, had entered Nalchik. The use of the word *Jama'at* on the Web site indicates that they were Militant Islamists. The Web site also described the armed group as being members of the Caucasian Front and used the term Mujahideen, an Arabic word for warriors. It also posted the following statement "...the subdivisions of the Caucasian Front were continuing to combat with the *Kafirs* and *Munafiqs* directly in Nalchik."[20] The latter Arabic terms, Kafirs, meaning nonbelievers and referring to the Russians, and *Munafiqs*, meaning traitors and referring to the local pro-Russian), clearly underscore the Caucasian Front's Militant Islamist orientation. The Kavkaz Center Web site also posted a statement on behalf of Shamil Basayev, who claimed responsibility for the Nalchik attacks. However, the militants claimed 217-armed *"Mujahideen"* carried out the attacks.[21]

Kabardino-Balkaria, along with other Caucasian Russian republics, has seen a rise in armed Militant Islamist movements, as noted before, and in violence targeting police, soldiers, and other law-enforcement officials linked to the festering, decade-old armed conflict in the Caucasus.

Russian President Vladimir Putin has ordered security forces to deal more severely with suspected Militant Islamist fighters in the south. Law-enforcement forces blockaded Nalchik, which has a population of 235,000, during a series of sweeps targeting suspected extremists in and outside Chechnya. Such measures had been undertaken before and created a period of false calm, but none of Moscow's actions have addressed the major regional problems, such as poverty, unemployment (estimated at 90%), and widespread official corruption.

MILITANT ISLAMISTS IN CENTRAL ASIA

It is important to underscore that the Militant Islamists in Central Asian nations in numerous ways are connected not only to militants in Afghanistan and Pakistan but also to the East Turkistan Islamic Movement, a group of Uighur and other ethnic non-Chinese Muslims who challenge the Chinese control of the northwestern province of Xinjiang, China. The East Turkistan Islamic Movement also maintains a presence in Kazakhstan and Kyrgyzstan. It appears that Uighur residents of Kyrgyzstan and Kazakhstan do sympathize with, and give financial assistance to, their political activist brethren in the cities of Urumchi (Urumghi) and Kashkar in Xinjiang—an autonomous Uighur province.

Chinese repression of the Muslim minorities in Xinjiang (home to the Central Asian ethnic groups, the Uighurs, Dungons, Tajiks, Kazaks, and Uzbeks, whoview themselves as Muslims) has contributed significantly to the increase in Islamist militancy in the region. According to Human Rights Watch and Human Rights in China, "China's attempts to suppress Islam as a motive force for separatism by confining it to tight state control is not only profoundly a violation of human rights, but is a policy that is likely to alienate Uighurs, drive religious expression further underground, and encourage development of more radicalized and oppositional forms of religious identity."[22] The Chinese authorities call practicing Muslims terrorists, which has heightened distrust between the Muslim community and the non-Muslim Han Chinese and further widened the existing division between the two communities in the Xinjiang province. The report further notes that, historically, Chinese authorities in the province have described practicing Muslims as feudal elements and as ethnic nationalists in the 1950s and 1960s, as counterrevolutionaries in the 1970s and 1980s, as separatists in the 1990s, and as terrorits since September 11, 2001. In September 2005, the Chinese Public Security Ministry said that more than 220 "terrorist" acts had been committed in Xinjiang in the past two decades, killing 160 and wounding 440 people. One July 9, 2008, Chinese authority reported that police shot dead five Militant Islamist separatists in a shoot-out in Urumqi, Xinjiang, and the next day arrested 82 Militant Islamists after breaking up five different militant groups, accusing them of planning to carry out attacks during the Beijing Olympics in the predominantly Muslim region of Xinjiang.[23]

Central Asians express increasing insecurity and disillusionment with the political and economic changes in their countries. The Central Asian governments appear to have no aims, and the main objective of the leadership in these countries is to perpetuate the existing political system. The people have lost confidence in their leaders and do not see anyone who can take their countries in a direction that would bring about positive political and economic development for the majority. However, unique to these societies is the absence of an overwhelming presence of Islam and adherence to Islamic tenets, in contrast to countries where Islam predominates or is practiced by many of the people. But the longer that disillusionment and widespread corruption and poverty exist in the Central Asian nations, the more likely it is that Muslim residents will be targeted for recruitment by the Militant Islamists.

In Central Asia, Kyrgyzstan and Uzbekistan are the most vulnerable to the growth of Militant Islamist groups, even though these nations lack well-established Islamic movements, except for the Islamic Movement of Uzbekistan (IMU). Another Islamist group in Central Asia is *Hizb ut-Tahrir* (Liberation Party). It was established in 1990 in the Ferghana Valley region of Uzbekistan and then spread to southern Kyrgyzstan, Kazakhstan, part of Tajikistan, and Pakistan. Its aim is to establish an Islamic state, with a return to the *Khalifa* and rule by the Islamic law, the *Shari'a*. It is a highly secretive group that claims it does not advocate violence. It is banned in all Central Asian countries (see Table 3.2).

Hizb ut-Tahrir and other regional Militant Islamist groups such as the Taliban and *al-Qa'ida* have similar ideologies, maintain some form of contact, and possibly cooperate with the Muslim movement in the Xinjiang province. The Muslim ethnic minorities of Xinjiang seek independence as the country of Eastern Turkistan. There have been numerous armed clashes between the Militant Islamists of the Eastern Turkistan Islamic Movement and the Chinese security forces in the Xinjiang province, specifically in the cities of Urumchi (Urumqi) and Kashgar from 1993 to 2002.[24]

Hizb ut-Tahrir maintains an office in the United Kingdom, in London. The party was founded in 1953 by a Palestinian judge, Taqiuddin Nabhani, who lived in East Jerusalem, then under Jordanian rule. He broke away from the Egyptian *Ikhwan ul-Muslimoon* "Muslim Brothers," militant Islamic group, rejecting its willingness to even consider cooperation with Egyptian struggle against the British, in order to establish an independent secular government. Germany outlawed an Islamic organization, citing the spread of anti-Semitic and anti-Israel propaganda to explain the third such ban since September 11, 2001. Little is known about the organization and structure of *Hizb ut-Tahrir,* but German authorities say the group advocates the destruction of Israel and disseminates anti-Jewish propaganda.

Russia's Federal Security Service said on June 9, 2003, that it had detained 55 members who were citizens of Kyrgyzstan and Tajikistan and confiscated their weapons and explosives. Uzbekistan's Supreme Court on February 16, 2004, convicted and sentenced to death a *Hizb ut-Tahrir* member with ties to *al-Qa'ida* for two deadly bombings in neighboring Kyrgyzstan. Azizbek Karimov, a 25-year-old man, was convicted of organizing and carrying out the bombings at a market in the Kyrgyz capital, Bishkek, in December 2002, and at a Western Union office in the southern Kyrgyz city of Osh in May 2003. This group is also active and growing in Tajikistan. Krygyz President Akaev warned the National Security Council that various forms of extremism threaten Kyrgyzstan's national interests, Akipress.org reported on October 25, 2003. The president singled out the banned *Hizb ut-Tahrir* as one of the most dangerous examples of "ideological terrorism." Noting that the movement's aim is to establish a caliphate in the Ferghana Valley, Akaev decried "so-called human rights advocates who try to pass off any prosecution of *Hizb ut-Tahrir* members who have broken the law as the persecution of dissidents."[25]

Hizb ut-Tahrir faces strong opposition in the former Soviet Central Asia, where it is banned and pursued as an extremist organization. In Uzbekistan, human rights groups say the majority of the country's 7,000 political prisoners are from *Hizb ut-Tahrir,* and the Uzbekistan government of President Islam Karimov continues to push the West to blacklist and ban the group. This organization, which has existed for more than four decades, does not limit its activities to this region. On March 25, 2004, an Egyptian court convicted 26 people, including three Britons, of trying to revive *Hizb-ut-Tahrir,* which is outlawed in Egypt, and sentenced them from one- to five-year prison terms. The three Britons—Ian Malcolm Nisbett, Maajid Nawaz, and Reza Pankhurst—were each sentenced to five years in prison. One of the 26 was convicted in absentia.[26]

The economic, political, and social conditions in the Caucasus and the Central Asian republics continue to produce an environment that is a breeding ground for Militant Islamists. Such conditions present more problems in the Caucasus than in Central Asia. The treatment of Muslims in the western Chinese province of Xinjiang and the Central Asian republics needs to be analyzed within the context of current and future developments in Afghanistan and Pakistan. Further deterioration or the lack of any improvement in the economic and political conditions in Afghanistan would have a direct impact on them.

CHAPTER 8

Militant Islamists in Lebanon and the Palestinian and Israeli Territories

In addition to the global network of Militant Islamists, there are those militants and terrorists who conduct attacks exclusively in Lebanon and the Palestinian and Israeli territories. The *Hizbullah*, whose name is Arabic for Party of God, and the Palestinian Islamic Jihad Movement (*Harakat al-Jihad al-Islami al-Filastini*) operate in Lebanon, particularly in the southern parts of the country, which is predominantly *Shi'a*. HAMAS (an acronym of the first letters of the Arabic words *Harakat al-Muqawamah al-Islamiyya*, meaning The Islamic Resistance Movement and also the acronym HAMAS meaning "zeal") was founded about 1979 and carries out terrorist acts in Israel. The activities of the two most active and important groups, *Hizbullah* and HAMAS, are explored here.

HIZBULLAH ACTIVITY IN LEBANON

The genesis of *Hizbullah* lies in the Lebanese civil war, which erupted in April 1975 when, after gunshots were fired at a church, Christian armed men ambushed a bus carrying Palestinians. This conflict arose because of a number of triggering events, particularly killings by one religious group against the other and the responses to those killings. The civil war involved different religious and nonreligious groups, such as Christian armed militia, Druze militia, leftists, and different armed Palestinian factions who lived in the refugee camps. The problems became a full-scale civil war after shots were fired at a church and armed men ambushed a bus filled with Palestinians. Palestinian armed groups joined Leftist-Muslims in clashes with the Christian armed militia, and the fighting eventually spread to most parts of the country. To help separate the factional combatants, the Lebanese President called for support from Syrian troops in June 1976, who were joined in the fall of 1976 by the Arab Deterrent Force. In 1978 the Palestine Liberation Organization (PLO) attacked a bus in northern Israel, and Israel retaliated by invading Lebanon in order to punish PLO and to intervene in the civil war. In response, the U.N. Security Council passed Resolution 425, which called for the immediate Israeli withdrawal of forces and created the U.N. Interim Force in Lebanon, which was charged with maintaining peace. Israeli forces withdrew but established the South Lebanon Army (primarily a Christian militia) inside Lebanon along the border with Israel, thus setting up a 12-mile "security zone" to protect northern Israel from cross-border attacks.

A cease-fire brokered by the United States in 1981 lasted for almost a year until June 6,1982, when with the support of Lebanese *Maronite* Christian leaders and militia, Israel invaded Lebanon in response to the PLO's rocket attacks on northern Israel and an assassination attempt on the Israeli Ambassador to the United Kingdom. In August 1982, U.S. mediation resulted in the evacuation of Syrian troops and PLO forces from Beirut. The agreement also provided for the deployment of a multinational force comprising U.S. Marines, along with French and Italian military units, while Israeli forces remained in the country. On September 14, 1982, the new president of Lebanon, Bashir Jemayel, who had been elected with the support of Israel, was assassinated. The next day, Israeli troops crossed into West Beirut to secure Muslim militia strongholds and stood aside as Lebanese Christian militias massacred almost 800 Palestinian civilians in the Sabra and Shatila refugee camps. With U.S. backing, Amin Jemayel, chosen by the Lebanese parliament to succeed his brother as president, focused anew on securing the withdrawal of Israeli and Syrian forces.

Factional fighting between the *Shi'a Amal* militia and the Palestinians armed factions brought Syrian forces back into Lebanon in 1988. In 1989 a conference held in Ta'if, Saudi Arabia, to resolve the civil war resulted in the Ta'if Agreement. This agreement was supported by the Arab League, and it ended the civil war in March 1991. In May 1991, all factions were disarmed. It is estimated that during the war 100,000 were killed and another 100,000 became handicapped. Nearly 250,000 Lebanese emigrated as result of the civil war.

The assassination of President Jemayel and the subsequent terrorist attacks were the initial signs of the radicalization of Muslim groups, who saw the successive Israeli and U.S. intervention in the country as an attempt to consolidate and serve the interests of Christians in Lebanon. The group responsible for the assassination as well as the attacks was the *Hizbullah,* which had secured the support of Syria and the Islamic

Republic of Iran. *Hizbullah* launched deadly attacks against its opponents in Lebanon and later against the Israeli forces and their South Lebanon Christian collaborators. In December 1981, *Hizbullah's* first major suicide terrorist attack occurred in Lebanon at the Iraqi embassy, killing 27 people and wounding more than 100 others. In September 1982 the group assassinated pro-Israeli Lebanese President Bashir Jemayel. A suicide bomber from *Hizbullah* drove his explosives-laden car into the U.S. embassy on April 18, 1983, killing 63 people, 17 of them Americans, including the senior CIA officer, Robert Ames.

Hizbullah also launched deadly attacks against its opponents in Lebanon and later against the Israeli forces and their Southern Lebanon Christian collaborators. In late October 1983, another suicide bomber drove a truck packed with explosives into the U.S. Marine barracks in Beirut, killing 241 American troops serving with the Multi-National Force (MNF) peacekeeping forces. Simultaneously, a building housing the French military members was also attacked; 59 French paratroopers died. Later, in early November, the headquarters of the Israeli military forces in the southern Lebanese city of Tyre was destroyed by a *Hizbullah* bomb that killed a number of Israeli troops and Palestinian and Lebanese prisoners kept there. Suicide bombing quickly became a regular tactic used by *Hizbullah* to achieve its goals in Lebanon while also striving to become a major political force.

Hizbullah's reputation soared with the Israeli withdrawal from southern Lebanon in May 2000 after 22 years of occupation. It has now become very active in Lebanese politics, fielding candidates for various offices and occupying 12 seats in Lebanon's parliament. Additionally, it owns television and radio stations, medical services, and many charity organizations. *Hizbullah's* main target is the Israeli military forces at the Lebanon and Gollan Heights borders. Tension has subsided since the Israeli withdrawal, but it has not disappeared. The possibility still exists that conflict will erupt between *Hizbullah* and Israeli forces.

Hizbullah's attraction and popular reputation are rooted in its nonmilitary activities. In the early 1990s, when southern Lebanon was in the midst of the civil war between the *Shi'a* militia and Israeli troops and the South Lebanon Army (which was primarily a Christian militia aligned with Israel), *Hizbullah* opened a 30-bed hospital that was available to all Lebanese. More than a decade later, the same hospital treats more than 50,000 patients annually, regardless of religious affiliation. The organization continues to fund the hospital, has grown to a 50-hospital network, and is expanding into northern Lebanon. In addition to providing health care, it runs schools and orphanages. Thus, *Hizbullah* is a major provider of social services and aid to thousands of Lebanese *Shi'a*s and others.

The group's welfare programs are arguably better than those provided by the state.

The Islamic Republic of Iran (IRI) remains a major supporter of the *Hizbullah*. The *Hizbullah* and Tehran confirm such support, but claim that funding is made by Iranian private charity organizations. This funding is not clandestine; rather, the government publicly reports that its funding is specifically given for social and health services.[1] Moreover, the *Hizbullah* leadership visits Tehran whenever the occasion arises.

It is important to note that the majority of the Lebanese population is *Shi'a*. Although Lebanon has not conducted a national census since the 1950s, observers believe an up-to-date count of the population would show that the majority of the Lebanese are *Shi'a*s. Moreover, not all Lebanese *Shi'a*s are members or loyal to *Hizbullah*.

During a debate on September 2, 2004, the U.N. Security Council approved the U.N. Resolution 1559 sponsored by the United States and France demanding that, along with the withdrawal of Syrian forces, Lebanese and non-Lebanese militias be disarmed, a tacit reference to *Hizbullah*. The *Hizbullah* leaders said they would not do so while Israel occupies Lebanese land, a reference to the disputed hundred-square-mile Shebaa Farms along Lebanon's southern border with Israel. Resolution 1559 requires all militias to lay down their arms, including *Hizbullah* and Palestinian armed groups. But the Lebanese government has so far made a distinction between *Hizbullah* and the rest, referring to *Hizbullah* as a "resistance" force against Israeli occupation.

On February 14, 2005, former Lebanese Prime Minister Rafiq al-Hariri was assassinated in a suicide bombing that also killed 17 others. Anti-Syrians within Lebanon and the international actors, the United States and France particularly, accused Syrian and Lebanese agents of the murder. This demonstration lasted for several days, and it, along with pressure from Lebanese and foreign political leaders, forced the Lebanese prime minister, Umar Karami, to resign on February 28, 2005. Then, on March 8, 2005, *Hizbullah* showed its clout by sponsoring one of the largest demonstrations in recent Lebanese history, bringing hundreds of thousands of largely Shi'a supporters into central Beirut to support the party's alliance with Syria and the presence of 14,000 Syrian troops in Lebanon. The Lebanese prime minister was reappointed by the Lebanese Parliament largely because of this demonstration by *Hizbullah* supporters.

These events in Lebanon rocked the country and reignited the fear of a possible outbreak of the sectarian violence of the 1975–1990 civil war. On March 19, 2005, a car bomb exploded in a Christian neighborhood, damaging a number of apartments. On March 23, 2005, an explosion in a shopping center in the Christian district of Kaslik, near the Lebanese port city of Jounieh, killed and wounded a number of people.

Since the end of the civil war, *Hizbullah* has become an important political force in Lebanon. Because *Hizbullah* also perpetrates terrorist acts, this has created a dilemma on several levels for the United States and the European Union. The United States has classified *Hizbullah* as a terrorist organization because of its military terrorist activities in Lebanon and against the Israeli forces. In contrast, the European Union, and in particular France, has believed that, although *Hizbullah* commits violent terrorist attacks, it is also a powerful political group, and thus a more fruitful approach to stabilization is to work within the political system of Lebanon.

The assassination of former Lebanese prime minister Rafiq al-Hariri on February 14, 2005, led to renewed debate as to whether *Hizbullah* should be designated as a terrorist organization. During January and February 2005, U.S. Secretary of State Condoleezza Rice, along with Germany and the United Kingdom, tried to convince the European Union to formally declare *Hizbullah* a terrorist organization and thus restrict its fundraising capability. However, the French government blocked these efforts. France cited the increasing instability in Lebanon, especially following the assassination of al-Hariri, as a reason for keeping the militant group off the terrorist list. Placing *Hizbullah* on the list now, France argued, could further destabilize Lebanon.[2] Similarly, Russian officials believed that *Hizbullah* should play a political role, as it is in the interest of Lebanon and the Middle East that *Hizbullah*'s political role be recognized and taken into account. A Russian official presented such a view after meeting opposition leader Walid Jumblatt of Lebanese Druze, a Muslim sect, in Moscow. The Druze chief has repeatedly urged dialogue with *Hizbullah* and said it should join any new government formed in Lebanon after Syrian withdrawal.[3]

Although the European Union perhaps prefers this approach, whether it will be possible is uncertain because not all European legislators agree. On March 10, 2005, European legislators branded *Hizbullah* a "terrorist" organization and urged European Union member governments to place the group on their terrorist lists, as the Union did with the Palestinian HAMAS organization in 2003. In fact, the European Union imposed restrictions on the transfer of funds to the Palestinian authorities after the installment of the HAMAS-led government at the insistence of Germany. Germany and the United States see eye-to-eye on the issue of the HAMAS-led Palestinian government, with both condemning its refusal to recognize the existence of Israel. Germany was a major player in pushing through a European Union boycott of the HAMAS-led government, including a freeze on direct funding to the Palestinian authorities worth 500 million ($630 million) a year. A German official said Chancellor Angela Merkel would tell U.S. President George Bush that the criteria for lifting HAMAS out of its isolation—including recognizing Israel and honoring the commitments of earlier Palestinian governments—must be adhered to. Israeli Prime Minister-designate Ehud Olmert lurged Germany to wield its influence with its European partners to maintain the boycott of HAMAS.[4]

The United States has acknowledged that *Hizbullah* is an important political force and its isolation would be more harmful to the Lebanese polity. President Bush gave *Hizbullah* an opening to be removed from the United States list of terrorist organizations when on March 15, 2005, he urged *Hizbullah* to give up its weapons and not obstruct the Israeli-Palestinian peace process. For its part, *Hizbullah*'s Secretary General and spiritual leader, Sheikh Hassan Nasrallah, said *Hizbullah* is not ready to disarm: "We are ready to remain a terrorist group in the eyes of George Bush to the end of time but we are not ready to stop protecting our country, our people and their blood and their honor." Nasrallah also said on March 16, 2005, that "They [U.S.] want to disarm us for Lebanon to stay defenseless—our force protects Lebanon." Nasrallah made the comments during a talk show aired on three Lebanese TV channels, including *Hizbullah*'s al-Manar TV station. "The U.S. and Israel have been exerting pressure since 2002 to disarm *Hizbullah*. They consider us a major threat for their projects in the region."[5] The direct quotations presented here are intended to present the reader with the opportunity to acquire knowledge about the *Hizbullah*'s leadership and what they attempt to gain not only in Lebanon but also throughout the Islamic world.

Nasrallah said *Hizbullah* does not get orders from Damascus or Tehran to carry out attacks against the Israelis. Rather, he likened the organization to a protective militia.

> "If you can convince me that there are other ways to protect Lebanon, I'm ready to listen. As long as Lebanon remains threatened, even if that lasts a million years, we will say to our children and to their descendants that their patriotic, human, moral and sacred religious duty is to defend their people and their fatherland...I'm holding on to the weapons of the resistance because I think the resistance...is the best formula to protect Lebanon and to deter any Israeli aggression...Hezbollah's arms will not be used domestically. Their only role is against Israel...We don't carry out operations in occupied Palestine...The Israelis say *Hizbullah* is behind the operations by Palestinian factions. This is not true...This is an honor that we don't claim," he added. Nasrallah also described UN Resolution 1559 as a "resolution to serve the interests of the United States and France."[6]

Hizbullah draws its support from Lebanon's large *Shi'a* population that is widely respected in the country and the Arab world for its military role in forcing Israel to leave southern Lebanon in 2000 after an 18-year occupation.

After the withdrawal of Israeli forces from Lebanon in 2000, *Hizbullah* came under continuous pressure to integrate its forces into the Lebanese army and focus on its political participation and social services, which it continued to do. However, *Hizbullah* maintained that it was a resistance force not only in Lebanon but in the region. Therefore, it maintained militia forces in the south on the Israel-Lebanon border. It insists that the Israelis must leave Shebaa Farms, which was occupied in 1967, and has been an area of clashes between *Hizbullah* militia and the Israel forces. *Hizbullah* receives continued wide support from the Lebanese for its position on Shebaa Farms. However, Israel with the backing of United Nations—based on a French map made during the French colonial occupation of Lebanon—claims that the Shebaa Farms are on the Syrian side, and thus are part of the Golan Heights, which Israel has occupied since 1967. Another cause of armed clashes cited by *Hizbullah* is the continued detention of thousands of Lebanese prisoners in Israeli jails.

After the withdrawal of Syrian troops from Lebanon in 2005 following large anti-Syrian protests in the wake of Lebanese Prime Minister Rafiq Hariri's assassination on February 14, 2005, *Hizbullah* became the most powerful armed force in Lebanon and also enhanced its political influence in the general election by gaining a seat in the Lebanese cabinet. This development was contrary to the aims of those who forced Syrian troops to withdraw. Nationally those actors included the Lebanese Prime Minister Fouad Siniora, the Druze leader Jumblat, the right wing of the Christian parties, along with the United States, France, and the oil-rich Persian Gulf Arab governments that were pleased with the Syrian withdrawal and promoted the capture of Lebanon for the West. However, the majority of the Lebanese remained the main source of support of *Hizbullah*.[7]

Hizbullah militia forces captured two Israeli soldiers and killed three others in cross-border attacks on July 12, 2006. Immediately, the Israelis demanded the release of the two soldiers or face military retaliation. *Hizbullah* expressed a willingness to swap the two Israeli soldiers for Lebanese prisoners, which was rejected by the Israeli government, which then immediately attacked the Lebanese civilian infrastructure and other targets. In retaliation, *Hizbullah* fired missiles at Israeli settlements, villages, and later the third largest Israeli city of Haifa. The Israeli air strike continued, and *Hizbullah* was able to put up a stiff resistance and fire missiles at the Israeli targets. *Hizbullah*'s military resistance and responses were the first ever by an Arab armed group or state since the establishment of the state of Israel. The confrontation, which involved the Israeli ground troops, lasted 34 days, and Israeli government and the military failed to secure the release of two soldiers, which was the principal reason for the war, in addition to disarming the *Hizbullah* militia.

Shortly after the outbreak of the war the governments of Egypt, Jordan, and Saudi Arabia—characterized by the Americans as moderate Arab governments—criticized *Hizbullah* for kidnapping the Israeli soldiers. King Abdullah sent his foreign minister Prince Saud and security advisor Prince Bandar—former Saudi ambassador—to the White House to persuade President Bush to pressure Israel to accept cease-fire. The foreign ministers of the three Arab "moderate" governments were invited to attend the Rome conference of July 26, 2006, in order to impose cease-fire, buth they also failed to persuade the Western governments in attendance, including the United States, once again. In Rome, the Western governments declined to intervene and stop the Israeli bombings. During a European Union foreign minister meeting in Brussels on July 24, there was a lengthy discussion that called on Israel not resort to "disproportionate action," which was a watered-down version of the original criticism of Israel after pressure from the U.K. and German governments, Israel's closest European Union allies.

In a private conversation picked up by an open microphone at the St. Petersburg G-8 summit, President Bush and the U.K. Prime Minister Tony Blair singled out the Syrian government for fueling violence in Lebanon, the Palestinian territories, and Iraq. Bush and Blair claimed that Damascus was trying to destabilize the region and prevent the spread of democracy. President Putin argued that "attacking Syria and Iran by name in the final communiqué would be counterproductive." But Bush disagreed by saying the root cause of the instability was *Hizbullah* and its relationship with Syria and Iran.[8] It should be noted that the Egyptian, Jordanian, and Saudi governments were the only Arab states to criticize *Hizbullah* for the capture of the two Israeli soldiers and start of the war. However, their criticism of *Hizbullah* sparked a wave of anger and street demonstrations in the Arab and other Muslim countries.

In a July 21, 2006, interview with Aljazeer's correspondent in Lebanon in connection with the Arab governments that criticized *Hizbullah* for starting the war and characterizing it as "miscalculated adventure," Nassrallah employed a famous Karbala—where the grandson of prophet Mohammad was killed along with his companions—quote to Muslims who let him meet his tragic fate: "Their hearts are with him but their swords are against him." Nassrallah added, "We don't want your swords or even your hearts. . .Just get off our backs."[9]

After his failure to persuade President Bush to impose cease-fire on the Israeli, King Abdullah of Saudi Arabia announced that he would give $500 million to Lebanon—obviously the government—to pay for reconstruction of the country, in addition to $1 billion for the Central Bank of Lebanon to support its economy and currency. Saudi Arabia has been a major supporter of Lebanon since the 1975–1990 civil war, which ended with the Taif peace deal. The Saudi king also announced that he would give $250 million to the Palestinians, who were suffering the effects of an Israeli onslaught following the capture of an Israeli soldier by Gaza-based militants. The king coupled his aid promises with an unusually forthright comment about the war. "Saudi Arabia warns everybody that if the peace option fails because of Israeli arrogance, there will be no other option but war," he was quoted as saying by the Saudi official press.[10] The king's statement was an effort to make up for his failure to convince the U.S. administration.

Shortly after the imposition of a cease-fire, the Qatari ruler—whose government has a friendly relationship with Israel—made a visit to Lebanon following his stopover in Damascus. His tour of the bombed areas was intended to show support and present his financial support of the Lebanese government in the reconstruction efforts, though no dollar figure was given. But *Hizbullah,* a popular grass roots organization specifically among the Lebanese *Shi'a* majority population, by then had begun its street-level, door-to-door assistance through its social and charity services, helping people who had been the target of the bombings by offering money for rents and household effects. No governments and businessmen—local and international—however rich, could match Hizbullah's grass roots network. Of course, *Hizbullah* would have the financial support of the Islamic Republic of Iran in its charity and social efforts.

Shortly after the cease-fire Nasrallah said on al-Manar TV:

> What I said in the first days of war (about reconstruction) wasn't to help you hang on...Today is the day to be true to these words and to deliver on the promise God willing, you won't need to ask favors of anyone or queue up or go anywhere (for financial assistance). Our brothers, who are your brothers will be at your service starting tomorrow morning everywhere in towns and villages.[11]

On August 28, 2006, in an interview on Lebanese TV, Nasrallah said, "Had we known that the kidnapping of the soldiers would have led to this, we would definitely not have done it." He added that neither side [*Hizbullah* and Israel] was "heading towards a second round" of fighting. "We did not think that there was a 1% chance that the kidnapping would lead to a war of this scale and magnitude." He added, "I would say no, definitely not, for humanitarian, moral, social, security, military and political reasons. Neither I, Hezbollah, prisoners in Israeli jails, nor the families of the prisoners would accept it." War left at least 1,287 people dead in Lebanon, nearly all of them civilians—30 percent of them children under 12—43 Lebanese soldiers and policemen, and 4,054 wounded. UNHCR reported at least 700,000 to 900,000 Lebanese were displaced. The cost of the damage for Lebanon, according to the government, was $2.5 billion, while others placed it at more than $7 billion. At least 160

Israelis were killed, mostly soldiers. The damage cost for Israel was estimated at $1.1 billion, and the number of displaced Israelis was estimated
at 500,000. Hizbullah casualties were reported at 74 dead, while its allied
Amal lost 17 members of its armed militia. U.N. Human Rights Chief
Jan Egeland accused Israel of "immoral use" of cluster bombs in Lebanon.
The report indicated that Israel dropped the bomblets during the last
72 hours of the war. U.N. inspectors found 100,000 unexploded cluster
bomblets at 359 separate sites, but a later report put the number of bomblets at 1 million in a region that has a population of 650,000. Egeland
added:

> Cluster bombs have affected large areas—lots of homes, lots of farmland.
> They will be with us for many months, possibly years—Every day, people
> are maimed, wounded and killed by these weapons. It shouldn't have hap-
> pened. Despite the return of the majority of the displaced people to the south,
> approximately 200,000 displaced people have not been able to rebuild their
> houses and livelihood destroyed by the Israeli bombings. Also an estimated
> 900,000 cluster bombs still after a year plague the land.[12]

However, in an interview with the Lebanese daily newspaper As-Safir
published on September 5, 2006, Nassrallah said, "The capture was
exploited [by the Israelis] for the timing of the war...but we think it has-
tened a war that was going to happen anyway and this was to our advantage and the advantage of Lebanon...I say we did not make a mistake in
judgment. Our calculations were correct and we do not regret it." The
Hizbullah leader argued that Israel was unable to achieve any of its
declared goals, including destroying *Hezbullah*'s rocket launchers
and infrastructure, pushing its fighters away from south Lebanon, and
freeing the two captured soldiers. He mocked Israeli Prime Minister
Ehud Olmert and said: "His only achievement was putting me in a shelter." Olmert rebuked Nasrallah on September 5, 2006, saying, "Someone
who doesn't come out of his bunker is not a person who thinks that
he's won."[13]

Naim Qassem, deputy general secretary of *Hizbullah,* said in an interview that armed militia would coordinate with the Lebanese army as it
moved into parts of south Lebanon dominated by *Hizbullah.* But *Hizbullah*
will not give up the concept of resistance against Israel on the grounds
that Israel continues to occupy the Shebaa Farms, holds Lebanese prisoners, and over-flies Lebanese territory almost every day. He said, "The jus-
tifications for ending it (resistance) are not yet there. When we agree on a
defense plan to confront Israel, defining the job of the resistance, the army
and the Lebanese people, then we will see what the rules and roles are."[14]
The refusal by Western countries to prevent the death and destruction of
the Lebanese would play a major role in the reception they would receive
in the predominately Shi'a south of Lebanon. It is not unusual for

Germany, the United Kingdom, and other Western supporters of Israel to decline any contribution of military forces for the U.N. peacekeeping troops in Lebanon.

The war against the *Hizbullah* and its stiff resistance to the bombings and ground attacks supported by the Western countries have for the first time placed it and Lebanese *Shi'a* not only in a direct confrontation with the Western countries, but also made it a hero in the Arab and Muslim world as the defender of the Islamic world against Israel. The war has also narrowed, if not removed, the long history of animosity between the Shi'a and Sunni—more than 90 percent of the world Muslims. Moreover, it has put the *al-Qa'ida's* world view on the back burner, or for that matter forced them to become more active.

HAMAS ACTIVITY IN THE ISRAELI AND PALESTINIAN TERRITORIES

In 1959 the spiritual leader of the Militant Islamist group HAMAS, Sheikh Ahmad Yasin, left Gaza for Egypt, where he spent a year studying in Ain al-Shams University. Yasin returned home influenced by Egypt's Muslim Brothers, an Islamist movement that inspired the ideological framework of HAMAS. However, the economic, political, and social conditions of the Gaza population were the principal factors influencing the ideology of HAMAS, which Sheikh Ahmad Yasin established in 1987. However, it should be noted that he registered *Al-Majma' al-Islami* (Islamic Association) in Israel in that year. The Muslim Brothers, who by then had established themselves in the occupied territories, created an underground movement by the name of HAMAS, which Israel viewed as counterweight to the PLO. Shortly after the first *Intifada* (uprising) in 1987, HAMAS became public and claimed itself as a challenge to the PLO in the occupied territories.[15]

The first Palestinian suicide bombing occurred on September 4, 1994, with an attack by a member of HAMAS and Islamic *Jihad* in Afula, Israel, in response to the Oslo Peace Accord.[16] Importantly, the first suicide bombing in Israel, in 1972, was perpetrated not by a Militant Islamist organization but by the Japanese Red Army, a radical leftist group that carried out terrorist acts in support of Palestinians. All the Palestinian suicide bombers have been Militant Islamists, not members of the Democratic Front for the Liberation of Palestine, a Marxist movement founded in 1969. HAMAS does not recognize Israel's right to exist and has been committed to destroying it. Since 1993, HAMAS has carried out numerous terrorist attacks against Israel. In 2000, it unleashed a deadly suicide bombing campaign in Israel for four years known as the *Intifada*, or uprising, which brought about widespread bombings, including suicide bombings, throughout Israel.

During a Friday prayer on December 27, 2002, just a day after the Israeli military forces killed nine Palestinians, HAMAS founder Sheikh Ahmed Yasin pledged, "The march of martyrs will move forward." He told approximately 40,000 HAMAS supporters at a Gaza City rally, "We have the right to defend ourselves with all means because the enemy is using all means to kill us. Jihad is our only way to win...Resistance will move forward, Jihad will continue, and martyrdom operations will continue until the full liberation of Palestine. The Zionist entity will fall within the first quarter of this century." With the rally, HAMAS marked the fifteenth anniversary of its founding.

The Israeli government of Prime Minister Ariel Sharon openly called for Yasin's assassination. On September 6, 2003, Yasin survived an attempt on his life when an Israeli F-16 fighter jet fired several missiles at a home in Gaza City. Then on March 22, 2004, the Israel military succeeded in assassinating him, along with nine other people. Yasin was replaced by Abdel Aziz al-Rantisi (a pediatrician) as the leader of HAMAS, but he, too, was assassinated just a month later on April 17, 2004, in Gaza City by an Israeli missile strike that also killed two others. Because of the previous assassinations of its leaders, Khaled Meshaal (who held a university degree in physics), became the HAMAS's overall leader and resided in Lebanon and Syria. Other prominent HAMAS officials who were killed by the Israelis include Ismail Abu al-Shanab, in August 2003, and Salah al-Shehada, the leader of Izzedine al-Qassam Brigades, in July 2002. Al-Shehada's successor, Mohammad al-Deif—whom Israeli authorities blame for the 1996 bombings—has managed to escape several attempts on his life. In the summer of 2003, Mahmoud al-Zahhar (personal physician of Sheikh Yasin) survived an Israeli air attack intended to kill him. His home was demolished and his son was killed.[17]

Although the Israeli government killed two previous HAMAS leaders, Mahmoud al-Zahhar, a senior HAMAS leader and spokesman for the movement, states that this will not deter HAMAS from continuing operations: "We try to take all possible cautions, but [are] never afraid. I was targeted twice. The first time, the mosque I pray in was bombed by an Israeli Apache helicopter. The second time, my home was demolished by bombs, [claiming] the life of my eldest son and seriously injuring my wife and my daughter besides myself. But fear never makes it to my mind, frightened leaders cannot lead people to victory."[18] The assassination of HAMAS leaders clearly indicates that Israeli intelligence and security forces have inside information regarding the whereabouts and the movements of these individuals.

Both the United States and the European Union formally list HAMAS as a terrorist organization; however, similar to *Hizbullah*, it has both military and political wings. In 2005 and early 2006, HAMAS successfully participated in the Palestinian political process, and thus, like *Hizbullah*, the U.S. administration and European Union officials may find it more advantageous to deal with HAMAS as an active political party.[19]

The European Union has some concern regarding its official contacts with HAMAS, which would make it difficult for it to influence HAMAS. However, the following development has made news, which may have some interesting implications since the death of Palestinian leader Yasser Arafat. European Union Foreign Policy Chief Javier Solana denied having had direct contact with the Palestinian militant group HAMAS since it was put on the European Union's list of banned terrorist organizations. Solana's office issued a statement clarifying an interview he gave to BBC Radio in which he appeared to confirm he had held secret talks with HAMAS a few months ago. "With reference to the BBC interview broadcast today, the office of the High Representative, Javier Solana, clarifies that at no time did Dr Solana wish to imply that direct contacts between himself and HAMAS had taken place," the statement said.[20] HAMAS announced on March 12, 2005, that it would end a long-standing boycott and participate in the Palestinian elections in July 2005. Its participation in the Palestinian political process will make the militant organization a major political force.

HAMAS boycotted the first legislative elections in the Palestinian territories in 1996 because of its opposition to the Oslo interim peace accords that mandated the ballot, and it refused in 2005 to put forward a candidate for the presidential election held in January, which saw Mahmoud Abbas elected to succeed the late Yasser Arafat as leader of the Palestinian Authority. The organization enjoys popular support among the Palestinian public, partly because of its fight against Israel but also because, like *Hizbullah*, it has provided welfare and social services to poverty-stricken Palestinians, especially since the start of the Intifada, when the Palestinian socioeconomic situation worsened. HAMAS's victory in the municipal July 2005 elections not only increased its political clout and popularity in the Palestinian territories, but also its power in the future peace negotiations with Israel.

The announcement that HAMAS would participate in elections came ahead of a meeting of all Palestinian factions in Egypt on March 15, 2005, where they discussed a cease-fire. The Palestinian national security authorities announced that all armed groups were ready to observe a truce following several months of an official period of calm.[21]

The success of HAMAS candidates in the local elections changed the view of outsiders, particularly the European Union, which dismissed the concerns of Israeli officials. On June 16, 2005, Israeli officials protested strengthening European Union contacts with HAMAS, which confirmed that its contacts with European Union diplomats were growing. Israeli authorities expressed their concern and encouraged the European Union member states to strengthen Palestinian moderates, meaning Abbas's *Fatah* party.

European Union states had reached no collective decision on whether to change its policy toward HAMAS and Palestinians in Gaza. HAMAS's growing clout is posing an increasing dilemma for the West because American and European Union agencies are locked into arrangements with Palestinian towns that are now run by newly elected HAMAS-backed mayors. However, the contacts between European Union officials and HAMAS leadership were carried out by low-level diplomats.[22]

The Bush Administration spent foreign aid money to promote the popularity of the Palestinian authority and its Fatah party against HAMAS candidates, who are popular among the Palestinians, on the eve of the January 2006 election in the Palestinian and Israeli occupied territories. HAMAS had already won a number of local municipal elections. The White House's backing of *Fatah* party candidates was a direct challenge to the Bush administration's program of "promoting democracy" in the region, as administration backing of the *Fatah* party was intended to alter the outcome of an open and transparent election.[23]

In connection with the August and September 2005 Israeli withdrawal from Gaza, Mahmoud al-Zahhar told Reina Frescó of Radio Netherlands, "We would give Israel a long-term truce if they withdrew from all occupied lands, stopped settlements and dismantled the existing ones, released all Palestinian detainees and, above all, if the Palestinian people were given a chance to live. But that does not mean that we will relinquish our rights in our land. We will never recognize the state of Israel or the occupation of a single inch of land." He contended that this is not only the position of HAMAS, but all Muslims. Reina Frescó posed the following statement to al-Zahhar: "If HAMAS were to win in the national elections and then take part in the Palestinian Authority, this would mean the HAMAS would have to lay down its arms." Al-Zahhar replied, "Our arms will turn to secure the achievements of our people . . .we will have national borders, an airport, seaport and holy shrines, which all need to be protected and secured. All liberation movements in the world turned their fighting movements to national armies after independence, why should HAMAS be an exception?"[24]

On the subject of whether HAMAS would stop targeting Israeli civilians after the August 2005 withdrawal from Gaza, al-Zahhar said: "The problem is definitely not HAMAS attacks, it is the continuation of occupation. Zionists occupied a part of the land in 1949 and took the rest in 1967. We have the right to resist the foreign occupation as do all other nations of the world, and calling that an attack on Israelis is simply not fair."[25]

In the January 2006 national election HAMAS won 76 of the 132 seats, beating the ruling *Fatah* party. President Bush, who said in 2003 that "in order for there to be peace, HAMAS must be dismantled," said after the 2006 election results that HAMAS is "a party with which we will not deal" unless it gives up violence and accepts Israel. The quartet of the United States, the European Union, Russia, and the United Nations,[26] which collectively drew up the road map, has also called on HAMAS to end violence and recognize Israel. On February 10, 2006, however, Russian President Vladimir Putin, during an official visit to Spain, announced that Russia issued an invitation to HAMAS leaders to visit Moscow in order to persuade the group to give up its radical policies, a deviation from the quartet's policy. The Russian invitation received the public backing of President Jacques Chirac of France, which infuriated Israeli officials, and created a crack in the European Union's policy toward HAMAS. Israeli officials said "it will not negotiate with HAMAS until it recognizes Israel's right to exist, renounces terror and accepts the Middle East peace process."[27]

The 2006 Palestinian parliamentary elections were free and fair, so HAMAS must be accepted as the legitimate winner of a majority of the seats. As responsible political players, they have to accept responsibility for running the day-to-day affairs of the Palestinian community, which includes participating in diplomatic negotiations, even those with Israel. At the same time, the United States and the European Union must accept the political reality that HAMAS is positioned to wield the greatest political power in the Palestinian territories. If it instead pursues a rejectionist policy by refusing to negotiate with HAMAS, this will do nothing to resolve the Palestinian-Israeli conflict. This conflict is one of the Militant Islamists's grievances with the West and U.S. policy in particular. Therefore, if progress is to be made on not only solving the Palestinian-Israeli question but also on quelling Militant Islamist terrorist action, the West must recognize that HAMAS, despite its terrorist activity, is also a legitimate political power.

On December 15, 2007, at least 300,000 Palestinians in Gaza turned out to mark twentieth anniversary of the founding of HAMAS—the biggest crowd since HAMAS seized power. Men, women, and children sang along with a popular HAMAS song, which starts: "HAMAS is not afraid of death." The turnout was intended to display the popular resolve of the Gaza Palestinians in the face of diplomatic and economic isolation of the HAMAS and the residents of Gaza. A large banner hung from a building near the scene of the rally that read: "We will not recognize Israel." The HAMAS prime minister, Ismail Haniya, whose government was fired by Mahmoud Abbas, said: "Your [participants in the rally] message today is that the movement will not surrender in front of such an embargo. We will not break. The root of the movement is like a good tree in good soil." On the occasion of the Muslim festival of Eid al-Adha (the festival of sacrifice), Haniya said, "is an Eid for an Islamic Arab Palestinian identity, an Eid for the project of Islamic Jihad." Khaled Mehal, the HAMAS political leader in exile in Syria, said the "Palestinians are capable of launching a third or fourth *Intifada* until victory is ours." He admitted that the anniversary came during "difficult circumstances and a painful situation for the besieged Palestinians in Gaza."[28]

The leaders of HAMAS continue to reject any negotiations with Israel or for that matter with Mahmoud Abbas and the *Fatah* organization, as the latter already began to negotiate with Israel following the Annapolis meeting sponsored by the Bush Administration and supported by the majority Arab and other Muslim governments. The "peace conference" did not invite HAMAS, thus setting the stage for further widening the division between the Gaza Palestinians ruled by the HAMAS and the West Bank dominated by Mahmoud Abbas's *Fatah* organization, which is backed financially and politically by the United States and the European Union and which continues to impose a collective boycott of the Gaza Palestinians.

On January 4, 2008, almost 20 days later, HAMAS leader Khaled Meshaal said on the occasion of the organization's twentieth anniversary: "some Europeans have offered us to meet indirectly with [the] Israelis to discuss a truce and we told them no and one thousands nos," adding that Palestinians have no choice other than "resistance." He did not identify the European government.

Meshaal also said he was ready to talk "unconditionally" with Mahmoud Abbas, the Palestinian president: "We are ready for an unconditional dialogue in which all issues will be discussed, including that of bringing forward elections. . .I say to the leaders of *Fatah* that our differences are political."

Meshaal reinforced that HAMAS rejects Abbas's rule of Gaza in current political, social, and economic conditions: "No Arab country has asked HAMAS to give up on the current situation in Gaza," adding that the government of Salam Fayyad, the prime minister appointed by Abbas, should "go. . .our people must stop this government from selling off Palestinian interests."

Mashaal also said that a recent U.S.-sponsored Israeli-Palestinian peace conference in Annapolis, Maryland, had not stopped the building of settlements in Palestinian territories nor improved the lives of Palestinians, noting that 560 Israeli checkpoints are still in place and still in force around the territories.

Mashaal said, "Give our people another alternative. As long as the horizons are closed and there are no other alternatives then there is nothing our people can do other than resistance." He said that since the time that HAMAS was founded in the late 1980s, its ability to hit Israel had improved. "HAMAS added momentum to the resistance with its special operations, whether martyrdom [suicide] operations, its performance, steadfastness or rockets."[29]

Israel's recent 22-day war on Gaza and HAMAS, similar to the July 2006 Israeli large-scale attack on Hizbullah, added to the credibility and stature of HAMAS's fervent ideology of resistance among the Arab public and Muslim nations in general. These events sparked widespread demonstrations, intensifying anti-Israeli sentiment in the region and throughout the world. Moreover, on December 27, 2008, Israel's military launched attacks, known as "Operation Cast Lead," on Gaza—a city with a population of 1.5 million—starting a sudden bombing campaign by Israeli jets, drones, and helicopters. The Israeli military targeted all government buildings, HAMAS leadership, mosques, private apartment buildings, and any site of manufacturing under the control of HAMAS. The military attacks, which were the bloodiest since the 1967 Israeli invasion of the Gaza Strip, were presented as a response to the rocket attacks by the HAMAS militia. However, the HAMAS militia rocket attacks started sometime in 1999. Apparently, the Israeli's massive land and air attacks were intended to stop HAMAS rocket attacks on Israeli towns and villages in close range of Gaza, but in fact their principal objective was to topple HAMAS—the de facto government in Gaza.

On January 18, 2009, after 22 days of war on Gaza, Israelis—acting under international pressure, particularly the UN Secretary General—declared unilateral cease-fire after 22 days of military invasion and attacks on Gaza that left more than 1,298 dead and over 5,000 injured.[30] The UN reported that the deaths included more than 400 children and 100 women. Arab leaders faced sharp criticism for the lack of action over Israel's offensive, and an emergency summit held in Doha earlier in the week revealed the sharp division among the Arab states. Egypt kept the Rafah border crossing closed to the Gazans during the Israeli attacks, and Saudi Arabia refused to attend the Doha meeting. The United States and European Union—which classify HAMAS as terrorists—did not take any steps to stop the attacks, and the two major Arab governments showed similar inaction.

Both Militant Islamist organizations emerged out of conflict with radical responses, such as suicide bombing and other forms of terrorism, toward achieving their "aims." After a long period of radicalism both organizations among all Arabs forced Israel to withdraw involuntarily from South Lebanon and Gaza. However, they also began to become politically involved, Hizbullah in Lebanon and HAMAS in the West Bank and Gaza territories, and both succeeded in winning elections, thus becoming more political rather than remain dedicated exclusively to arms struggle.

A number of parallels exist in the evolution of *Hizbullah* and HAMAS. Both emerged from conflicts with other groups and the foreign occupation, in this case the Israeli military, and both sought to achieve their aims through armed struggle and terrorist actions, particularly suicide bombings. Eventually, their activities forced Israel to withdraw from South Lebanon and Gaza. Both groups also effectively provided important social services to the population in their regions. Recently, the groups have become politically active, fielding candidates in and winning offices at the local and national levels in free and fair elections. As a result, the West and Israel must now determine how to deal with the two, particularly HAMAS, not solely as terrorists but also as legitimate political parties that now have responsibilities to their own communities and the world. However, the June 2007 armed clashes in Gaza that resulted in the ouster of Palestinian Authority from Gaza and subsequently the dismissal of the HAMAS-led prime minister have changed the picture in the Palestinian territories. Such developments were immediately welcomed and supported by the United States, Canada, and European Union by offering the *Fatah* government financial assistance. Such an approach is predicated on the assumption that the isolation of HAMAS would ultimately succumb to the international pressure.[31]

The Arab governments specifically and the Muslim countries in general are dominated by corruption and ruled by repressive regimes, assisted in this effort by the *Mukhaberrat* (secret police) and hired thugs (officially-named institutions to control public social and political behavior), while failing miserably to deliver services. However, *Hizbullah* and HAMAS have earned the reputation of being honest and efficient in delivering numerous services to their constituents. Thus, despite their Militant Islamist world view, they continue to play an important role in their respective lands even though they are characterized by the international actors (e.g., the European Union and the United States) as terrorists. In fact, their political, social, and armed actions in their respective lands have gained them respect among the Arab and Muslim public.

CHAPTER 9

Militant Islamists in Europe

The face of Militant Islamist terrorism has changed. It has become ideological, sometimes apocalyptic, highly mobile, and does not recognize national borders. In other words, it has become transnational. While it has become ideologically global, it acts locally and uses and exploits the latest informational technology tools. At the same time, Militant Islamists use the Muslim community to deal with those states that are labeled as a threat to Islam and Muslims in general, particularly those individuals who believe in or promote the "clash of civilizations" paradigm and view Islam and Muslims as the enemy of the West. Have such mutations in the Militant Islamist world view and terrorist activities developed to adjust to the modes of protection implemented by the Western states? Do the security threats emanate from within the Western nations or do they come from external forces?

Developments in Algeria in the past decade have had a direct impact on the development of Militant Islamists in the country and consequently on the militants activities in Europe, among them the Algerian *al-Salafi* Group for Call and Combat (GSPC) and other Militant Islamists who have been directly involved in the European militant activities. Since 2002 hundreds of people have been detained and nearly a hundred have been placed under investigation and jailed in suspected terrorism-related cases or activities. Beginning in 2005 at least 19 radical Muslim clergy were expelled from France.

French authorities cracked down on militant Algerian groups, especially the "almost psychotically violent" Armed Islamic Group (AIG). During the same time, the Algerian military government imprisoned or forced into exile many leaders of the militant Islamist party, FIS. As a result, the Algerian Islamic movement broke up into numerous militant groups. Among those groups that have taken responsibility for terrorist attacks are the AIG, the Movement for an Islamic State, the Army of the Prophet Muhammad, the United Company of Jihad, and the Armed Islamic Movement (AIM). Reports indicated that a number of militant Algerians had crossed into the United Kingdom because of its somewhat liberal political asylum system, which allows asylum seekers to stay in the country while their cases are processed.[1]

The GSPC is the principal group of Militant Islamists in Algeria's Islamist rebellion that has killed approximately 150,000 civilians, soldiers, and Militant Islamists since 1992. Such development came shortly after the Algerian intervention in the national election, which gave majority seats to the Islamist party. Algerian Militant Islamists are mostly followers of the *al-Salafia* Islamic school, which was developed in medieval times and is derived from the Arabic *al-Salaf al-Salih* ("the venerable forefathers," referring to the Prophet Muhammad and his companions. The school of thought believes Islam has been corrupted and seeks to restore its purity. The group was linked to the 2005 kidnapping of 32 European tourists, most of them Germans, in southern Algeria. It appears that the GSPC was responsible for a January 3, 2005, attack that killed 19 Algerian soldiers. According to authorities, the GSPC has between 300 and 500members and has become the only organized extremist group still operating in the country following the breakup of the AIG, once considered the deadliest radical movement fighting secular authorities. On January 3, 2005, Algeria's government reported that its security forces killed the AIG's leader in July 2004, which led to the "almost total collapse" of the group. It said that action by security forces had reduced the AIG to approximately two dozen and that the organization had split into two groups. The Algerian authorities claimed the end of the AIG, but continuing events and arrests indicate that the GSPC has, in fact, expanded its armed activities to other countries.[2]

In September 2007 the GSPC announced joining *al-Qa'ida* and changing the group's name to *al-Qa'ida* in the Islamic Land of Maghreb (AQLIM)—meaning in Libya, Tunisia, Morocco, Algeria, and Mauritania. The group increased its violent suicide terrorist attacks in 2007, which killed at least 156 people. In an attack on December 11, 2007, two separate suicide car bombers—one in the Ben Aknoun district near the country's Constitutional Council and the other close to the United Nations offices in the capital city Algiers—killed at least 37 people and wounded 170 others and destroyed many cars and buildings. The 63-year-old grandfather suicide bomber in one of the attacks changes the stereotype of the terrorist as a malleable, impulsive youth.[3] But a more concerning issue beyond that day's violence was whether the AQLIM's agenda extended beyond Algeria. The next day AQLIM claimed responsibility for the bombings and posted photos of the suicide bombers. Undoubtedly, AQLIM is connected to the global Militant Islamists "*Al-Qa'ida.*" This is worrisome for the European countries, especially the connection between the North African AQLIM and the European Militant Islamists. AQLIM is connected with the sub-Saharan networks of Militant Islamists as well, which has been detected by U.S. military intelligence.

Further indication of the spread of the AQLIM groups in North Africa and their aim on Europe is evident in the Moroccan court ruling of January 4, 2008, against a number of Militant Islamists who have been in custody for some time. The court convicted 50 Militant Islamists, including four women, for plotting bombings and robberies and sentenced them to prison terms from 2 to 25 years. The defendants were identified as members of the *Ansar al-Mehdi* (Companions or Partisans of Mehdi) organization, who were rounded up in 2006. The Moroccan security forces seized explosives and laboratory equipment.

All the defendants pleaded not guilty. The Moroccan authorities said the group, which planned to declare *Jihad* (holy war) in northeast Morocco, had recruited members of the police and the military and planned to rob banks and convoys and use the money to buy more explosives. The court found the defendants guilty of plotting to bomb government buildings and tourism landmarks in Casablanca and other cities and of belonging to an illegal group, collecting money to fund terrorism, and undermining state security and public order. Moroccan authorities claimed that they have broken up more than 50 cells and arrested about 3,000 people since 2003, when suicide bombings killed 45 people in Casablanca.

Morocco and the neighboring *Maghreb* governments have been on alert for attacks since AQLIM stepped up suicide bombings and other attacks in 2007. These governments feared a broad upsurge in violence in the region after AQLIM called on the other Militant Islamists to link up in the region and use it as a base for bombing European targets. Algeria has suffered a series of deadly bombings since early 2007, including a December 11 attack that killed 37 people. In Morocco, six Militant Islamist suicide attacks were carried out in Casablanca alone in 2007.[4]

Moreover, on January 4, 2008, the Dakar rally that goes through Morocco and Mauritania was cancelled for the first time in its 30-year history after threats from what organizers called "terrorist organizations." In Mauritania, three attackers suspected of links to *al-Qa'ida* killed four French tourists and wounded a fifth on December 24, 2007. Armed men killed three soldiers three days later on December 27 in a remote area in northern Mauritania, near the border of Algeria and Morocco's disputed Western Sahara territory in connection with the Militant Islamists and their European agenda.

Arrests and convictions of Militant Islamists in European countries continues unabated since the bombings and other attacks in the countries. Of the 18 suspects arrested or detained, 12 were Algerian, and all had applied for asylum. The British government had paid the rent on the raided apartment in Manchester because the tenants were asylum-seekers. The asylum system has generated several debates in the British Parliament, in which Liberals have defended the tradition of granting asylum while Conservatives criticized it. However, most of the estimated 9,000Algerians who began coming to the United Kingdom in the mid-1990s to seek asylum are thought to have legitimate cases, many of which are still pending.

French officials complained about the failure of the British to extradite or investigate militants posing as asylum-seekers. The militants, the French said, had congregated in mosques in London, Manchester, and Leicester. The French also said that the Algerians were setting up a network and raising money to support groups that were carrying out attacks in Algeria and France and were sending fighters to train for war in Afghanistan and Chechnya. It was there in the late 1990s, according to reports and French officials, that Algerian Militant Islamists began forming an ideological alliance with *al-Qa'ida.* That movement sought to unite disparate, angry, and Militant Islamists—from Maghreb countries to Southern Thailand, the Philippines, and elsewhere—and to channel their anger toward the United States, their ultimate enemy.

Despite the political finger-pointing and past intelligence service rivalries, the French and British intelligence services have improved cooperation in order to be more effective, and cooperation would demonstrate the importance of sharing intelligence more effectively as both countries increase their antiterrorism efforts.

MILITANT ISLAMISTS IN THE UNITED KINGDOM

In the United Kingdom police raided an apartment on January 5, 2003, as part of a sweeping investigation into what French and British counter-terrorism officials say was a cell of Algerian Muslim militants ideologically linked to *al-Qa'ida* and operating on both sides of the English Channel. Investigators say they think the group was plotting to develop the deadly toxin ricin[5] for a terrorist attack.

A Special Branch police officer was stabbed to death and three other officers were wounded while trying to arrest three Algerians, whom authorities have been questioning since their detention. One has been charged with murder in the stabbing. The officer's death and the arrests or detention of 18 North African suspects in London, Manchester, and Bournemouth to the south, reflected that Algerian militants had a broad presence in Britain. The Militant Islamists had spent years building a network of terrorist "sleeper cells" that went undetected, despite warnings from French and Algerian officials and at least one of the British government's own informants.

The head of Britain's MI5 domestic security service said on November 8, 2004, that Britons face a serious and sustained threat of terror attacks at home and abroad, despite the arrest and killing of many *al-Qa'ida* leaders. The Militant Islamists continue to inspire others. Moreover, the Militant Islamist cells are inventive, adaptable to the environment, and capable of changing their tactics. The British arrests suggest that with improved cross-border coordination, police are beginning to crack the Algerian terror cells that, authorities say, have grown in Britain in recent years, as Algerians have escaped a crackdown in France. The case, as with other arrests in France and Germany, points to progress in European efforts against potential terrorism.[6]

On November 22, 2004, British ITV television, quoting a senior official, said Britain had foiled an *al-Qa'ida* plot to fly planes into London's Heathrow Airport and the Canary Wharf financial district. The government recognized the severity of the Militant Islamist threat, so it announced a range of new measures to fight global terrorism and organized crime. The measures include the introduction of identity cards (which feature biometric details such as fingerprints and iris scans that were slated to be phased in during 2007 and 2008 as people apply to renew their 10-year British passports) and the establishment of a special police force similar to the FBI in the United States. British officials have long sought to introduce national identity cards, which are commonplace in most of Europe but have not been used in Britain since the end of the Second World War.[7]

Britian's Scotland Yard announced on August 10, 2006, that "A plot to blow up planes in flight from the U.K. to the U.S. and commit 'mass murder on an unimaginable scale' has been disrupted." British Home Secretary John Reid announced the arrest of more than 20 British Muslims of Pakistani origins, including two convert Muslims, from London, Buckinghamshire, and High Wycombe. Security officials believed that the aim of the terrorists was to smuggle explosives onto airplanes in hand luggage and to detonate them in flight. Their intended targets were flights from the United Kingdom to the United States. On August 11, 2006, the British authorities announced the arrest of 22 people by antiterrorism police. It was reported that the suspects were planning to blow up several planes by using liquid explosives carried in soft-drink bottles and detonators disguised as electronic equipment. On August 10, 2006, Pakistan announced it had made a number of arrests in connection with the investigation. Pakistani authorities reported the arrest of two British nationals of Pakistani origin in Lahore and Karachi a week earlier in connection with the alleged plot. The suspects were rounded up in raids in London, High Wycombe in Buckinghamshire, and the West Midlands. All were being held in London. Searches continued at several addresses, and people were evacuated from some homes in High Wycombe. Armed police were deployed in many airports, and passengers are no longer allowed to take their hand luggage into the cabin. Many flights on August 11 were grounded.[8] U.S. authorities viewed the plot as having an international scope, with the aim of carrying out the plan by using a number of aircraft.[9]

Security forces arrested 14 Muslims on September 1 and 2, 2006, after raiding a Chinese restaurant frequented by the Pakistanis, and the Manchester police arrested two others in northwest England. Police officials arrested the British Muslims under the Terrorism Act 2000, and police said they suspected the men had been involved in training and recruiting for terror attacks.[10]

Attacks in London, 2005

On July 7, 2005, three coordinated bombings were executed in the London underground train system and one on a double-decker bus. The bombs killed at least 52 people and injured more than 700 others. The London terrorist attacks came almost 16 months after the Madrid bombing of March 11, 2004. Four London bombers were Britons and three were of Pakistani descent. The immediate responses to the bombings ranged from utter anger to those who called for dealing with the root causes of terrorism perpetrated by the Militant Islamists. In an interview with CNN on July 9, 2005, King Abdullah of Jordan highlighted the Israeli-Palestinian conflict as one of the major sources of discontent among the Militant Islamists and labeled it as one of the root causes of actions by the Militant Islamists. The freedom of Palestinians and the freedom of Iraqis is used as a recruiting ground.[11]

On the other hand, British Prime Minister Tony Blair condemned the bombings on July 16, 2005, in a speech to the Labor Party and characterized the al-Qa'ida world view as an "evil ideology." One of Blair's former cabinet members, Clare Short, who resigned her post over the Iraq war, said in an interview broadcast on July 17, 2005, that she had "no doubt" the London bombings were connected to the war. "Some of the voices that have been coming from the government talk as though this is all evil, and that everything we do is fine, when in fact we are implicit in the slaughter of large numbers of civilians in Iraq and supporting a Middle East policy that for the Palestinians creates this sense of double standards—that feeds anger."[12]

On July 21, exactly two weeks after the July 7 bombing, four explosions occurred simultaneously in London—three blasts in the underground and one explosion in a double-decker bus. None caused any casualties, but they seemed to be a carbon-copy of the earlier bombings. Reports indicate that the perpetrators of the first bombing died in the explosions. It appears that the people involved follow the same Militant Islamist ideology as the earlier suicide bombers. Despite the amateurish nature of the second round of bombings, its psychological impact on Britain and possibly other target countries, such as Denmark and Italy, which were named in a Web site threat that came out immediately after the July 7, 2005, bombings, would be much larger. Thus, the message that the July 21 bombings conveys is more important than the limited physical consequence.

Al Jazeera television aired a video of one of the four July 7 London bombers, which he had taped before his suicide bombing. In the video Muhammad Sidique Khan, a Briton born in West Yorkshire, said, "Your [the West's] democratically elected governments continue to perpetuate atrocities against my people all over the world. Your support for them makes you directly responsible...until we feel security, you will be our targets. Until you stop the bombing, gassing, imprisonment and torture of my people, we will not stop." He continued, "We are at war and I am a soldier. But our words have no impact on you, therefore we will talk to you in a language you understand. Our words are dead until we give them life with our blood...I and thousands like me have forsaken everything for what we believe." Apparently foreshadowing his suicide bombing plan, he said, "I'm sure by now the media has painted a suitable picture of me. Its predictable propaganda machine naturally will tack a spin on things to suit the government and scare the masses to conform to their power—and wealth-obsessed agenda." This tape accompanied al-Dhawahiri's tape, mentioned above.[13]

An investigation of those behind the July 7 suicide bombers appears to have not produced any substantive information to assist the police authorities with preventing new groups from organizing and planning future bombings. Three of the suicide bombers were young Pakistani Britons who grew up in northeast England. The fourth was a longtime British resident of Jamaican origin. Shortly after the bombings, authorities searched for those who might have recruited, trained, or supplied the men. The official investigation, which took British investigators to Pakistan, led nowhere. Security forces had more success catching the group that attempted the July 21 copycat attacks in London. Four men were charged in the attempts, and a dozen others were accused of aiding them. Prime Minister Tony Blair had made battling terror and cracking down on those who spread radical ideologies a top priority since the July 7 attack.

After the bombings, Blair announced plans to work with moderate British Muslims on countering radical ideologies that have taken root among young people. He targeted militant preachers spreading a gospel of hatred, proposing legislation that would ban the glorification of terrorism and moving to deport some extremists. The revelation regarding the background of the bombers highlighted the problem that had been simmering for years—the alienation and economic marginalization of minority Muslim youth from mainstream British life. Many are children and grandchildren of immigrants from South Asia who embraced their new country's values. Authorities do not have any information concerning the number of radicalized young British Muslims. The alienation, marginalization, and the reluctance of the larger British community to accept the young generation of Muslims, along with the invasion of Iraq, the Palestinian-Israeli conflict, and the United Kingdom's unquestionable coat-tailing of U.S. foreign policy and military action in support of Arab authoritarian regimes, have contributed to their desperation and even disillusion toward their parents and community. Being cognizant of the system, however, Militant Islamists choose their friends from those they know well and maintain a very small group of close friends, thus making it difficult, if not impossible, to infiltrate militant groups even if the infiltrator is an immigrant and speaks a native tongue, such as Urdu or Arabic.

Britain's Home Office, in connection with the bombings, released reports that stated that there is "as yet no firm evidence" or direct verification of *al-Qa'ida*'s role, if any, in organizing the attacks which killed 52 commuters and four bombers. However, the suspected ringleader, Mohammed Sidique Khan, and accomplice Shezad Tanweer traveled to Pakistan in 2003 and between November 2004 and February 2005, respectively, and it is "likely that they had some contact with *al-Qa'ida* figures," said a second report by the Intelligence and Security Committee to a panel of nine British lawmakers.

In September 2005, Khan, the 30-year-old suicide bomber, made a farewell videotape that aired posthumously on Al Jazeera television. Khan said he was inspired by *al-Qa'ida* leader Usama bin Ladin, his deputy Ayman al-Dhawahiri, and by Abu-Musab al-Zaaqawi, leader of *al-Qa'ida* in Iraq, who was killed in Iraq.

The association of the *al-Qa'ida* leaders and Khan was considered to be the strongest link to the terror organization in the attacks. Britain's Home Office reported on May 11, 2006, that the inquiry was continuing. According to one of the reports, no links were found between the July 7 bombers and the group that mounted the failed bombing attempts against the London transport system on July 21. According to the report, security forces were surprised to learn that each of the two groups had members of Pakistani descent and one member originally from Jamaica. Security official said it appeared the attackers were motivated by "fierce antagonism to perceived injustices by the West against Muslims," and the intelligence officials have discounted claims that a foreign terrorist acted as a mastermind.[14]

This revelation is not unique to the United Kingdom and holds true for those Western European countries where a large Muslim population resides and works, such as France, Germany, Denmark, and the Netherlands. In publicly talking about the racial and religious problems that Muslims in Britain face, however, the British prime minister provided an opportunity for public discussion and debate about the problem. The measures that are introduced to deal with terrorism are of the utmost importance. Harsh and punitive governmental strategies against resident Muslim populations may play directly into the hands of Militant Islamists. At the East London Mosque, which has a large moderate congregation, director Dilowar Hussain Khan said the prime minister's efforts to crack down on militancy were likely to backfire and added, "Trying to push through this tough legislation, the government is playing into the hands of the extremists who say, 'See, they don't want you in their country.' " Some Muslims say they sense other Britons' wariness of them since the bombings. The brutal killing of an innocent Brazilian by the London undercover police in the underground metro after the July 21 bombing heightened the tension among the Muslim community.[15]

Failed car bombings, 2007

On June 29, 2007, British police discovered two cars—both Mercedes—containing petrol, gas cylinders, and nails in two locations in central London, Piccadilly Circus and Cockspur Street. Both cars were towed away by the police and had failed to explode. The next day, on June 30, a burning Jeep Cherokee loaded with flammable material rammed into Terminal 1 of Glasgow Airport. Scottish police arrested two men (Dr. Billal Abdullah) and one severely burned (Kafeel Ahmed, who holds doctorate in aeronautic engineering, who died of his burns in August) at the scene. Australian police arrest Dr. Mohammed Haneef at Brisbane Airport when he was on his way to India. On July 27, 2007, the Australian prosecutor dropped the terrorist charges against Mohammed Haneef after four weeks and he was released conditionally. The Glasgow attack apparently would have been a suicide car bombing if it would have succeeded. Immediately, the authorities raised the terror alert to red in the United Kingdom. Police linked the car attack to the Mercedes cars and classified them as attempted terrorist attacks. Police also said the new tactics of car bombing by terrorist cells are imminent in the United Kingdom. It should be noted that these were failed attacks, which occurred on the second anniversary of the 2005 London terrorist attacks that killed 52 people.

On July 1, the British security forces arrested eight people, including two in Glasgow, Dr. Mohammed Jamil Abdulkader Asha (a 26-year-old Jordanian) and his wife Marwa Daana Asha (a 27-year-old who was released a few days later with charge) who were picked up on the M6 Motorway. Others arrested in connection with the failed terrorist attacks of July 2 included Dr. Sabeel Ahmad, arrested near Liverpool's Lime Station, and Dr. Bilal Abdullah (Iraqi) and Dr. Mohammad Haneef, both arrested in Brisbane, Australia. A 28-year-old man and a 25-year-old man, thought to be medical students or doctors from Saudi Arabia, were arrested in Paisley. (On July 15 they were released with charges.) The unique feature of this attempted terrorist attack specifically at Glasgow Airport involved the highly educated as perpetrators, in this case physicians.[16] The failed attacks are clear evidence of a homegrown threat in the country, rather than looking far away for possible attacks.

ATTACKS IN SPAIN AND THE MARCH 11 MADRID ATTACKS

On January 24, 2003, Prime Minister of Spain José María Aznar announced that Spanish police officials had arrested 16 militants suspected of links to *al-Qa'ida*, breaking up two cells and confiscating electronic material and containers of unidentified chemicals. Those arrested were ready to commit attacks with explosives and chemical materials.[17] Police described the early morning raids on a dozen sites in the eastern provinces of Catalonia as an important move against a terror network linked both to *al-Qa'ida* and the AIG. The prime minister did not disclose the potential targets of the foiled attacks.

A statement issued by the Spanish officials said the suspects, members of a militant *al-Salafi* group that broke away from the Algerian GSPC, had bought communications equipment that was intended to be sent to Chechnya or Algeria and had shown interest in buying a transmitter with a range of more than 1,800 miles. Spanish authorities hoped the new arrests would make many people realize that the Spanish government is not talking about hypothetical or remote dangers.

The operation was carried out in close coordination with British and French intelligence. Spanish police said they found large quantities of chemical and explosive material, including time-switches, remote control detonators, and barrels of a suspicious recin. Officials were also reported to have found chemical warfare and electronics manuals and electronic equipment for forging documents and producing credit cards, as well as powerful radio transmitters.

The March 11, 2004, bombings of Madrid commuter trains killed 191 and wounded 2,000 people. The attacks were one of the deadliest terrorist assaults against the civilian population in modern Spain. Official statements issued shortly after the Madrid attacks identified ETA as the prime suspect, but the group, which usually claims responsibility for its actions, denied any wrongdoing. Later evidence strongly pointed to the involvement of the Moroccan Islamic Combatant Group.

Some 116 people were arrested, and in 2006 24 remained jailed in connection with the March 11 attacks on charges that included terrorism and mass murder. The others were freed, although they are still considered suspects and remain under court supervision. On February 1, 2005, Spanish authorities arrested a family of four Moroccans suspected to have links to the Madrid train bombings and issued an arrest warrant for a fifth Moroccan who might be the *al-Qa'ida* spokesman in the video who claimed responsibility for the attack.

The Spanish authorities also said on February 1 that investigations in Belgium had led Spanish investigators to think the spokesman in the video might be Youssef Belhadj, a 28-year-old Moroccan, who was later arrested in Belgium in March 2004 on suspicion of belonging to the extremist Moroccan Islamic Combatant Group. That group is believed to be tied to *al-Qa'ida* and was blamed for the May 2003 suicide bombings in Casablanca, Morocco, the Spanish Interior Ministry said.

The Casablanca targets included a Jewish community center, a Spanish social club, the Belgian consulate, a Jewish-owned restaurant, and a major hotel. The blasts killed 33 victims and 12 attackers. The family detained on February 1, 2005 (a married couple in their 40s and their two sons) were arrested in the Madrid suburb of Leganes, the Interior Ministry said. The family is believed to have helped two other suspects from the train attack flee after a collective suicide on April 3, 2004, by seven of the suspects, including several ringleaders, the Ministry said. The men killed themselves in an apartment in Leganes as police moved in to arrest them. The family was identified as Allal Mousatten, his sons Brahim and Mohamed, and their mother Safia Belhadj. It is not known whether the mother is related to Youssef Belhadj, the man sought in the arrest warrant.

The Spanish authorities believed the family also has links to Hasan al-Haski, a 41-year-old Moroccan arrested in the Canary Islands in December 2004. Al-Haski is suspected of helping prepare the Madrid bombings and of being a prominent member of the group blamed for the Casablanca bombings, according to the judge leading the probe into the March 11, 2004, attacks. After a two-year investigation, officials concluded that the Madrid attacks were carried out by a local Islamist cell inspired but not directed by *al-Qa'ida*. The court charged five people with 191 counts of terrorist killings and 1,755 attempted murders, while another 23 people were charged with collaboration. In comments on the 1,471-page report, a court spokeswoman said the Islamist cell had been inspired by an Islamic essay published online: "It [the Militant Islamist cell] took its inspiration from a Web site that called on local Islamists to stage attacks in Spain before the 2004 general elections to prompt withdrawal of troops from Iraq.["18]

The Madrid attack was a clear example of the localization of Militant Islamist terrorism, and perhaps signaled that *al-Qa'ida* was no longer a centrally operated organization. A terrorist campaign on the scale of the Madrid attack requires long-term planning to recruit, organize, and execute. Thus, *al-Qa'ida* may have been dismantled shortly after the invasion of Afghanistan, or even when the news of the invasion of Afghanistan was being discussed in public, but it has remained as an inspirational world view. However, the existence and spread of Militant Islamist cells remain the majority terrorist threat for the country. Spanish police arrested 15 people, 13 of them Moroccan, during a raid on May 28, 2007, on charges of sending money and recruiting fighters for Afghanistan, Iraq, and Africa. Eleven suspects were arrested in Barcelona and in two other northeastern towns. Two others were arrested in the central town of Aranjuez, and one in the southern city of Malaga. The spokesman said the police operation was continuing and that there could be more arrests. Spanish police arrested dozens of terror suspects since the September 11, 2001, attacks in New York and Washington, and again after the 2004 train bombings in Madrid. Currently, 29 suspects, mostly Moroccans, are on trial in the Spanish capital for their alleged roles in the Madrid train attacks.[19] The arrests are clear evidences that Spain is part of the global Militant Islamist terrorism campaign in Europe.

A two-year investigation of the Madrid train bombings concluded that the Islamic terrorists responsible for the attacks were homegrown Militant Islamists who acted on their own rather than receiving instructions or a directive from *al-Qa'ida*, two senior intelligence officials said. Spain remains home to a network of Militant Islamists of Algerian, Moroccan, and Syrian groups committed to carrying out attacks—and aiding the opposition groups against U.S. troops in Iraq—a Spanish intelligence chief and a Western official intimately involved in counterterrorism measures in Spain told the Associated Press. The Spanish intelligence could not find any phone calls between the Madrid bombers and *al-Qa'ida* and no trace of a transfer of funds. The plotters had links to other Islamic radicals in Western Europe, but the plan was homegrown, hatched and organized in Spain.

The Spanish authorities believe the ideological mastermind for the Madrid bombings was Serhan Ben Abdelmajid Fakhet, a Tunisian who blew himself up along with six other suspects when police surrounded their apartment three weeks after the bombings, and that Jamal Ahmidan, a Moroccan who also died that day, was a planner. At least three others— Said Berraj, Mohammed Belhadj, and Daoud Ouhane—are sought by authorities, although all are believed to have fled Spain long ago. The intelligence official said the top planners are all either dead or in jail.

The intelligence official also believed that the Madrid attackers were likely motivated by Usama bin Ladin's October 2003 call for attacks on European countries that supported the U.S.-led invasion of Iraq. However, no evidence of contact among them and *al-Qa'ida* were uncovered.[20] Most of the plotters were Moroccan and Syrian immigrants, many with criminal records in Spain for drug trafficking and other crimes. They paid for explosives used in the attack with hashish. That is a far cry from the September 11, 2001, attacks on the United States—allegedly planned by *al-Qa'ida* operatives such as Khalid Sheikh Mohammed and Ramzi Binalshibh and funded directly by *al-Qa'ida* through international wire transfers and Islamic banking schemes.

The absence of any trace of phone calls or transfer funds clearly supports that *al-Qa'ida* is not and never was a hierarchical and centralized organization. It was and still is an ideology, and those who had adhered to it even during the anti-Soviet war in Afghanistan were volunteers, and the acceptance of carrying terrorist missions was based on the same principles. However, it is important to note that the Madrid plotters were undoubtedly inspired by the *al-Qa'ida* ideology. Paul Wilkinson cautioned that the absence of a direct link between the Madrid terrorists and *al-Qa'ida* "doesn't mean none exists...If security officials knew everything that was going on, we would have caught Usama bin Laden by now."[21]

It appeared, and continues to be true today, that the authorities could not keep up with terrorists groups and individuals who continue to recruit new ones. What Western Europeans are concerned with in particular is understanding the recruitment and radicalization processes, the broader issues of the failure of social integration within many European states, and preventing the next generation from heeding the calls that bin Laden and al-Dhawahiri continue to make. Arrests clearly support the idea that local Militant Islamist movements have emerged throughout Europe. On January 12, 2005, Spanish police said they had detained Omar Nakcha, a 23-year-old Moroccan whom they suspected of being the leader of two extremist groups recruiting volunteers to fight in Iraq. He is described as "the head of two cells based in Spain and dismantled this week," and was picked up near Santa Coloma de Gramanet in the Catalonia region of northeast Spain. On January 9, 2005, Spanish police arrested 20 people in three towns believed to belong to cells that were recruiting volunteers to be sent to fight in Iraq and that have links with *al-Qa'ida*.

Nakcha was also sought in connection with the Madrid train bombings, the Spanish Ministry said. An Algerian suspect, Larbi bin Sellam, said Nakcha had organized the departure from Spain of at least two bombing suspects, the Ministry said. These were Mohamed Afalah, Mohamed

Belhadj, and "probably" Daoud Ohnane, who managed to flee an apartment at Leganes, in the suburbs of Madrid, although police had surrounded it. Seven of the suspected bombers died in the apartment in an explosion on April 3, 2004. Police said they had ties to the Moroccan Combatant Islamist Group and the Algerian GSPC, both linked to *al-Qa'ida*. They were also in touch with sympathizers in Algeria, Belgium, France, Iraq, Morocco, the Netherlands, and Syria.[22] The Madrid terrorist train bombings were Europe's worst terrorist attacks since the 1988 Pan Am 007 flight disaster over Lockerbie, Scotland.

At a three-day conference in 2005 in Madrid, the United Nations Secretary-General Kofi Annan said the commemorations were also for "the victims of September 11, 2001, and those of other terrorist attacks in Dar el-Salaam, Nairobi, Tel Aviv, Bali, Istanbul, Riyadh, Casablanca, Baghdad, Bombay, Beslan—indeed, all victims of terrorism everywhere, no matter what their nationality, race, or creed." Annan said the United Nations's strategy to fight terrorism comprises five elements:

- To dissuade disaffected groups from choosing terrorism as a tactic to achieve their goals.
- To deny terrorists the means to carry out their attacks.
- To deter states from supporting terrorists.
- To develop state capacity to prevent terrorism.
- To defend human rights in the struggle against terrorism.[23]

THE NETHERLANDS

On November 2, 2004, Dutch police stormed a flat in The Hague after a 14-hour standoff in which four officers were wounded, arresting two people and elsewhere five more, all suspected of links with a network of Militant Islamists. Hundreds of police had laid siege to the building after a predawn raid in which the suspects resisted arrest and threw a grenade. Four officers were hurt, one of them seriously, when the grenade exploded. Police had originally said three were wounded. Han Moraal, chief public prosecutor, said the two arrested were suspected of plotting murder with a "terrorist intent" and were charged with attempted murder or homicide of policemen. Police said one of the suspects was shot in the shoulder when a special police unit entered the apartment. A spokesman for the prosecutors office said four people in Amsterdam and one in the central town of Amersfoort were detained, in addition to the pair held after the siege in The Hague. "The investigation is into a network of radical Muslims," a Dutch official told a news conference, but declined to give the nationalities of those detained. Police said the raid was not linked to an investigation into the murder on November 2, 2004, of filmmaker Theo Van Gogh by an Islamic extremist, but was part of a separate investigation into suspected terrorists.

Dutch filmmaker Van Gogh was assassinated by a 26-year-old suspected Dutch Moroccan militant Muslim. Van Gogh was knocked off his bicycle by the bullet shots fired from a 9mm handgun. He struggled to the other side of the road, where he collapsed in front of a shop. The Militant Islamist assailant crossed the road to where Van Gogh lay, and opened fire again. Eight bullets were later found in his body. The assailant continued his heinous crime by affixing a five-page letter to the corpse by thrusting a knife into Van Gogh's chest. The letter was addressed to Ayaan Hirsi Ali, the author of a film that suggested that the *Qur'an* sanctioned domestic violence. Following a shoot-out with police, Mohammed Bouyeri, a second-generation Moroccan, was arrested nearby. In the note found with Van Gogh's body, Bouyeri warned "There will be no mercy for the wicked, only the sword will be raised against them." In another note, written as a last testament, which the police found on Bouyeri, he said, "These are my last words, riddled with bullets...smeared with blood...like I hoped."[24] Van Gogh had enraged Muslims with a film accusing Islam of promoting violence against women. Police arrested 10 people in the Van Gogh investigation and as of May 2006 were still holding six, including the prime suspect who is also charged with links to a group with terrorist plans. Prosecutors said they were looking for other militant cells and possible links with international Militant Islamist groups.

The 47-year-old Van Gogh had made a controversial film, *Submission,* which was critical of Islamic culture. The 11-minute film is about Islamic violence against women. The film was written and narrated by Ayaan Hirsi Ali and directed by Van Gogh. Van Gogh's and Ali's aims were to illustrate domestic violence in Muslim societies and to denounce oppression of women in the name of the Qur'an. Ayaan Hirsi Ali is an immigrant born in Somalia and a member of the Dutch Parliament who was already under police protection at the time of Van Gogh's murder. Because of threats made against her after the film's release, Hirsi Ali was encouraged by the Dutch government to leave the country and travel to the United States for three months.

Submission denounces the barbaric treatment of women in many Islamic societies, focusing attention on forced marriage and the penalization of rape victims under the guise of adultery. The film featured images of *Qur'an*ic verses daubed on semi-nude women's legs, stomachs, and backs. In this film Hirsi Ali, calls the Prophet Muhammad a "lecherous tyrant," Islam a "backward religion," and the Koran [sic.] "in part a license for oppression." Theo Van Gogh dubbed Muslims "goat-fuckers," a radical Islamic leader "Allah's pimp," and Islam a "retrograde and aggressive" faith.

Their film was broadcast on Dutch national television in August 2004. It depicts, among other scenes, a beautiful young Muslim girl addressing Allah in a mosque. She wears a veil that covers her face, but her naked body is clearly visible through a transparent gown. "All praise to Allah, the Lord of the Worlds," says the text that scrolls across the actress's throat and down her breasts which is the *al-Fatiha,* or opening of the-*Qur'an.* Other scenes portray a Muslim woman who is forced into an arranged marriage, abused by her husband, raped by her uncle, and then brutally punished for adultery. In a third, a woman's bruised and beaten shoulders are covered with lines from verse 34, chapter 4 of the *Qur'an:* "Men are the maintainers of women because *Allah* has made them excel...The good women are therefore obedient. Those on whose part you fear desertion, admonish them, and leave them alone in the sleeping-places, and beat them." Damning Islam as a "backward, twelfth-century religion," a "medieval, misogynist cult incapable of self-criticism and blind to modern science," Hirsi Ali said orthodox Muslim men routinely indulge in domestic violence against women as well as incest and child abuse. To make matters worse, she argues, their behavior is invariably hushed up. The film was a potent, if undeniably provocative, interpretation of Hirsi Ali's thesis.[25]

The hideous murder act—as Van Gogh writhed on the ground, the murderer cut his throat and left him with two knives protruding from his body—happened almost 15 years after Ayatollah Khomeini, the founder of the Islamic Republic of Iran, issued his fatwa against Salman Rushdie, which was the first cultural war between a Muslim cleric and the West. However, there is no precedent for the slaughter of a prominent artist in broad daylight on the streets of Amsterdam, in the Netherlands, one of the most tolerant of European cultures and nations since the Dutch revolt against Spanish rule four centuries ago. The crime resonates not only in the Netherlands but also throughout Europe, if not the world.

Dutch authorities are investigating a radical Muslim group they suspect is linked to the man accused of killing Van Gogh and to the 2005 Casablanca bombings discussed earlier in this chapter. Dutch authorities confirmed that 13 young Muslims who were arrested on terrorism charges in the Netherlands after the murder of filmmaker Van Gogh are members of a radical Islamic group with international links and a Syrian-born spiritual leader. Dutch intelligence calls the group the "Hofstad Netwerk," and the 43-year-old Syrian Redouan al-Issar, the alleged spiritual leader, has disappeared without a trace.

The assassination prompted politicians and government leaders, including then Chancellor Gerhard Schroeder, to send a message to

Muslims immigrants: learn German, fit in, and commit to democratic rules. More than anything, politicians and law enforcement officials worry that Muslims who reject German culture are more susceptible to radical Islam. After the assassination of Van Gogh, Dutch police discovered a Militant Islamist cell with a "death list." Since the discovery, police are taking seriously the threats against those whose names appeared on the list.

Dutch Interior Minister Johan Remkes and Justice Minister Piet Hein Donner told parliament in a 60-page letter that Bouyeri, charged with murdering Van Gogh, assisted a radical group under observation since summer 2002. A group of young Muslims of North African origin was centered in Amsterdam and often met at the home of Mohammed Bouyeri. He was charged with killing Van Gogh, conspiracy to murder a politician, and as a member of a group with "terrorist" plans.

The member of the group had visited Pakistan, possibly for training in Militant Islamist terrorist campaigns, and had contact with a man suspected by the Moroccan officials of involvement in a May 2003 killing of some 45 people who was arrested by Spain in October 2003. Dutch officials pointed out that these Militant Islamists are believed to have been under the influence of the Redovan al-Issar for many years. However, officials believe those who think and act in terms of actual violence in the Netherlands are small in numbers. However, the ideology is widespread among thousands of Muslims.

Al-Issar went by several names, including "Abu Khaled," the Justice Ministry official said. An *al-Qa'ida* fugitive, Muhammad Bahaiah, who is a known courier between bin Ladin and European cells, uses the same name. Al-Issar had sought asylum in Germany beginning in 1995, but has not been seen there since May 2004. The Dutch secret service realized in spring 2003 that al-Issar was "a leading figure" who preached at fundamentalist gatherings at Bouyeri's Amsterdam home. Al-Issar is characterized as charismatic and therefore exercises great influence on the Muslim youth, especially those involved in the network. Thus, the authorities remain worried that there would be another attack similar to the one that killed Van Gogh because the Dutch are part of the Western target of the Militant Islamists.[26]

On December 23, 2004, the Netherlands intelligence service, known by its acronym AIVD, released a report, "Violent Jihad in the Netherlands," warning that radical Islamic ideology was spreading to thousands of young Dutch Muslims through Internet sites and online chat rooms. The spread of radical Web sites as an alternative to traditional outlets of Islamic teaching, such as mosques, makes it harder for authorities to isolate potential threats. These Web sites contribute to the spread of radical ideology among Muslim communities in the country.

The agency identified the potential threat in an overview of domestic radical Islamic movements compiled for the Home Affairs Ministry in the wake of the country's first terrorist attack. The publication came out nearly two months after the murder of Van Gogh and said a variety of sources of Muslim radicals pose a threat to the country, ranging from *al-Salafi* mosques openly preaching anti-Western, antidemocratic ideas to an underground political movement backing violent Militant Islamists. It points out that the Netherlands has been confronted with extreme violence and goes on to highlight the Madrid train bombings on March 11, 2004, and Van Gogh's murder on November 2, 2004. The report lists 20 guidelines for reducing the threat of radicalization, such as promoting positive role models and the emancipation of Islamic women, but it warns against focusing on terrorist groups and ignoring the social problems that lead some young people to militancy. It also sees problems in "al-Dawa" movements, which are not violent but promote a radical Islamic ideology. Al-Takfir (state of unbelief) movements, which seek to convert immigrant Muslims in the West back to the fundamentalism of the Muslim community of the seventh century, are also seen as problematic.[27]

The AIVD said fighting extremist Muslims demanded much more subtlety and that concentrating only on Usama bin Ladin and *al-Qa'ida* Militant Islamists was a mistake, as many militants operated outside any formal group structures. The intelligence service, which had previously said it is monitoring about 150 suspected Militant Islamists in the Netherlands, now claimed that "several thousand" Muslims, mostly youngsters, were vulnerable to the appeal of radical Islam. "Classical ways of fighting terrorism without consideration for processes of radicalization and prevention will have little effect in the long-term. . .Preventing, isolating or containing radicalization is an important way of fighting terrorism durably. . .Recruitment of Dutch youths with mostly foreign roots for the armed radical Islamic struggle is rather a trend than an incident in the Netherlands."[28]

Relations between the native Dutch population and the Muslim community have been strained since Van Gogh's murder, which prompted a wave of attacks and counterattacks on mosques and Christian churches. There are roughly 1 million Muslims in the Netherlands.

Militant Islamists have threatened their targets through the use of information technology. Sometimes the threats come by e-mail, and other times warnings show up on Internet chat sites. Occasionally they appear in the form of short video clips. A video that appeared in 2005 has a soundtrack of an Arabic song and automatic-weapons fire, and it calls for the beheading of Dutch lawmaker, Geert Wilders, and shows a photograph of the intended target. In Arabic, the speaker says, "He is an enemy of Islam and he should be beheaded. . .and you will earn a place in paradise." Wilders's response was, "I've been threatened many times. We've never experienced this before. It's something that nobody wants to live with." He is among the more provocative critics of radical Islam and immigrants in the Netherlands. He wants the preemptive arrest of suspected terrorists, whom he calls "Islamo-fascist thugs." He wants immigrants expelled from the country for even minor infractions. Wilders's transgression, according to the radical Muslims, is his insulting of Muslims in the Netherlands, with frequent denunciations of Islam. He has said, "Islam and democracy are fully incompatible...They will never be compatible—not today, and not in a million years."[29]

The degree of fanaticism of the Militant Islamists in the Netherlands became clear when Van Gogh's assassin, Mohammed Bouyeri, stunned the courtroom on July 12, 2005, in the final minutes of his two-day trial, when he told Van Gogh's mother,

> I don't feel your pain...If I were released and would have the chance to do it again...I would do exactly the same thing...What moved me to do what I did was purely my faith....I was motivated by the law that commands me to cut off the head of anyone who insults *Allah* and his prophet.[30]

The assassination led to an intense national debate over the integration of Muslims, who make up 6 percent of the Netherlands' 16 million people. Bouyeri was born in Amsterdam to Moroccan parents. Bouyeri's court statement was his first public comment since he had been arrested after the slaying. He had not mounted a defense during the trial and ordered his lawyer not to speak.

According to the AVID report, despite the arrests and in some cases the convictions of members of the "Hofstad" group, there is not much optimism about the decline of terrorist threats in the Netherlands. Radio Netherlands quotes the report as saying, "The radicalization of young Muslims, most of them from a Moroccan background, continues unabated; terrorist networks are growing more diffuse and hence more difficult to keep tabs on. The AIVD also warns that, in the worst-case scenario, Dutch society could risk falling apart along ethnic and religious lines." Radio Netherlands reports that "The AIVD's later report points to a change that has taken place since 2003 within radical Islamic groups operating inside the Netherlands. Up until 2003, some mosques provided their main source of inspiration. There was also a strong foreign influence from, for example, veterans of the jihad who'd fought in places such as Afghanistan and Chechnya, and from foreign 'preachers', including Radwan al-Issa, regarded as the man who inspired the members of the Hofstad group. The AIVD report in fact employs a new term for the final 'step' some may take to a violent course of action: 'jihadization'."[31]

However, the AIVD report points out the differing pattern of radicalization in the Netherlands, in broad terms, from that found in other European countries. The Militant Islamists in the Netherlands seem to be interested more in individual targets, such as Van Gogh, Ayaan Hirsi Ali, and Geert Wilders, rather than attacking buildings or infrastructures. In addition, the advanced level of female emancipation in the Netherlands also seems to be finding echoes in the Militant Islamist circles, despite the fact that these circles so fiercely reject Dutch society. In the Netherlands, young Muslim women play a significant role, while in other European countries Muslim women do not seem to be playing any role in the violence perpetrated by the Militant Islamists.[32]

Clearly, the invasions of Afghanistan and Iraq have contributed to the spread of the *al-Qa'ida* ideology and Militant Islamist activities in Western Europe. However, Dutch observers contend such influence and particularly the Salafi groups in the Netherlands have been limited.[33]

MILITANT ISLAMISTS IN GERMANY, FRANCE, AND ITALY

Germany has one of the largest Muslim populations in the European countries and has been involved in a number of international conflicts, specifically Afghanistan and its close cooperation with the United States in foreign policy. German authorities believe that three arrested Iraqis on December 3, 2004, were members of *Ansar al-Islam fi Kurdistan,* a Militant Islamist terrorist group that originated in Kurdish areas in northern Iraq and which the United States has held responsible for numerous suicide bombings in Iraq. All three suspects were held due to their alleged membership in *Ansar al-Islam.* A German intelligence official said that the three had been under observation for at least several months. Mullah Krekar, the founder of *Ansar al-Islam,* had been questioned in Oslo by German police before the arrests.

German security officials believe that the suspected assassination plot was a sign that for the first time, Iraqi Militant Islamists were attempting to organize attacks outside their own country, which is a clear indication of the existence of Militant Islamist terrorist cells in the country who are looking for opportunity. German authorities had several members of the German-based al-Tawheed in their custody. In fact, German federal prosecutor Kay Nehm said *Ansar al-Islam* has about 100 supporters in Germany, and the United States has linked the group, which has claimed responsibility for a series of attacks in Iraq, to *al-Qa'ida.* Germany has been investigating the group's activities, which Nehm said included fund-raising, trafficking, and propaganda.

Lokman Mohammed, a Kurd who has lived in Germany since 2000, joined *Ansar al-Islam* in the first half of 2002. The group has said it killed soldiers in the U.S.-led coalition and abducted foreigners working in Iraq. Ansar al-Islam was founded in northern Iraq in September 2001 with the aim of building an Islamic state there modeled on the Taliban administration that ruled Afghanistan from 1996 to 2001, the prosecution said. The group renamed itself *Jaiysh Ansar al-Sunna* after the 2003 U.S. -led invasion of Iraq and said it carried out several attacks, including bombings, shootings, and kidnappings. German police said the defendant was active in logistics, financing, and recruitment. Lokman helped recruits living in Germany move to Iraq to join the insurgency, arranged for wounded fighters to have medical treatment in Europe, and sent donations, passports, medical equipment, and computers to Iraq, the court said. Germany introduced new antiterrorist laws in 2002 after discovering that four of the hijackers in the September 11 attacks had lived in Hamburg.[34]

Following the December 3, 2004, arrests, German police took 22 suspects into custody on January 12, 2005, during nationwide raids of a network of Muslim radicals that uncovered Militant Islamist propaganda and forged passports. Authorities said the roundup at mosques and homes in five German states included supporters of Ansar al-Islam, which security officials classified as top security risks, but there was no evidence that the group had planned imminent attacks. Police said the suspects, aged 17 to 46, included German citizens and nationals of Egypt, Tunisia, Algeria, Libya, and Bulgaria. Thus, it appears that some Militant Islamist cells in Europe are multinational, while others recruit among those with close ethnic affiliation.

German authorities immediately increased their monitoring of Muslim radicals, focusing on *Ansar al-Islam*, which is suspected of recruiting for Iraq from Germany and other European countries. Evidence indicated that besides *Ansar al-Islam*, members of the network also had links to the radical Palestinian group al-Tawheed.[35]

A German Muslim convert by the name of Abdul Gaffar al-Amani, known as Eric B. and a member of Islamic Jihad Union (IJU), posted an Internet message on June 10, 2008, claiming responsibility for a suicide attack in the eastern Afghan city of Jalalabad. This suicide bomber, according to the Internet message, went by the *norm de guerre* Said Kurdi. Eric B. is believed to be an active member of IJU, and in the same iInternet message claimed responsibility for training Guneyt Ciftci, a German-born Turkish citizen who is believed to have been the first German-born suicide bomber responsible for the early 2008 bombing of the government building in the Khost province of Afghanistan.[36]

As part of the same development in Germany and other Western European countries, security official adopted a more aggressive approach toward radical imams as part of an increasing effort to monitor and restrict militant imams across Europe. Authorities stepped up surveillance of militant imams in several countries, including Germany and France. French officials deported an imam after officials said he was inspiring men to join the jihad. Concerns are that militant imams may encourage young Muslims to join radical causes and movements throughout the world, including Iraq.

Although the dimensions of the recruitment effort from Europe to Iraq are not clear, there are indications that it is intensifying. The German arrests of January 12, 2005, were part of an ongoing investigation, in cooperation with the United States, of recruitment and other terrorist activities in Europe. German security officials said that, like their counterparts in Britain, they have seen indications of an increase in attempts by Muslim groups in Germany to recruit young Muslim men to travel to Iraq to fight. Officials say some men have planned to go to Iraq to carry out suicide bombing missions.

Italian investigators say several recruits from Italy carried out bombing attacks in Baghdad. Swiss officials say they are concerned that several militant clerics have openly urged men to become terrorists, and in Jordan senior officials say they have recently arrested several dozen men who intended to cross the Iraqi border to serve as foreign fighters.

According to the French intelligence officials, an imam was deported from France to Algeria for encouraging young men in a working-class neighborhood of L'Ariane, outside Nice, to join the Militant Islamists.[37] As part of the ongoing investigation, French security agents from DST, a domestic intelligence agency, detained five men and two women on January 24, 2005, who were suspected of involvement in a network recruiting French Militant Islamists to go to Iraq. DST officials announced that this operation allowed security to completely smash this network. This is the first operation of its kind, and an important one. The fight against radical Islamic groups is one of the top priorities for the Interior Minister. The arrests were the result of an investigation that began on September 22, 2004, to determine whether a network existed in France for recruiting and sending Muslim Militants to Iraq to fight American-led forces. The investigation was opened after the bodies of several French citizens were discovered in Iraq. There have been numerous arrests of members of suspected *al-Qa'ida*-linked Militant Islamist cells in France. Militant Islamist campaigns in France are not new; in fact, they have been involved in several terrorist campaigns, specifically those in 1995. A series of attacks were carried out in the summer of 1995 by Armed Islamic Group, when it bombed the Paris Metro on July 25, killing eight people and injuring 100 others. On August 17, a bombing at the Arc de Triomphe wounded 17 people, and on September 3 a bomb malfunctioned in Paris and injured four. In a final attack on September 7, a car bomb at a Jewish school in Lyons injured 14 people.

French police, probing a ring of young French Muslims, who allegedly recruited other young French Muslims to fight in Iraq against the U.S.-led forces, arrested six men in the Paris area on September 19, 2005. The suspects were in their twenties and thirties. This was the second raid of suspected Militant Islamists cells by French security forces, following an operation in Paris in January 2005 that resulted in the arrest of 11 suspects. French authorities believe young Muslim immigrants from North African countries were enlisted to join the opposition fighters in Iraq often on an individual basis in prayer rooms or through family members. French security officials say that 21 young French Muslim men were identified as having participated in combat in Iraq in 2004. Six were killed either fighting U.S.-led forces or in suicide bombings, three were taken prisoner, and the fate of a dozen others remains unknown.[38]

A direct threat to Europe and particularly France came in a video. Ayman al-Dhawahiri, the second in command of *al-Qa'ida*, on the occasion of the fifth anniversary of the September 11, 2001, terrorist attacks on the United States, urged the Algerian Militant Islamist group GSPC—the Salafist Group for Preaching and Combat—to punish "Crusader nation" France, even though it vehemently opposed the U.S.-led war in Iraq. The term Crusader refers to medieval military campaigns waged in the name of Christendom to recapture the Holy Land from Muslims and is frequently used by the Militant Islamists and other radical Muslim circles to designate enemies of Islam. The GSPC emerged from the Armed Islamic Group (see Table 3.2), which was blamed for a massacre of civilians during a bloody insurgency against Algeria's military-backed government in the 1990s. Close French intelligence links with its former North African colonies combating Militant Islamists and its role in NATO operations in Afghanistan against the Taliban militia have placed France as a "Crusader nation." France has also dispatched some 2,000 troops to join a peacekeeping force in its former protectorate Lebanon, putting it in the front line of a mission that Dhawahiri has denounced. On September 11, 2006, the head of the DST domestic security service said the threat of terrorist attack remained "very high and very international."[39]

Moreover, on the eve of the *al-Qa'ida's* threatening video came Pope Benedict XVI's statement made while visiting Germany. In his speech at Regensburg University, the German-born Pope explored the historical and philosophical differences between Islam and Christianity and the relationship between violence and faith. Stressing that they were not his own words, he quoted Emperor Manuel II Paleologos of the Byzantine Empire, the Orthodox Christian empire that had its capital in what is now the Turkish city of Istanbul. The emperor's words were, he said,

"Show me just what Muhammad brought that was new and there you will find things only evil and inhuman, such as his command to spread by the sword the faith he preached." Benedict said "I quote" twice to stress the words were not his and added that violence was "incompatible with the nature of God and the nature of the soul...The intention here is not one of retrenchment or negative criticism, but of broadening our concept of reason and its application." He added in the concluding part of his speech, "Only thus do we become capable of that genuine dialogue of cultures and religions so urgently needed today."[40]

His statement generated mild to very harsh responses from the Islamic world. In fact, the Vatican's statement failed to quell criticism of the Pope from Muslim theologians, politicians, and others throughout the Islamic world. The Pope's statement—while occupation of Afghanistan and Iraq remain and the Palestinian-Israeli conflict continues, in addition to the cartoons of prophet Mohammed —undoubtedly will fuel and present opportunities to the Militant Islamists. Meanwhile, the "hostile" remarks drew a demand for an apology from a top religious official in Turkey.

Ali Bardakoglu, Turkish minister of religious affairs, recalled atrocities committed by Roman Catholic Crusaders against Orthodox Christians and Jews as well as Muslims in the Middle Ages. In Egypt, Muslim Brotherhood head Mohammed Mahdi Akef said the Pope's words "do not express (a) correct understanding of Islam and are merely wrong and distorted beliefs being repeated in the West."

The 57-nation Organization of the Islamic Conference also said it regretted the Pope's remarks. The head of the Muslim Brotherhood said the Pope's remarks "aroused the anger of the whole Islamic world." Pakistan's parliament passed a resolution demanding that the Pope retract his remarks "in the interest of harmony between religions." The derogatory remarks of the Pope about the philosophy of jihad and Prophet Mohammed "have injured sentiments across the Muslim world and pose the danger of spreading acrimony among the religions," the AFP news agency quoted the resolution by the country's national assembly as saying.[41] This particular development will have not only regional (Europe), but also global impact on the Christian and particularly Catholic and Muslim relations. A collection of responses and reactions to the Pope's expression of "sorrow" and "regret" in connection to his speech would be useful for this study.[42]

French counterterrorism officials continue to focus on the North African Militant Islamist groups operating in Europe as they attempt to not only recruit from within Europe but also "import" recruits. Antiterrorism police arrested 11 people in coordinated raids in France and Italy as part of a probe into the financing of Islamic extremist groups, sources close to the investigation told *Agence France-Presse*. Five of the suspects were arrested by French police near the Mediterranean port city of Marseille, while Italian authorities arrested six others around Naples, the sources said. France's DNAT antiterrorism investigators and Italy's DIGOS anti-terrorism forces are investigating groups suspected of financing Islamic terror groups via a range of criminal activities including forgery, the sources said. The Italian news agency Ansa reported that raids had also taken place in the southern town of Caserte and in Milan in the north, targeting both Italian and Algerian nationals.

Investigators are trying to determine whether the activities in Italy benefited Islamist extremists, particularly Algeria's *al-Salafi* GSPC, according to a French diplomat in Rome. The diplomat said the suspects—for whom European arrest warrants have been issued—are thought to be linked to illegal immigration activities. Ansa reported that forged identity documents were being sent on an almost weekly basis from Naples to Marseille via couriers on tourist buses, to be sold in the French city.

Naples prosecutors have issued arrest warrants for two Italians and five Algerians, two of whom are already in jail, Ansa said. France stepped up its terrorism alert after the July 7, 2005, bombings in London, and French government ministers have warned repeatedly that Italy is seen as a target by Militant Islamists. Investigators take seriously a threat from the GSPC, which in a September 2005 statement had identified France as its "enemy number one." Italy, which has frequently received threats from extremist groups via the Internet for maintaining its 3,000-strong military contingent in Iraq, also stepped up security in the wake of the London bombings.[43]

Senior European counterterrorism officials say the movement of young men from Europe has not come close to the levels seen in the 1980s, when at least 10,000 men traveled to Afghanistan to fight against the Soviet occupation. So far, there seems to be little coordination of the recruitment efforts across Europe's borders, and French officials emphasize that the cells they reported dismantling were local.

Counterterrorism officials said there was no concrete evidence that Iraq's active terrorist groups and organizations were involved in the recruitment, or that Ansar al-Islam, a European-based terrorist group once located in northern Iraq that later expanded its operations into Baghdad and maintained loose ties with the notorious al-Zarqawi (killed in a U.S. air strike on June 7, 2006), was aiding the effort.

Investigators say they are reluctant to estimate how many people have left Europe to join the insurgency. American military officials in Iraq also admit they do not know the precise number of outside fighters, although French intelligence officials estimate that there are 2,000 to 3,000 Iraqi and foreign fighters in Iraq. The number of foreign fighters in Iraq is difficult to estimate with certainty. The French daily *Le Monde* in December 2004 quoted intelligence services as saying there were about 1,000 to 2,000 fighters, mostly from Jordan, Syria, Saudi Arabia, Yemen, and Kuwait.[44]

German federal prosecutors said police arrested two suspected *al-Qa'ida* members on January 23, 2005, whom they said were involved in planning a suicide attack in Iraq. Police arrested Ibrahim Mohamed K., a 29-year-old Iraqi living in Mainz, on suspicion of recruiting suicide attackers in Germany and providing logistical help to the terrorist organization. He also is believed to have tried to obtain uranium in Luxembourg. The other arrested suspect, 31-year-old Palestinian Yasser Abu S., planned to carry out a suicide attack, according to Kay Nehm, a German chief federal prosecutor .

The Iraqi suspect, according to the prosecutor, trained multiple times in camps in Afghanistan before the September 2001 terror attacks in the United States, and then spent a year in Afghanistan fighting American forces after the U.S. invasion of Afghanistan. The prosecutor said Ibrahim Mohamed K. had contacts with high-ranking *al-Qa'ida* leaders during his time in Afghanistan. "This convinced him not to seek the original aspiration of martyrdom as a suicide attacker, but rather to recruit suicide attackers in Europe," prosecutors said in a statement. He recruited a Palestinian in September for a suicide attack in Iraq and purchased more than $1 million in life insurance for him, with the aim of faking the man's death in a car accident in Egypt, prosecutors said. The German authorities said the majority of the collected insurance payoff was to be used to fund *al-Qa'ida* activities.[45]

According to the Norwegian Defense Research Institute (FFI), since September 11, 2001, at least 15 major terrorist attacks have been prevented in Europe. In an interview with Radio Netherlands, a spokesman for the EFI claimed that the discovery stopped the attacks that would have caused many casualties. The FFI is the chief adviser on defense-related science and technology to the Ministry of Defense and the Norwegian Armed Forces. The 15 foiled attacks were "mass casualty attacks" designed to take a great number of lives for maximum impact, according to an FFI spokesman, who refused to give further details to Radio Netherlands. The Dutch intelligence and security service AIVD disclosed that at least three major attacks had been foiled in the Netherlands since 2000. In addition, several arrests had been made in an alleged plot to blow up the U.S. Embassy in Paris.

In a response to the Norwegian estimate, terrorism expert Glenn Schoen, of the U.S. security firm Transecur, pointed out that the number of foiled terrorist attacks could be between 20 or even 30, depending on the definition of "major attack." More specifically, Schoen listed five thwarted attacks in France and an equal number in Spain, three each in Germany and Britain, and one apiece in Belgium, Italy, and the

Netherlands. These 19 cases are only about which the authorities chose to release details.[46]

While the individual European states have strategies to deal with Militant Islamists, Europe as a whole does not have a clearly stated strategy to combat terrorism. NATO is the only multinational defense organization that could implement such a strategy. However, NATO's secretary general, de Hoop Scheffer, in a public speech said that "...in Europe, we still have complicated discussions...of how far governments could go in the relationship with their citizens in the fight against terrorism." On the other hand, as General James Jones, NATO's supreme commander, noted at the 2005 NATO defense ministers meeting in Romania, NATO has a force of 17,000 advanced military forces that can be deployed rapidly to address a variety of situations early in a crisis or to support national authorities in time of natural disasters. Some battalions were used to help with the security at the Summer Olympic Games of 2004 in Athens and at the Afghan elections in early November 2004.[47]

A study compiled by the European Monitoring Center on Racism and Xenophobia indicated that Muslims across Europe are confronting a rise in "Islamophobia" ranging from violent attacks to discrimination in job and housing markets. The 117-page study urges European countries to strengthen policies on integration, but at same time it noted that Muslims need to do more to counter negative perceptions driven by terrorism and upheavals, such as the backlash to cartoons depicting the Prophet Muhammad. The study presents the many divides between the European Union mainstream and the estimated 13 million Muslims—which comprises more than 3 percent of the 25-nation bloc's population—and seeks to offer a street-level view of the complexities blocking efforts to bridge the differences. The report, however, noted that "data on religiously aggravated incidents is collected on a limited scale." It noted that only Britain publishes a hate-crime list that specifically identifies acts against Muslims. Since the September 11, 2001, attacks, many Muslims feel "they have been put under a general suspicion of terrorism...The key word is 'respect,'." People need to feel respected and included." The report also said Europe's Muslims are "often disproportionately represented" in poor housing conditions, unemployment statistics, and in lower education levels. "Islamophobia" ranges from verbal threats to physical attacks on people and property.[48]

The terrorists' violent actions in the Europe have double-edged consequences in European countries that have large populations. Militant Islamists are well aware of the ethnic, religious, political backlash, and stigmatization of Muslims and Muslim nations that has occurred since September 11. The violent attacks, the Madrid bombings, the assassination of Theo Van Gogh, and theLondon bombings, in addition to the failed attacks in London and Glasgow, have heightened tensions, nurtured anti-Islamic and anti-Muslim sentiments in the Western European countries, fostered a breeding ground for polarization, and, ultimately, made Militant Islamist world views seem more attractive to some Muslims in Europe. Thus, Militant Islamist violence in European countries could further the existing racism, isolation, economic marginalization, and alienation of Muslims in Europe. Denying such developments is very dangerous. Thus, the consequences and reactions pose the most important and serious challenges to the Muslim communities as well as to the government officials and political leaders in these countries.[49]

It is important to underscore that the killer of Van Gogh and the London bombers were born and raised in the countries where they committed their terrorist acts. Such a development clearly presents a new picture of European Militant Islamists, making it difficult, if not impossible, to profile the probable Militant Islamist or terrorist in Europe. Also, the new homegrown European Militant Islamist cells do not receive orders from above, such as *al-Qa'ida*, or for that matter from someone in a distant Muslim country. The new European Militant Islamist cells may not even become suicide bombers, but may still commit terrorist acts in the target country and would therefore be able to carry out numerous terrorist acts.

Danish intelligence agents arrested eight alleged Islamic militants with links to leading *al-Qa'ida* figures on September 4, 2007, and said the suspects were plotting an attack involving explosives. Denmark officials reported that the country's PET intelligence services arrested eight alleged Militant Islamists—six Danish citizens and two foreigners with residence permits—allegedly linked to *al-Qa'ida* who were plotting an attack involving explosives. Authorities reported that the suspects are of Afghan, Pakistani, Somali, and Turkish origin who were under surveillance for a year, and that the arrests prevented terrorist attacks. Such surveillance of Muslim youth in the country began after a Danish newspaper published 12 cartoons of the Prophet Mohammad, triggering fiery protests in Muslim countries in early 2006. The arrests in Europe point to the current homegrown Militant Islamists. Direct involvement of the Western European states on the side of the Arab states and Afghanistan perpetuates the alienation of European Muslim youth from their societies, making them vulnerable for terrorist recruitment.

Sentiments of perceived or real threat and insecurity generated by terrorism of the Militant Islamists is not limited to the civilians and governmental agencies, but rather it has penetrated the worldwide business boardrooms as well. Peter Levene, chairman of Lloyd's of London, in a press conference on May 9, 2007, presented the result of the insurance company's survey. He said more than one-third of international businesses surveyed reported fear of becoming victims of terrorist attacks. The report indicated that some 36 percent of companies surveyed predicted their facilities could be targeted by terrorists in the next five years, and close to half of them thought it highly likely their IT infrastructure could come under attack. Almost two-thirds of them admitted lack of enough knowledge about their exposure of terrorism and political violence.

Of those surveyed who have developed a plan to counter terrorism, 20 percent said it covered chemical, nuclear, or radiological attacks, despite the British and French police having discovered poison gas attacks in the past five years. Nearly one-third of the European and more than half of the North American respondents cited religious extremists, such as *al-Qa'ida* and other Militant Islamists groups, as a major threat. Nearly 50 percent of the 154 surveyed business leaders from around the world thought the United States would see a rise in political violence or terrorist activity over the next five years, while 39 percent thought Western Europe would as well.[50]

U.S. program of Extraordinary Rendition (EOR) and European involvement: An added controversy

Extraordinary Redition (EOR) is a program in which those who are suspected of involvement or collaboration in terrorism are seized and sent to other countries, where torture is practiced, for interrogation. A few dozen of the terrorism suspects seized have disappeared since the September 11 attacks. This section presents several cases and evaluates the consequences and reaction to the EOR program.

Reports point out that Italian, German, Swedish, and other European authorities are investigating whether U.S. Central Intelligence Agency (CIA) agents broke local laws by kidnapping and detaining suspected terrorists on European soil and taking them to other countries that are less opposed to torture, such as Afghanistan, Azerbaijan, Cyprus, Egypt, Jordan, Morocco, Pakistan, Poland, Qatar, Saudi Arabia, UAE, and Uzbekistan. As part of the U.S. "war on terrorism," this practice, euphemistically known as rendition, has been sanctioned by the United States, as confirmed by the Swedish authorities, who claim that at least one plane allegedly linked to the CIA landed in France twice (in 2002 and 2005) and in Sweden three times since 2002. Denmark confirmed 14 flights with suspected CIA ties entered its airspace since 2001; Norway has confirmed three such flights; and Icelandic media reported 67 such landings. The *Guardian* reported on December 1, 2005, that it had seen navigation logs showing that more than 300 flights operated by the CIA had passed through European airports as part of a network that could be involved in the clandestine detention and possible torture of terrorism suspects.[51]

The practice of EOR has created widespread disillusionment among the U.S. and European media and also the public in general. The following interaction among the U.S. officials presents the controversial nature of the practice, as this author believes it would be helpful to the reader. It should be noted that the relationship between European countries is so important that it would be in many ways difficult, if not impossible, for the Europeans not to cooperate with the United States, despite public denial.

The then-CI.A director told the U.S. Senate Arms Services Committee, in connection with the treatment of the detainees and despite the renunciation of torture: "Professional interrogation has become a very useful and necessary way to obtain information to save innocent lives, to disrupt terrorist schemes and to protect our combat forces...Terrorists brought the war to our soil. We have taken the war to them. Sometimes this requires what we euphemistically call a kinetic solution on foreign soil. We have to be able to use all the tools at our disposal and understand the consequences of how we use them." When Senator Carl Levin of Michigan asked about the Agency's policy toward rendition, the CIA director hesitated, saying he preferred to discuss it in closed session. When Levin pressed him on how vigorously the CIA checked complaints from people who have been subjected to rendition, the director replied, "Again, this is the kind of question that is complicated and would need to be answered in closed session...But I can assure you, that I know of no instance where the intelligence community is outside the law on this...Torture is not...it's not productive...That's not professional interrogation. We don't torture." Between 100 and 150 terror suspects are believed to have been flown by American authorities to Egypt, Syria, Saudi Arabia, Jordan, Pakistan, and other countries for questioning, supposedly after those countries had given assurances that the people being questioned would not be tortured. During a visit to the United States in May, Egyptian Prime Minister Ahmed Nazif said the United States has dispatched 60 to 70 Egyptian detainees to their home country since the attacks of September 11, 2001.[52]

In Germany, a 41-year-old German citizen named Khaled el-Masri told authorities that he was locked up at the Macedonian border during a vacation in the Balkans and flown to Kabul, Afghanistan, in January 2004, where he was held as a suspected terrorist for four months. He said that only after his captors realized he was not an *al-Qa'ida* suspect did they take him back in May 2004 to the Balkans and released him on a hillside along the Albanian border near an Albanian border checkpoint, where guards returned his passport and cash. Masri reported his captors spoke English with an American accent.[53]

In connection with el-Masri's case, however, reports indicate that the U.S. Department of State had already begun to inform the German authorities about the case, with the stipulation that the German authorities would not reveal anything about it. In May 2004, the White House sent the U.S. ambassador, Daniel R. Coats, to visit the German interior minister. "Coats informed the German minister that the CIAhad wrongfully imprisoned one of its citizens, Khaled el-Masri, for five months, and would soon release him...There was also a request: that the German government does not disclose what it had been told, even if Masri went public. The U.S. officials feared exposure of a covert action program designed to capture terrorism suspects abroad and transfer them among countries, and possible legal challenges to the CIAfrom Masri and others with similar allegations."[54] German Chancellor Angela Merkel said on December 6, 2005, that the American administration had admitted that el-Masri had been erroneously taken, adding that she would ask Foreign Minister Frank-Walter Steinmeier to report to a parliamentary control body about the case. She also said the German authorities had discussed the one case, which the government of the United States had accepted as a mistake.[55]

Similar action by the intelligence officers were carried out in Italy as well. A radical Egyptian cleric Hassan Mustafa Usama Nasr, known as Abu Omar, was walking to a Milan mosque for noon prayers on February 17, 2003, when he was grabbed by two men, sprayed in the face with chemicals, and put in a van. After being imprisoned, he was released for a short time on house arrest in 2004 and then returned to prison immediately after he talked to his wife in Milan, Italy, by telephone. His phone call violated the terms of his house arrest. As of mid-August 2006, he is being held in Wadi Natrun prison north of Cairo, which is used for security prisoners. Before his arrest, Abu Omar took refuge from Egyptian authorities in Albania, but moved to Germany and then to Italy in 1997. That period coincided with a U.S. operation, in cooperation with Albanian secret police, to watch and eventually round up a cell of suspected Egyptian radicals. He was released from prison in Egypt in February 2007. He claimed to have been tortured in jail all the time, except for a few week in 2004.[56]

In Sweden, a parliamentary investigation found that CIA agents wearing hoods orchestrated the forced removal in December 2001 of two Egyptian nationals on a U.S.-registered airplane to Cairo, where the men claimed they were tortured in prison. One of the men was later exonerated as a terrorism suspect by Egyptian police, while the other remains in prison in Egypt. Details of the secret operation have shocked many in Sweden, a leading proponent of human rights.

The CIA usually carries out such rendition operations with the help or blessing of friendly local intelligence agencies. The CIA has kept details of rendition cases a closely guarded secret, but it has defended the controversial practice as an effective and legal way to prevent terrorism. The Bush Administration has received backing for extraordinary renditions from Muslim governments that have been criticized for their human-rights records, including, Egypt, Jordan, and Pakistan, where many subjects are taken for interrogation. European authorities investigating the practice face many practical and legal hurdles to filing criminal charges against U.S. agents, including whether they are protected by diplomatic immunity and determining their identities. Prosecutors in Italy and Germany have not ruled out criminal charges against the U.S. agents.[57]

The secretary-general of the Islamic Commission of Spain issued its fatwa [religious edict] to coincide with the first anniversary of the Madrid attacks. The Islamic commission's secretary-general, Mansur Escudero, said the fatwa had moral, rather than legal, weight and hoped it would spur similar pronouncements from Muslim communities worldwide. "We declare...that Usama bin Laden and his *al-Qa'ida* organization, responsible for the horrendous crimes against innocent people who were despicably murdered in the March 11, 2004, terrorist attack in Madrid, are outside the parameters of Islam...The terrorist acts of Osama bin Laden and his *al-Qa'ida* organization...which result in the death of civilians, such as women and children...are totally prohibited and are the object of strong condemnation within Islam," the Islamic Commission proclamation said in a statement, quoting extensively from religious texts.[58]

The invasion of Afghanistan immediately following the September 11 terrorist attacks forced out the Taliban regime and their allies, *al-Qa'ida* leaders and fighters. For more than two years there were celebrations of the end of *al-Qa'ida* and its possible threat to the West, based on the thesis that *al-Qa'ida* was a centralized organization. Then on March 11, 2004, the dreadful terrorist train bombing attacks in Madrid, and a few months later the killing of Theo Van Gogh, on November 2, 2004, in the middle of street in Amsterdam, somewhat cast a shadow on the persisting view of *al-Qa'ida*. The two attacks, particularly the Madrid one, proved the earlier view was false. The London bombings and the failed bombings in United Kingdom in 2007 began to present the view known as "homegrown" Militant Islamists who are committed to carrying out terrorist attacks. As evidence and evaluations in this chapter indicate, the threat of the homegrown Militant Islamists is widespread throughout the Western European countries.

No evidence exists of a direct connection between Usama bin Ladin or Ayman al-Dhawahiri and the European Militant Islamists involved in terrorist attacks, but it would be impossible to deny that the "homegrown"

Militant Islamists were and continue to be strongly inspired by the *al-Qa'ida* ideology. Similar to any inspired individuals, the Militant Islamists will continue to emerge, and out of close-knitted individuals will emerge leaders who would ultimately carry out the terrorist attacks. The London bombings of July 2005, the failed bombings of 2007, and continued arrests of suspects in European countries are clear evidence of the ever lurking threat of Militant Islamists.

In fact on January 10 and 11, 2008, several European governments reported receiving and intercepting telephone and short-wave transmitted threats of possible attacks by the Militant Islamists to blow up the Eiffel Tower and the German Ministry of Justice as well as against the lives of the former prime minister of Italy and his brother for anti-Islamic articles printed in the Il Giornale newspaper. The former prime minister Silvio Berlusconi—who has been singled out as the enemy of Islam by the Militant Islamists—received a threatening letter containing two blank bullets warning he would face the same fate as Benazir Bhutto. Subsequently, the security services of these countries were put on high alert, even though France had been on red alert for while because of renewed violence and demonstrations by Muslim youths. It is believed such threats of possible attacks are in retaliation to the jailing of two Lebanese in Germany and the anti-Islamic postures and statements made by the French president as well as current and former Italian prime ministers. These threats came shortly after the posting of messages from Usama bin Ladin, Ayman al-Dhawahri, and Adm Gadahan—also known as Azzam Amriki, an American convert to Islam—that called on Muslim fighters to welcome George W. Bush to the Middle East on January 6, 2008, with bombs. In January 2005 French police arrested three French-born Algerian suspected of plotting to blow up the Eiffel Tower. However, such threats and warnings in the past had always turned out to be wrong. But the question remains: cCan the security officials ignore such threats?

A national survey conducted by the National Committee for the Dutch Remembrance and Liberation Days (celebrated on May 4 and 5 in the Netherlands), whose mandate included linking national events to present-day social discussions on freedom, solidarity, and tolerance showed that "terrorism and war are the two international issues that Dutch people are most concerned about, followed by the environment and health."[59]

CHAPTER 10

The United States-Led Invasion of Iraq and Its Consequences

In March 2003, two years after it invaded Afghanistan in retaliation for the September 11 attacks, the United States led an invasion of Iraq with the objective of war against Militant Islamist terrorism, among other reasons. Shortly afterward, a number of Militant Islamist groups emerged and began to take terrorist actions not only against the U.S.-led coalition forces, but also against those in the Iraqi government, and later against Iraqi *Shi'a*s and Kurds, including ordinary civilians. Some of these groups claim they were established by the "Afghani Arabs," who are veterans of the Afghanistan war against the Soviets and worked directly with the Taliban regime, and thus are connected to *al-Qa'ida* and Usama bin Ladin. Over the next several years, the frequency and viciousness of the attacks escalated as militants kidnapped and killed their victims, sometimes by beheading, and destroyed shops, restaurants, passenger buses, and even mosques and shrines. These events and those similar to them show that the invasion of Iraq has led to that country becoming a new training ground for Militant Islamists. Attacks in Iraq, Kuwait, Saudi Arabia, Turkey, and Indonesia, among others reveal that the targets are Western interests rather than specific governments, although in some countries (for example, Algeria, Egypt, and Saudi Arabia), Militant Islamists commit terrorism also because they oppose the national government.

In an audiotape aired on Al Jazeera television on February 11, 2003, bin Ladin warned against the possible invasion of Iraq and called on Muslims to attack U.S. and U.K. targets if Iraq was attacked. He went to say, "We also stress to honest Muslims that they should move, incite, and mobilize the [Islamic] nation, amid such grave events and hot atmosphere so as to liberate themselves from those unjust and renegade ruling regimes, which are enslaved by the United States. They should also do so to establish the rule of God on earth. The most qualified regions for liberation are Jordan, Morocco, Nigeria, Pakistan, the land of the two holy mosques [Saudi Arabia], and Yemen."

Local, very tight, small networks, or micro-cells, are emerging and staging violent attacks at their choosing. Therefore, whether the top fugitive *al-Qa'ida* figures are killed or arrested may have limited impact on Militant Islamist activity because the world view and the agenda of *al-Qa'ida* has taken a stronghold in many parts of the world. Since the U.S.-led invasion of Afghanistan, the Militant Islamists ceased to exist as a single centralized organization, and instead its ideological message has reached many Muslim communities if not all.[1] The invasion of Iraq, the Palestinian-Israeli conflict, the inability of Islamic and Arab states to bring about a solution to the problems of the invasion, and U.S. unilateralism in connection with the Palestinian-Israeli conflict have contributed vastly to the spread of local Militant Islamist cells.

The burgeoning *al-Qa'ida*-associated groups in Iraq are clearly a consequence of the invasion. One of the most notorious groups is the *al-Qa'ida* Group of Jihad in the Land of Two Rivers (*Tanzim Qa'edat al-Jihad Fi Bilad al-Rafidayn*). This group is directed either by a Jordanian, Abu Musab al-Zarqawi, or its "field commander" in Iraq, Abdullah bin-Rashed al-Baghdadi, who has taken credit for beheadings, suicide bombings, and armed attacks against the American forces and the newly recruited Iraqi police officers. The organization may have replaced al-Zarqawi with al-Baghdadi in early 2006 because of several mistakes he made.[2]

Most present-day Militant Islamists discussed in this book are Sunnis, except for the *Hizbullah* in Lebanon, who adhere to the Islamic world view of the Muslim Brothers and Usama bin Ladin. Some of these individuals are *al-Salafis*. The *al-Salafis* (which translates as the Ancestors) are scriptural literalists who contend that the most pure or original form of Islam existed during the first 40 years of the Islamic system of Umma, or community of believers. They are puritanical Islamists who call for steadfast emulation of Islam's seventh-century founding *Khalifa*. The *al-Salafis* are blamed for most of the militant bombings, kidnappings, and killings in Iraq, and Militant Islamists recruit mainly from this Islamic school of thought, especially for suicide bombing campaigns. Usama bin Ladin, Ayman al-Dhawahri, and Abu Musab al-Zarqawi are considered *al-Salafis*. The Militant Islamists in Iraq also tactically cooperate with the former Ba'thist opposition and Iraqi nationalists. It seems that the opposition is made up of those who represent the disappointed, desperate, or humiliated, and those who face social and economic disaster as a consequence of

American invasion. [3] The backbone of the suicide bombings in Iraq are the Militant Islamists.

In Iraq, the Militant Islamists have been able to create hostile and dangerous religious and ethnic divisions in the population by targeting *Shi'a* and Kurdish communities and accusing them of collaborating with and militarily supporting the American and coalition forces. Using audiotapes and the Internet, particularly Islamic Web sites, Militant Islamists have also increased the number of public attacks and insults against non-Sunni communities. Moreover, U.S. military and political actions in the country have further polarized Iraq, giving the Militant Islamists additional power to persuade potential recruits.

The audio and videotape messages posted by the Militant Islamists in Iraq and other conflict areas are the principal means by which they convey rhetorical, condescending, and sometimes exaggerated claims about their activities. In one such audio statement that contained anti-*Shi'a* diatribes, which was posted on the Internet on January 20, 2005, Abu Musab al-Zarqawi claimed that a large number of military forces from other countries participated in the battle of Fallujah in November 2004. The *al-Qa'ida* Group of Jihad in the Land of Two Rivers posted the message. He said, "It is known that 800 Israeli soldiers...participated in the battle; just like the participation by the Jordanian military, whose officers contributed to the planning and the military assault against the city." The statement coincided with the first day of a Muslim holiday, *Eid al-Adha* (the Feast of Sacrifice, established by Prophet Abraham), a time when people focus on the religious aspects of Islam. Al-Zarqawi also claimed that Israeli soldiers in Fallujah "were accompanied by 18 rabbis, some of whom were killed, as newspapers and Israeli media announced." He also claimed that *Shi'a*s participated in order to kill Sunnis: "The battle of Fallujah removed the ugly mask of the doomed '*Rafidha*' meaning "the Rejectors" [a derogatory term for Shi'as], whose hatred [for Sunnis] was manifested in this battle...They [Shi'as] participated in the military campaign for the battle against Fallujah with the blessing of the imam of infidelity and apostasy, Sistani [referring to Ayatollah al-Sistani]...They played a big role in the massacre, the looting, the sabotage, and the spilling of innocent blood among children, women, and the elderly," he added. Al-Zarqawi charged that *Shi'a*s "occupied (Sunni) mosques, sticking on their walls photos of their Satan, al-Sistani, and writing with hate: 'Today (we take) your territory, and tomorrow your honor...'90 percent of the (Iraqi) national guard is composed of hateful *Rafidha* and 10 percent *Peshmerga* [Kurdish armed militia]."[4]

Three days later, on January 23, 2005, another audiotape by the same group was posted on the same Web site frequented by the Militant Islamists. The tape surfaced as rumors spread in Iraq that al-Zarqawi had been captured. In this statement, al-Zarqawi accused *Shi'as* of engaging in a plot with Washington to seize absolute power. He said, "Oh people of Iraq, where is your honor? Have you accepted oppression of the crusader harlots...and the rejectionist pigs?...Four million Rafidha have been brought in from Iran to take part in the elections so that they realize their aim of taking most seats in the pagan assembly." The *Shi'a* Iraqis, he said, were poised to spread "their insidious beliefs" to Baghdad and *Sunni*-dominated areas of Iraq.

An Iraqi security official told journalists in 2004 that he estimated there are more than 200,000 active opposition fighters and sympathizers in Iraq. His assessment included 30,000 to 40,000 full-time fighters—he calls them terrorists—who receive support from about 200,000 Iraqis. He added that others were also likely to be providing everything from intelligence to logistics and shelter. The numbers far exceed any figure presented by the U.S. military in Iraq, which has struggled to control the country since ousting the former government in April 2003. Past U.S. military assessments have been increased from 5,000 to 20,000 members, most recently in October 2004. An intelligence report that was quoted on September 15, 2005, gave an estimate of 16,000 Sunni Muslim fighters, of whom 6,700 were hard-core Islamic fundamentalists who were now supplemented by a possible further 4,000 members after an amalgamation with *Jaiysh* Muhammad (Army of Mohammad), a group loyal to the former Ba'athist regime.[5]

The opposition forces enjoy wide backing in the provinces of Baghdad, Babil, Salah al-Din, Diyala, Nineveh, and Tamim. According to the reports, the opposition gained strength through Iraq's tight-knit tribal bonds and links to the former 400,000-strong Ba'thist Iraqi army, which was dissolved by the U.S. occupation in May 2003. This development is due to the problems created after two-years of occupation without seeing any progress in the people's daily life. Of course U.S. officials dismissed the figure, although General George Casey, commander of all forces in Iraq, pointed out in January 2005 that 15,000 insurgents had been killed or captured, indicating that the total number likely exceeds the October 2004 estimate of 20,000.[6]

Georges Malbrunot, a journalist with the French daily Le *Figaro,* who was kidnapped along with Christian Chesnot (who speaks Arabic) of *Radio France Internationale* on August 20, 2004, and released on December 21, 2004, described the Iraqi opposition forces as a well-organized movement that had a clear strategy. It became clear to the French journalists that the opposition forces included former supporters of the Ba'thists alongside Militant Islamists. Oppositions regardless of ideological orientation continue to cooperate while maintaining separate organizations and strategies.[7]

The Iraqi opposition forces have demonstrated the capability to strike at the heart of the country's leadership to undermine the government. On January 4, 2005, Ali al-Haidri, the governor of the Baghdad province and a secular *Shi'a,* was assassinated. Witnesses described how masked gunmen cleared the streets before the attack and then opened fire when al-Haidari's BMW drove past, followed by three four-wheel drive cars filled with his guards.[8] Because opposition forces, particularly former Ba'thists and secular nationalists, have infiltrated the Iraqi security forces, the assailants probably had access to inside information about the governor's itinerary from a sympathizer within his own circle.

A statement apparently from the *al-Qa'ida* Group of Jihad in the Land of Two Rivers said the governor was killed for being an "American agent." The shooting of Ali al-Haidri in a street ambush showed the opposition's power to strike at the heart of the governing class and raised new doubts as to whether security forces can protect politicians, who must travel in heavily guarded motorcades. Hours earlier, a suicide bomber killed eight Iraqi policemen and three civilians at a checkpoint near the high-security Green Zone, which houses the interim government and foreign embassies. On January 3, 2005, a suicide car bomber killed two people while trying to crash through a roadblock near the headquarters of the Iraqi National Accord—the party of Iyad Allawi, the interim prime minister at the time. This bombing happened shortly before the party was due to announce its list of candidates for the January 30, 2005, parliamentary elections and suggests that the opposition groups had penetrated Iyad Allawi's party.[9]

However, the clearest indication of Militant Islamist infiltration came on April 12, 2007, when a suicide bomber killed two, including one member of Parliament, and wounded 22 in the cafeteria of the Iraqi Parliament, located in the heavily fortified Green Zone where the U.S. embassy is located. This suicide bombing was carried out in the ninth week of the U.S. military crackdown in Baghdad. The U.S. military security drive has brought down the rate of sectarian murders, but it has not stopped the bombings.[10]

Since the February 22, 2006, bombing of the al-Askari shrine, killings increased in a manner that had not been seen since the invasion. Hundreds of bodies of people who had been handcuffed, blindfolded, shot, and had showed signs of torture turned up in Baghdad and other towns.[11] As noted before, opposition fighters, including Militant Islamists, have a multi-target strategy in Iraq as well as outside of Iraq. In Iraq they hit target at every level, attacking security forces, political figures, i American forces, and those of U.S.-led forces all over the country.

The ongoing terrorist attacks and revenge killings have spread to include women and children, professionals, academics, judges, and their extended families. Iraqi officials issued 1,294 death certificates in March and 1,155 death certificates in April 2006.[12]

However, the opposition groups are under pressure and suffer from the military campaign against them. A posting on an Islamic Web site on December 24, 2004, made a rare admission of significant casualties among opposition members fighting U.S. forces in Iraq, saying 24 guerrillas, most of them non-Iraqi Arabs, were killed in battles in Fallujah on December 23, 2004. The statements said three hours of fighting in Fallujah resulted in the "martyrdom" of 24 fighters from different Militant Islamist factions, with 19 being from Saudi Arabia, Kuwait, Bahrain, Egypt, Syria, and Jordan, and the rest being Iraqis. However, it is not clear which Militant Islamist group posted the statement.[13]

The escalation of violent opposition by the Militant Islamist in Iraq clearly indicates that local militant groups and cells have grown in strength and that *al-Qa'ida* has a less central position in directing global terrorism. In an effort to maintain his role as the spiritual leader of the Islamist militancy, Usama bin Ladin, in a video aired on October 29, 2004, by the Al Jazeera television network, for the first time admitted that he was directly involved in the planning of the September 11 attacks and took credit for killing nearly 3,000 Americans. Previously, bin Ladin had denied having any involvement with the attacks. He stated, "We had agreed with the September 11 'commander' Mohamed Atta, may God rest his soul, to carry out all operations in twenty minutes—before Bush and his administration could take notice."[14] It is important to note that the conspiracy theorists in the Arab and the Muslim world had repeatedly accused the Israeli Mossad and the CIA of being responsible for the attacks. He also threatened Americans with future attacks. The videotape was delivered to the Al Jazeera television network office in Pakistan, which indicates Pakistan remains a haven for Islamist Militants, despite the government's campaign against them.

Another Islamist Militant group, *Ansar al-Islam fi Kurdistan* (supporters of Islam of Kurdistan), which emerged in September 2001, is based in the Kurdish-controlled northern provinces of Iraq close to the border of Iran. The Kurds are supported by the United States. *Ansar* challenges the two main Kurdish political and armed organizations, the Patriotic Union of Kurdistan (the PUK) and the Kurdish Democratic Party (KDP). Iraqi authorities believe that Ansar al-Islam members are terrorists who have declared war against all Kurdish political parties. In February 2002, Ansar al-Islam fighters assassinated Franso Hariri, a Kurdish Christian politician. In spring 2002, the group attempted to assassinate Barham Salih, a PUK member. Salih survived the attack, but five of his bodyguards and two attackers were killed.[15]

On February 27, 2003, an *Ansar* suicide bomber killed four people, including a high-ranking official of the PUK, his bodyguard, and a taxi driver. On March 13, 2003, it carried out another suicide bombing and ambush, which killed 42 PUK *Peesh-Margan* (plural for *Peesh-Marg* the armed Kurdish militia) and officials, thus establishing itself as a formidable group. It took place on a street behind the home of Kosrat Rasool Ali, a top official in the PUK. On February 1, 2004, two suicide bombers who wore explosive belts, similar to the Palestinian suicide bombers, struck the PUK and KDP offices in near-simultaneous attacks as hundreds of Iraqi Kurds gathered to celebrate an Islamic holiday. The attacks killed more than 100 people and injured more than 200 others, including a number of PUK and KDP officials.

Allegedly, the Ba'thist regime supported *Ansar al-Islam.* The United States has accused the group of harboring fugitives from *al-Qa'ida,* but these allegations have not been substantiated. Formal connections between the former Iraqi Ba'thist regime and *Ansar al-Islam* are unlikely because the Ba'thists are secularist whereas *Ansar* has a strong Militant Islamist view. Rather, *Ansar al-Islam*'s behavior and militancy indicate that its main support comes from Sunni Militant Islamist supporters in the Persian Gulf and North African countries.

The KDP and PUK had hoped that the invasion of Iraq by the United States-led forces would eliminate the threat of Ansar al-Islam. However, a new Iraqi Militant Islamist opposition group, *Jaiysh Ansar al-Sunnah* (Army of the Defenders of Tradition, or *Sunnah,* of the Prophet Mohammad), claimed responsibility for a series of suicide bombings in January 2004 in Iraq. Whether *Jaiysh* is a faction that broke away from *Ansar al-Islam* or *Ansar al-Islam* renamed itself because several groups agreed to merge to form a new entity is uncertain. *Jaiysh al-Ansar al-Sunnah* appears to have become the most active terrorist group in Iraq and has widened its militant campaign throughout the country, particularly in the Kurdish areas and the Sunni Triangle, which refers to the three adjacent provinces of Anbar, Ninewa, and Salaheddin. The group cooperates with Militant Islamists, Iraqi nationalists, and others who resist occupation. Evidence indicates that *Jaiysh* has become a major terrorist group that carries out myriad terrorist attacks, including suicide bombings, kidnappings, beheadings, and assassinations in predominately *Shi'a* areas such as Najaf and Karbalah, but its targets even include Sunnis who collaborate with the regime or U.S.-led forces. The group is directly involved in armed resistance in the towns of Fallujah, Anbar, Samarra, and Mosul, among many others.

Jaiysh Ansar al-Sunnah first made the Western news when it claimed responsibility for twin suicide bombings in the Iraqi city of Arbil in February 2004 that killed more than 100 people, mostly Kurdish officials gathering on a religious holiday. The attack was the deadliest against the Kurds since the U.S. invasion of Iraq; the fact the Kurds were targeted appears to link the group to *Ansar al-Islam*, but *Ansar al-Sunnah* claimed responsibility. On December 21, 2004, a bombing of a U.S. military dining tent during lunch near Mosul left 22 dead, including 14 U.S. soldiers, four American civilian contractors, three Iraqi soldiers, and one unidentified person. At least 72 people were injured, including 51 American soldiers and support employees. The attack was the work of a suicide bomber who had managed to enter the dining tent. According to the U.S. commander in Mosul, the suicide bomber was probably wearing an Iraqi military uniform. The strike was the second major bombing inside a military zone in two months, after a double suicide bombing in Baghdad's Green Zone (home to the U.S. embassy and Iraqi government) killed six in October 2004. These bombings were much more sophisticated than previous ones in Iraq.

Shortly after, *Jaiysh Ansar al-Sunnah* claimed responsibility and issued a statement reiterating it was a suicide bombing. "God enabled one of your martyr brothers to plunge into God's enemies inside their forts, killing and injuring hundreds," the group said on its Web site, posted on December 23, 2004. "We don't know how they can be so stupid that until now they have not figured out the type of the strike that hit them."[16]

On December 26, 2004, *Jaiysh Ansar al-Sunnah* issued a videotape about the bombing and identified the suicide bomber as Abu Omar al-Museli. The videotape posted on the group's Web site showed what appeared to be the dining hall explosion at the Mosul camp. A later shot, apparently taken from a car driving along the base's perimeter, showed the destruction. The video showed a map of the base with the dining hall clearly marked as a militant pointed to various areas with an army knife. A masked attacker also was shown embracing other group members before leaving on his mission, while a speaker urged God to accept the bomber as an Islamic martyr. The attacker's name, al-Mousli (likely a nom de guerre) suggests he was from Mosul. A statement read on the tape by a masked man said the blast was aimed at "striking fear in the hearts of the crusaders (the term is used by the Militant Islamists for US-led forces in Iraq) and their apostate lackeys."[17] However, on January 3, 2005, the Associated Press quoted the London-based and Saudi-owned newspaper *al-Sharq al-Awsat* as identifying the suicide bomber as a 20-year-old Saudi medical student, Ahmed Said Ahmed al-Ghamdi. The paper reported that the al-Ghamdis are a large Saudi clan, and that three members of the clan were among the September 11 hijackers.[18]

Ansar al-Islam has denied that its spiritual leader, Mullah Krekar, has had any role in the attacks in Iraq, including the car bombing that killed Ayatollah Hakim, and the attacks on the Jordanian Embassy and U.N.

headquarters. Mullah Krekar was arrested in September 2002 at Amsterdam's Schiphol Airport and held for four months for allegedly financing terrorist activities in Iraq before he was deported in January 2003 to Norway, which had previously granted him asylum in 1991. Krekar, whose name is Najm ul-Deen Faraj Ahmad, was born in 1956 in Sulaimaniyah, Iraq. While under the custody of Dutch authorities, Krekar was interrogated by the FBI.[19]

German police also interrogated Mullah Krekar in Oslo in late November 2004, and he is thought to be linked to at least one of several men arrested on December 2, 2004, on suspicion of planning attacks during Iraqi Interim Prime Minister Iyad Allawi's visit to Germany in 2004. Krekar, who has lived in Norway since 1991, founded *Ansar al-Islam* in September 2001, but insists that he has not been its leader since May 2002. He confirmed that German police wanted details of his client's European contacts. The telephone number of one of the arrested suspects was found in Krekar's possession. Krekar's brother, Khalid Faraj Ahmad, told the NTB that Krekar's interrogation was in connection with an old case and that the interview had been planned for months. Krekar was questioned as a witness in a case concerning several Kurds who were arrested in Germany a long time ago.[20]

Dia Rashwan, an Egyptian expert on Muslim militants, has argued that U.S. security practices, such as raiding homes and mosques where militants are suspected to be hiding, have stoked anger among Iraqis, prompting some of them—driven by religious or nationalist zeal—to volunteer for suicide attacks. Rashwan said that by killing themselves, bombers try to make up for the difference between the militants' lesser armaments and those of the U.S. military.[21]

Before the American invasion of Iraq, Egyptian President Hosni Mubarak said in connection with the invasion that, "...if it is over, this war will have horrible consequences." He further stated that this invasion would result in creating "...100 bin Ladins."[22] From Morocco to Indonesia, warnings against invasion by religious and secular leaders were widespread, and the invasion was considered not only to be illegitimate in connection with the "war on terrorism," but also an attack on Muslims. The invasion and the consequences along the ongoing developments since 2003 have added to the existing conflict issues highlighted and used by the Militant Islamists.[23]

The violence in Iraq and the consequent spread of Militant Islamist ideology and terrorism led Pope John Paul II, who opposed the U.S.-led invasion of Iraq and the Bush administration's policy of preventive war, on January 10, 2005, to criticize the policy, characterizing it as an "arrogance of power" that he said should be countered with reason and dialogue. "Recourse to arms and violence has not only led to incalculable material damage, but also fomented hatred and increased the causes of terrorism," the Pope said. "The arrogance of power must be countered with reason, force with dialogue, pointed weapons with outstretched hands, evil with good." Retired cardinal and former papal envoy Cardinal Pio Laghi said President Bush had assured him on the eve of the Iraq invasion that the war would be short. Cardinal Pio Laghi, speaking during a broadcast on the Vatican's official Telepace service in connection with the invasion of Iraq and his March 5, 2003, conversation with Bush, Laghi said "When I went to Washington as the Pope's envoy just before the outbreak of the war, he told me, 'Don't worry, your eminence. We'll be quick and do well in Iraq. Unfortunately, the facts have demonstrated afterward that things took a different course—not rapid and not favorable. Bush was wrong." Laghi's comments reflected the Pope's often-stated view.[24]

Since the invasion of Iraq, and particularly after May 2003 when the White House declared "mission accomplished," casualties among the occupying coalition forces have been a major concern of both the occupation and Iraqi authorities. The bombing of the Jordanian Embassy on August 7, 2003; the bombing of the Iraq U.N. office on August 19, 2003, which killed Sergio de Vieira de Mello, the United Nations' special representative for Iraq; and the bombing near to the Shrine of Imam Ali in the city of Najaf on August 28, 2003, which killed the leader of the Supreme Council for the Islamic Revolution in Iraq, Ayatollah Mohammed Baqir al-Hakim, were all attributed to Militant Islamist terrorists or ex-Ba'thists. The chaotic environment of Iraq and lack of border security have created a haven for the terrorist groups.

The U.S. invasion of Iraq was justified as both an action to protect the region and the world against the development of weapons of mass destruction by the Ba'thist regime of Iraq and later as a response to the regime's inhumane treatment of the Iraqi people. Since the invasion in March of 2003, the occupying forces have failed to discover any weapons of mass destruction. The ensuing destruction and chaos, in addition to the apparent absence of weapons of mass destruction and the continuing staunch U.S. support of Israel despite its policy of demolishing homes and building security walls and barbed wire fences in the occupied Palestinian territories, have further humiliated the Arab and tIslamic worlds. Such actions and events have enabled the Militant Islamists to successfully recruit locally and have given Arab-Afghan militants reason to enter Iraq. The bombings of the British Consulate and HSB bank on November 20, 2003, in Istanbul, Turkey (see Chapter 2) are evidence of such success in a country that the West considers a secular state.

Perhaps most importantly, a number of insurgency groups in Iraq do not share the world view of the Militant Islamists—their goals even may be antithetical to each other. However, one factor unites all of them, and that is to expel the American and the coalition forces from Iraq. The primary objective of Militant Islamists is to force the United States out of the Arab countries and to bring about regime change in particular Arab nations. Therefore, for tactical purposes the Militant Islamists do not hesitate to work with other opposition groups in Iraq to accomplish this objective.

KUWAIT

The terrorist and armed campaigns by the Militant Islamists are not limited to Iraq and Saudi Arabia, although the media most often reports terrorist events in these two countries. Other Middle Eastern and the Persian Gulf states have also been hit by local Militant Islamists. In Kuwait, Western expatriates have been targeted in a number of attacks since late 2002. The country is home to 25,000 American military personnel and is used as a transit point for U.S. and other coalition troops headed for Iraq. Some 13,000 American civilians also live and work in Kuwait, as do about 9,000 Europeans and about 1,000 Australians.[25]

In the southern Kuwaiti city of Umm al-Haiman, a gunman was killed, another arrested, and two Kuwaiti policemen wounded when security forces clashed with militants on January 15, 2005. The incident followed a shoot-out on January 10 in a Kuwait City suburb between Militant Islamists and state security in which two members of the security forces and one Militant Islamist were killed. According to the Kuwaiti authorities, at least one gunman was captured, as were a cache of weapons, explosives, and munitions during the firefight in Umm al-Haiman, near the town of Arfijan, which has a U.S. military logistics center and also is home to Kuwait's largest refinery. The dead gunman was identified as Saudi national Hamada al-Inezi. It was the first time a Saudi was identified as having been involved in such an incident in Kuwait.

Following the clash on January 15, Kuwait put its security forces on full alert and formed a joint operations center to coordinate raids by various security agencies on suspected hideouts. The Interior Ministry said Kuwaiti forces had raided desert camps near Umm al-Haiman on January 14, 2005, and information from the arrested militants led security forces to the group involved in the firefight. The prime minister and other top Kuwaiti officials visited the scene, indicating that Militant Islamist activity is a serious problem in the country. Kuwait controls 10 percent of global petroleum reserves, but security sources said there was no indication the attack was aimed at any oil facilities. However, evidence shows that the armed campaigns of the Militant Islamists have become sporadic.[26]

On January 30, 2005, the Kuwaiti special forces raided a housing complex in the al-Salmiya district, where many foreigners live, about 14 miles east of Kuwait City. One Kuwaiti police officer, three suspected gunmen, and a Bahraini civilian were killed, and three others were wounded. The interior ministry spokesman reported that three Militant Islamists were also arrested in the raid.[27] The militant actions in Kuwait are carried out by the local Militant Islamists who agree with the world view of *al-Qa'ida*. Reports also indicate that the Militant Islamists in Kuwait had a larger plan. On February 6, 2005, Kuwait officials confirmed a report that suspected militants captured in recent police raids confessed that they had planned to use ice cream trucks packed with explosives to attack U.S. military convoys traveling to Iraq.

Forty Militant Islamist suspects have been handed over to Kuwaiti prosecutors since the January 2005 armed battle with Militant Islamists. The suspects in custody include two women—the wife of the ringleader, who allegedly helped him prepare explosives, and the wife of one of the five suspects who surrendered to police in the Sulaibiyah area on February 5, 2005. Among the arrested militants were two Saudis and three Jordanians; the rest were Kuwaitis. The other captured woman was later identified as a "non-Kuwaiti," who was "hiding a machine gun under her *abaya*," according to an official, referring to the black head-to-toe traditional cloak that some Muslim women wear. This was the first incident in which women participated in armed confrontation with Kuwaiti forces.[28]

SAUDI ARABIA

Terrorist attacks in Saudi Arabia did not begin with the invasion of Iraq. In fact, one of the major attacks came on June 25, 1996, near Dhahran when a bomb destroyed a housing complex, killing 19 servicemen. It should be noted that bin Ladin had arrived in Afghanistan from Sudan in May 1996. Between May 2003 and the end of 2004, more than a year after the invasion of Iraq, at least 87 policemen and civilians, many of them foreigners, were killed in shootings and suicide bombings in the country that is the world's largest oil exporter and birthplace of Islam.[29]

A series of attacks started in 2003, shortly after the invasion of Iraq, when car bombs exploded at three expatriate housing compounds in Riyadh, killing 35 people, including nine suicide bombers. Later that year, a suicide car bomb killed 17 people and wounded 122 others at a compound for foreign workers, also in Riyadh.

In May 2003, Militant Islamists killed 20 people, including 19 foreigners, when militants took over an expatriate housing complex in Khobar and held hostages for 25 hours. In the city of Yanbu that month, militants stormed the offices of Houston-based ABB Lummus Global Inc., killing six Westerners and a Saudi. All four attackers in Yanbu died in a shoot-out after an hour-long police chase, in which they dragged the body of an American from the bumper of their car. In June, militants in Riyadh kidnapped and beheaded Paul M. Johnson Jr., an engineer for a U.S. defense company. About 170 people, including foreigners, security forces, and militants, were killed in attacks and clashes since the first suicide bombings in Riyadh in May 2003.[30]

On May 12, 2003, attackers shot their way into three Riyadh housing compounds mostly occupied by foreign employees—among them British, German, French, and Australian citizens as well as Arab citizens of other countries—then set off suicide car bombs, killing and wounding a large number of people. The bombings were carried out just hours before the arrival of U.S. Secretary of State Colin Powell. This attack, too, was traced back to *al-Qa'ida*.[31] Saudi Interior Minister Nayef Ibn Abdul Aziz Al-Saud reported that the suicide bombers were members of a larger Militant Islamist armed group. The Saudi government sought 19 suspects in this case, including Saudis, a Yemeni, and an Iraqi with Kuwaiti and Canadian citizenship who were believed to have received orders directly from bin Ladin. If this connection is confirmed, it would clearly indicate that *al-Qa'ida* is still capable of mounting coordinated attacks in a strictly policed country. However, no group claimed responsibility for this incident.

Shortly after the May attacks in Riyadh, five coordinated terrorist attacks took place on May 16, 2003, in Casablanca, Morocco's largest city. Two international restaurants, a hotel, and two Jewish centers were hit, and 33 people and a dozen suicide bombers were killed. A connection between the attack in Riyadh and the one in Casablanca may be difficult to establish, but the probability seems very high because of timing, the nature of the political systems in the countries, and their close relations with the United States and thus the invasion of Iraq. The bombers, all Moroccans, were *al-Salafis* and were allegedly involved in the kidnapping of 32 Europeans in the Sahara in 2003. Following the attacks, Moroccan authorities arrested 634 suspects in connection with them; a French convert to Islam and 33 other suspected Muslim militants were put on trial on August 25, 2003.

While the Militant Islamists in Saudi Arabia have focused on U.S. and European targets, they have made clear in Internet postings and other statements that their goal is to overthrow the House of Saud, which they view as corrupt and beholden to foreigners. Usama bin Ladin, who has long been hostile to the monarchy, is from a wealthy Saudi family. *Al-Qa'ida* has tried to draw support from religiously conservative Muslims who are strongly opposed to the U.S. presence in the Middle East as well as the U.S. policy toward the Israel-Palestinian conflict and the invasion of Iraq and try to persuade them to approve and possibly finance the opposition against the U.S. military in Iraq. Usama bin Ladin accuses the West, particularly the United States, of seeking to destroy Islam and criticizes the Saudi royal family for its alliance with Washington. Saudi and U.S. officials have blamed *al-Qa'ida* for all major militant attacks in the kingdom since May 2003.

In November 2004, 26 prominent Saudi clerics, who are undoubtedly very conservative, jointly issued a *fatwa,* or religious edict, calling on Iraqi Muslims to fight "the invader occupiers" in their country and stating that armed resistance was "a legitimate right." Two former religious mentors to bin Ladin, Salman Ouda and Safar Hawali, were among those who issued the edict. This fatwa clearly revealed conservative religious attitudes. Moreover, because it provided clear support for the Militant Islamists in Iraq, it sent a strong message to young men who were dismayed with the Saudi ruling family and those undecided as to whether to join the Militant Islamist movement.

On December 6, 2004, armed Militant Islamists threw explosives at the gate of the heavily guarded U.S. consulate in Jeddah, then forced their way into the building, prompting a gun battle that left seven people dead and several injured before the three-hour crisis was brought under control. Three attackers were among those killed, while two others were injured and arrested, the Saudi Interior Ministry announced. Saudi security officials also said four of their forces were killed. The ministry statement did not mention hostages, although Saudi security officials said several had been taken.

The statement, carried by the official Saudi press agency, said a "stray bunch" (a reference to *al-Qa'ida* and Militant Islamists) had attacked the U.S. consulate. Saudi security forces engaged the attackers, killing three aggressors and capturing two others after they were hit. This attack was one of the boldest in Saudi Arabia since the Militant Islamists initiated attacks in the kingdom. The magnitude of this assault on the consulate was surprising, which led Crown Prince Abdullah bin Abdul Aziz,the current king,to issue a statement condemning the attack and restating the government's determination to fight terrorists and hunt them down. The consulate, like all U.S. diplomatic buildings and other Western compounds in Saudi Arabia, has been heavily fortified and guarded since 2003, when a series of bombings against expatriate housing compounds occurred. Guard posts are located at the corners of the compound.[32]

Since May 2003 when Militant Islamists attacked the Khobar expatriate housing compounds and killed 20 civilians, according to Saudi officials, at least three successive Saudi leaders of *al-Qa'ida* have been killed. In June 2003, Prince Turki al-Faisal, the former head of Saudi intelligence and the Saudi ambassador in London, in 2004 told Jane's Intelligence

Review that *al-Qa'ida* was severely disrupted inside the country: "Only one al Qaeda cell remains operational...Even now, it's in the process of being dismantled."[33]

Daring daytime attacks on targets like the U.S. consulate in Jeddah call into question one of the basic precepts of Saudi security strategy: that killing or capturing enough militants will eventually bring security back to the troubled kingdom. The consulate attack indicates that not only are the Militant Islamists more widespread and operating in small independent cells, but also that they have the ability to recruit and train new members to achieve their goals. Because of the paucity of information and data, it is difficult to speculate on the extent and number of recruited Militant Islamist Saudis who cross the border into Iraq to fight the occupying forces. Young Muslims who share a general sense of dissatisfaction with the ruling elite and government in particular and who perceive an increase in moral decadence often are attracted by Militant Islamist groups. Moreover, those who start a Militant Islamist terrorist cell commonly gain authority and respect among their peers because they are challenging authority and the legitimacy of the ruling Saudi royal family.

On December 29, 2004, Riyadh was again the site of an attack. Two car bombs were detonated in the city center, and the ministry of interior was the target. One person was killed by the first bomb, which was set off after a failed bid to storm the ministry itself. A second bomb exploded, hurting four people, after a car driver attempted to ram into a center for special security forces. Security forces later raided a house in the capital and killed seven suspects in a shoot-out.[34] The attack came a week after the second in command of *al-Qa'ida*, Ayman al-Dhawahri, and Usama bin Ladin warned in a video that Washington must change its policies or face further attacks by Militant Islamists. In the video, bin Ladin praised those who carried out the consulate attack in Jeddah and urged his followers to attack the kingdom's oil installations to weaken both the West and the Saudi royal family.

The Militant Islamists in Saudi Arabia stated on the Ansar al-Islam Web site that the attack on the U.S. consulate was one of a series of operations carried out by *al-Qa'ida* in its war against "the crusaders and the Jews to chase the infidels out of the Arabian Peninsula." The five gunmen claimed membership in what they called the "al-Fallujah Brigade"—a reference to the U.S. attack on Fallujah, the Iraqi city which was almost destroyed—in a call to the authorities made shortly after they entered the U.S. consulate in Jeddah, said Adel Al-Jubeir, foreign affairs advisor to Saudi Crown Prince Abdullah. *Al-Qa'ida* in the Arabian Peninsula claimed responsibility for the attack on the U.S. consulate in Jeddah in which nine people died. The *al-Qa'ida* in Saudi Arabia stated, "The squadron of the martyr Abu Anas al-Shami carried out the blessed Al-Fallujah attack by storming one of the bastions of the crusaders in the Arabian Peninsula; it does not mean exclusively Saudi Arabia rather includes the other Persian Gulf Arab countries,. . .from where the land of the two holy places is ruled. . .and spies and traitors dispatched far and wide."[35] Militant Islamists use the term Arabian Peninsula to refer to Bahrain, Kuwait, Oman, Qatar, Saudi Arabia, United Arab Emirates, and Yemen. Thus, its use indicates that their target is regional. Moreover, reference to the Iraqi town of Fallujah—which was attacked by U.S. military forces and resulted in extensive damage and loss of life—signifies that the attackers directly relate their terrorist campaigns in Saudi Arabia to the war in Iraq.

The attacks indicate that contrary to the Saudi government's claim, the Militant Islamists are still active in the country, are gaining recruits, and can mount armed operations against their chosen targets. It also questions the effectiveness of Saudi security forces and suggests they may have been infiltrated by Militant Islamists. The Saudi government's pro-American policy and regional problems, the Palestinian-Israeli conflict, and the violence that continues in occupied Iraq increases the attractiveness of Militant Islamist movements in the kingdom. Thus, the problem continues to make the Saudi ruling family uneasy, particularly because it could become a threat to the country's oil industry.

The seriousness of the Militant Islamists prompted 40 conservative Saudi clerics, academics, and public figures to sign a declaration released on January 16, 2005, that condemned those who incited the violence in Saudi Arabia beginning in 2003. The document said the violence was against Islamic law and specifically warned against potential attacks on Saudi Arabia's oil infrastructure. The signatories called on Muslims to close ranks and condemn the terrorists and the ideology, which were characterized as anti-Islamic. The signatories included Tawfiq al-Qussayir and Khalid al-Ujaimi, two university professors briefly detained by the authorities in March 2004 for signing pro-reform petitions, and prominent moderate clerics such as Muhsin al-Awaji and Safar al-Hawali.[36]

The Muslims' Hajj pilgrimage also presented an opportunity for Saudi religious leaders to address the issue of the terrorist campaign against the nation. On January 19, 2005, Saudi Arabia's senior Wahhabi cleric, Abdul Aziz bin Abdullah al-Sheikh, in his sermon for 2 million Hajj pilgrims characterized the terrorists violence as evil and warned them against assisting the enemies of Islam who wish to weaken Islam. At the same time he made references to the military invasion of Muslim lands (Afghanistan and Iraq), which he characterized as terrorism and as part of a campaign against Islam.[37]

On December 27, 2005, two Saudi Militant Islamists shot and killed five Saudi policemen in a gun battle in Buraidah, the capital of the Al-Qassim province, which had previously been the site of several shoot-outs with Militant Islamists. Both gunmen were captured; one died later from his injuries and the other, 26-year-old Abdul Rahman al-Mutaeb, was later killed by security forces. The former gunman was named by a Saudi-owned television network as 23-year-old Mohammed bin Abdulrahman al-Suweilmi and was described as an Internet specialist who had helped post militant statements on Web sites linked to *al-Qa'ida*. He was one of those on a list of 36 wanted insurgents linked to *al-Qa'ida* and terrorism in Kuwait. However, previously on September 6, 2005, Saudi authorities had announced that they had captured al-Suweilmi after a firefight in the eastern town of Damman. It was determined later that the militant captured on September 6 was not Suweilmi. In fact, in a message posted on the Web site shortly after the Damman clash, al-Suweilmi characterized the Saudi security forces as "clerics of the apostates" who were "living on the blood of our martyred brothers in order to please the principal tyrant, the fool [Saudi king] Abdullah bin Abdel Aziz." Al-Suweilmi announced that he would continue the fight against all unbelievers and apostates. The September 6 shoot-out was the bloodiest one in the previous three months as security forces stormed a major *al-Qa'ida* hideout in Dammam and killed all five armed Militant Islamists inside, ending a three-day gun battle. Four security men were also killed and 10 were wounded.[38]

The Saudi government has been further enriched by higher oil prices starting shortly after the invasion of Iraq in 2003. Oil revenues for 2004 were estimated at almost double the 2002 revenues of $61 billion, providing a financial windfall that was needed to help stabilize the political, economic, and security conditions in the kingdom. Obviously the increased oil revenue pleased the ruling Saudi family, but it also affected the security forces because they were given bonuses equal to two months' salary. From the early 1990s to 2003, a budget deficit was the hallmark of the annual government fiscal reports, along with high unemployment and declining social services and other state subsidies. Many observers had speculated that a crisis was imminent in the kingdom. However, the increased wealth does not solve the problem of the Saudi youth who have much money but are alienated and frustrated by the U.S. and European travel restrictions that make travel to other countries to pursue higher education and spend their money very difficult, if not impossible. The latter development is a consequence of new security measures against the Militant Islamists that particularly target young Muslim men. Such restrictions have become an additional source of frustration and anger, increasing the possibility that Militants Islamists will recruit them.[39]

In August 2005, Saudi King Abdullah vowed in his first television interview as monarch to eliminate *al-Qa'ida* even if the battle took decades to win, condemning the terror network as "the work of the devil (referring to the Militant Islamists)."Abdullah, who became the Saudi king in August 2005, insisted in the interview (with the American television channel ABC) that Saudi Arabia was doing all it could to halt terror following the September 11, 2001, attacks. Despite the public pronouncements by the Militant Islamists in Saudi Arabia that their objective is to overthrow the Saudi government, the Saudi Militant Islamists are not a threat to the reign of the House of Saud, whose family members number at least 6,000 and who control every aspect of the political, economic, and military system and apparatus of the country.

The invasion of Iraq and the subsequent developments remain a major concern of the Saudi ruling family, and it remanins watchful of possible recruitment by the Militant Islamists in Saudi Arabia to terrorist campaigns.[40]

LEBANON

The arrest of nine Lebanese Sunnis on April 10, 2006, was an important development as it signaled that sectarian violence in Iraq could spill over into Arab countries with significant *Shi'a* populations. A senior *Hizbullah* official said the nine men were charged with plotting to assassinate the leader of the Lebanese Shi'a Muslims as revenge for the killings of Sunnis in Iraq. The target of the alleged assassination plot, *Shi'a* leader Sheikh Hassan Nasrallah, is striving to avert any rift between *Shi'a*s and Sunnis. He urged all Lebanese to work together on "civil peace, coexistence and state-building." A top *Hizbullah* official told the Associated Press on April 14, 2006, that the nine men arrested are *al-Salafist* who saw Sheikh Nasrallah as a good Shi'a target to avenge the death of Sunnis in Iraq. In Iraq the *al-Salafi*s are the Militant Islamists who are blamed for most of the bombings, kidnappings, and killings of Iraqi *Shi'a*s, coalition forces and those who cooperated with the coalition forces and government in Iraq. Usama bin Laden, Ayman al-Dhawahri, and Abu Musab al-Zarqawi are considered al-Salafi.

Sheikh Hassan Nasrallah has had little direct connection to the conflict in Iraq, which intensified after the February 22, 2006, attack on the al-Askari Shrine with a cycle of revenge killings between *Shi'a*s and Sunnis. An attempt to kill him in the name of Sunni revenge could suggest a troubling turn for two Lebanese communities that have been divided for centuries. *Shi'a*s are a minority in most Arab states, but they are a majority in Iraq, and the defeat of Saddam Hussein's Sunni-led regime has heightened tensions over religion as the Iraqi *Shi'a*s have gained power. Egyptian President Hosni Mubarak angered *Shi'a*s across the region recently by saying they are more loyal to *Shi'a*-dominated Iran than to their own Arab nations.

The assassination of Nasrallah also would be a heavy blow to the delicate stability of Lebanon, an ethnically and religiously diverse nation where a fragile balance among *Shi'a*s, Sunnis, and Christians has been strained by a devastating 15 years of civil war that ended in 1990 and the 2005 assassination of former Prime Minister Rafiq al-Harriri, a Sunni. Still, *Shi'a* leaders have sought to lessen friction with the Sunnis, who along with *Shi'a*s account for about two-thirds of Lebanon's 3.5 million people. To calm the tension Ayatollah Mohammed Hussein Fadhlallah, the country's *Shi'a* leader, insisted in an Associated Press interview that *Shi'a*-Sunni violence in Iraq would not have any impact on Lebanon.[41]

The existing calm situation in Lebanon is superficial and fragile; eruption of violence within the Palestinian-Israeli conflict, increased tension in the Iraqi insurgency, and the involvement of Iran and Syria in Lebanon are all factors which could potentially disrupt Lebanon's stability.

PAKISTAN

Pakistan's involvement in the development of *al-Qa'ida,* the Taliban, and Militant Islamists goes back to the Soviet invasion of Afghanistan. As discussed in Chapter 2, Pakistan along with the United States, the United Arab Emirates, and Saudi Arabia had a direct role in the emergence of these groups during the Soviet-Afghan war. Pakistan also is home to many Militant Islamist cells. Many of the Taliban and their supporters escaped into Pakistan when the United States invaded Afghanistan, strengthening support for militants already in the country. Moreover, the problem of Indian-administered Kashmir, which revolves around the question of an independent Muslim territory within the disputed region, has over the years created a radical Muslim community that since the September 11 attacks has provided training ground for Pakistani Militant Islamists. Thus, the U.S. invasion of Afghanistan and Iraq has exacerbated an already volatile situation and fueled Militant Islamist activity in Pakistan.[42]

On October 4, 2004, Pakistani President Pervez Musharraf claimed that the country's security forces had eliminated the major sources of terrorism. Such a declaration was made in connection with the death of Amjad Hussain Farooqi, who was killed after a two-hour battle with Pakistani security forces in the city of Nawabshah in southern province of Sindh. Farooqi is said to be the man who masterminded two assassination attempts on Musharraf in 2004 and 2005 and was connected to the beheading of *Wall Street Journal* reporter Daniel Pearl in 2002. Pakistani officials described Farooqi as the chief *al-Qa'ida* contact in Pakistan and the key link between Usama bin Ladin and Pakistan's homegrown militants. He funded and recruited some of Pakistan's most extreme Militant Islamists (see Table 3.2). Farooqi was linked to a suicide bombing in 2002 at Karachi's Sheraton hotel, which killed 11 French engineers, and to a subsequent attack on the U.S. consulate, which resulted in the death of 12 Pakistanis. He also was linked to two failed attempts on Musharraf's life in December 2003, one of which killed 16 people. It is believed that his militancy has its roots in Pakistan's support for Kashmiri rebels in Indian-administered Kashmir in the 1980s and for the Taliban in the 1990s.[43]

On January 11, 2005, Pakistani officials announced that Mushtaq Ahmad, a militant sentenced to death for his role in an *al-Qa'ida* plot to kill President Musharraf, still had not been found since he escaped from jail in November 2004. He had been in the custody of the Pakistani Air Force near Rawalpindi, Islamabad's twin city. Authorities told *Agence France-Presse* that Mushtaq Ahmad is from a lower middle-class background and speaks English, Urdu, and Persian.[44] The attack, in which the would-be assassins blew up a bridge in Rawalpindi as Musharraf's motorcade passed, was the first of the two failed *al-Qa'ida*-linked attempts on the president's life in December 2003. A Pakistani official said that Ahmad was a member of the Jaish-e-Mohammed, a Militant Islamist group that provided logistical support to those who carried out the bombing. Five bombs were planted on the bridge, according to security officials, who said a hi-tech jamming device on his car delayed the explosions and possibly saved his life. Musharraf survived a second attack in the same area on December 25 when two suicide bombers rammed his motorcade, killing 15 people.

Musharraf had previously blamed the attack on a group of low-ranking army and air force officers who were led by *al-Qa'ida* militants and Muslim clerics. Whether Ahmad's escape was an inside job is an important question. Such a development would not be unusual in a country where Militant Islamist sympathizers permeate every aspect of government and society.

Occasionally the government announces the killing or the arrest of a Militant Islamist who is characterized as the leader of the *al-Qa'ida* in Pakistan. Despite this, the Militant Islamists maintain their activity without interruption. Many Pakistanis who supported the Taliban regime and the Taliban who survived the American military campaign in Afghanistan returned to Pakistan. These individuals work to enlist new recruits in a country that already is strongly oriented toward a radical Islam.

On December 17, 2004, Pakistani intelligence officials, in connection with Pakistan's military campaign against the militants, killed or arrested the leaders of *al-Qa'ida* and pro-Taliban forces. However, they accused the

United States of giving faulty intelligence reports about the concentration of *al-Qa'ida* and pro-Taliban elements during recent military operations in its tribal North and South Waziristan area. Authorities told ISN Security Watch that of the U.S.-provided information on terrorist hot spots only about 5 percent of it was credible. Nonetheless, security forces do pursue all the tips that are provided to them. The official said that on the ground, they could corroborate only 44 of the targets described in U.S. intelligence reports. Speaking to reporters, the official described U.S. intelligence assistance to Pakistani security forces in the tribal areas of North, South Waziristan, and Baluchistan provinces as becoming more problematic. According to the official, 6,000 to 7,000 soldiers were needed for any single operation in the rugged and hostile mountainous areas in the Wana region of Waziristan. For example, in an incident in which U.S. intelligence officials alerted them to a "huge concentration" of "foreign militants" belonging to *al-Qa'ida,* this "huge concentration" was actually a *Jirga,* or tribal meeting, in which local tribal elders were attempting to solve a community dispute.

Pakistan's military-led government has admitted to having lost over 200 soldiers and officers since March 2004, and independent sources put the number of civilian deaths at more than 1,500 and internally displaced persons at over 40,000. Moreover, both American and Pakistani officials have failed to kill or arrest a single known or wanted *al-Qa'ida* operative. In 2004, President Musharraf played down any prospects of finding bin Ladin in the tribal areas. Pakistani officials also told reporters that Pakistan military forces established 665 checkpoints along its side of the 600 Durand Line on the Afghan border—a border agreement between Afghanistan and British India in 1893—whereas U.S.-led coalition forces and the Afghan National Army have only a combined total of 69 checkpoints on the Afghan side. Pakistan has some 75,000 troops deployed along the Durand Line, but only 25,000 U.S.-led and Afghan troops are stationed on the Afghan side.[45]

In an interview with a *Washington Post* reporter, Pervez Musharraf's responses indicate that he has little understanding of not only the Militant Islamists in his country but also of the capture and elimination of the *al-Qa'ida* leadership that is the cornerstone of the U.S.-Pakistan military campaigns. The following portion of the interview reveals that Pakistan remains a source of Militant Islamists:

Q: U.S. officials contend that terrorist groups are still raising money and recruiting in Pakistan under different names in spite of your ban. To what extent are you willing to crush domestic terrorism?

A: We are cracking down in all possible ways. They are banned, and as far as recruitment, that is also totally banned. Groups may do it clandestinely but previously they had offices and recruiting centers all over. Their accounts have frozen and offices sealed.

Q: Don't these groups have ties to al Qaeda?

A: Within these extremist groups are masterminds, invariably from al Qaeda. [The masterminds] get an extremist Pakistani to plan operations and recruit people. Therefore, we are hitting the masterminds so that we dry up the planner.[46]

Musharraf urged his nation on February 26, 2005, to combat Militant Islamists and stop those who misuse mosques and religious schools. Speaking to thousands of people at a rally in the central city of Multan, Musharraf said eliminating extremism was vital to turn Pakistan into a prosperous and progressive country. He called on the Pakistani to stop those who use mosques and religious seminaries (*Madrassah*s) to spread Militant Islamist ideology and encourage terrorism, not in Pakistan but in other places. Musharraf made it his mission to fight religious extremism in the country after he sided with the United States in the global war on terrorism after September 11, 2001. After the numerous assassination attempts on Musharraf's life, this rally was held amid tight security with thousands of troops and police deployed across the city. Military vehicles patrolled the main roads, cellular phones were not allowed within the rally venue, and participants were thoroughly scanned with electronic detectors before entering.[47]

Many Afghanis, including the active Taliban and their sympathizers who fled the country after the U.S. invasion, found refuge in the Pakistani province of Baluchistan, which borders Afghanistan. Baluchistan is the home to approximately 250,000 Afghan refugees.[48] Although top-level Pakistani officials seem to be firm American allies since the September 11 terrorist attacks, Pakistan refuses to allow American troops in the country. It has maintained that it can deal with any Taliban seeking refuge in its territory, especially since Pakistan is where the movement began. Reuters reports that of the thousands of Taliban members who fled into Pakistan from the bombing and subsequent occupation of Afghanistan, not a single important Taliban member was arrested. The deputy police chief of Quetta, the capital of the province of Baluchistan, explained with a shrug, "You cannot arrest everyone wearing a turban."

Despite Pakistan's lack of success, the United States praised Musharraf and gave Pakistan a significant amount of financial aid in 2004 for continuing to campaign against *al-Qa'ida* and Militant Islamists. Musharraf also waged a military campaign with the deployment of 70,000 soldiers to the tribal area of Waziristan against tribesmen he accused of sheltering foreign Militant Islamist fighters. The border provinces of North and South Waziristan and Baluchistan are on the front lines in the hunt for the *al-Qa'ida* and Taliban fighters. According to official figures, the army has killed 300 militants in Waziristan, more than 100 of them foreigners, and has suffered more than 170 injuries among military forces. In Quetta, where there is strong hostility toward Islamabad and specifically Musharraf's pro-American stance, many young militants were recruited for the movement in the city mosques and Islamic *madressah*. (*Madressah* refers to any school, not just those that provide exclusively religious education for those who would become, for example, imams, or religious leaders in their communities.) It should be noted that most, if not all, religious *Madressahs* are built on public lands and funded by the government in Pakistan as well as by countries such as Saudi Arabia. Some of these religious *Madressahs* have thousands of students.

Pakistan's hunt for Militant Islamists in Baluchistan is complicated by the fact that the province has been beset by separatist-related violence for decades. The rebels seek greater autonomy as well as royalties from Baluchistan's natural gas fields. Baluchistan covers more than 44 percent of Pakistan, yet has just 5 percent of the population of approximately 163 million. A bomb exploded near an army truck in a crowded market in Quetta on January 20, 2005, killing eight civilians and a soldier. In 2004, rebels disrupted gas production with rocket and mortar attacks that killed eight people. A series of attacks also badly damaged gas facilities and a gas pipeline, disrupting supplies to industry and homes across Pakistan. As a result, the military established a new base in the province close to Quetta. Attacks on rail lines in the area have forced the government to bar trains from moving in the province at night, and large numbers of troops are hunting rebel tribesmen in the province.[49]

Pakistani paramilitary forces razed more than two dozen houses belonging to Bugti[50] tribesmen in the Baluchistan city of Sui, in retribution for a rocket attack that seriously damaged the country's largest natural gas reservoir. Over 100 people were arrested in a house-to-house search, which continued even during the Muslim Eid-ul-Adha holy celebrations. According to the Switzerland INS, the gas reservoir was attacked after an army captain and his colleagues allegedly gang-raped a female doctor in Sui. The angry tribesmen fired rockets and opened fire on gas installations and military posts between January 7 and January 12, 2006, after the local officials allegedly tried to cover up the crime.

Musharraf, who publicly committed his government and the Pakistani military to the "war on terror," has issued a stern warning to tribal chieftains, describing those behind attacks against government targets as little more than warlords. The province has unexplored mineral wealth ranging from oil and natural gas to gold and uranium and is the most underdeveloped region of Pakistan. Politicians and former military commanders largely oppose any kind of military operation in the poor but strategically important province, as any oil and gas pipelines from

Central Asia to the Arabian Sea or from Iran to India would have to pass through Baluchistan, and unrest has already scared off potential investors.[51] Consequently, because the Pakistani government has neither dealt directly with the local Militant Islamists nor with tribal demands and needs, this inaction has given the Taliban and their sympathizers the opportunity to ally with one another against the Pakistani government.

Since the deployment of tens of thousands Pakistani troops in 2004—under pressure from the White House—their aggressive tactics in the "war on terrorism" have backfired. The military forces alienated the public with their heavy-handed tactics, air strikes, and use of missiles. In response to the sheer military force, people have turned to their traditional way of dealing with the problem by supporting the local Militant Islamist (Taliban and *al-Qa'ida*) fighters. The Pakistani army has suffered numerous casualties since it entered the tribal areas in 2004. There have been repeated bloody clashes with tribal militiamen and, more recently, a spate of roadside bombings and one suicide bombing that targeted an army convoy.

The local Pakistani Talibans who have close ethnic and theological links to the Taliban across the border in Afghanistan have attracted new recruits and sympathizers and have become new power centers. In fact, developments have resulted in the Pakistani loss of the North Western Frontier Provinces (NWFP) and Baluchistan. The *al-Qa'ida*, Militant Islamist, and the Taliban fighters act freely in the areas. The people welcome them and the youths idolize them. There is no government, only the security forces who kill people. The Taliban settle disputes and deliver justice on the spot. The tribal areas are becoming recruiting school for the Taliban, and the army can't stop it.[52]

The impact of the U.S.-led invasion of Iraq on Pakistan is clearly evident in many areas, such as in the further radicalization of the Islamic institutions as well in the use of suicide and other forms of bombings. The bloody end to the military siege of the radical *Lal Masjid* (Red Mosque) and two attached *Madressahs*—one for men and the other for women—in Islamabad on July 7, 2007, that killed at least 102 and wounded many civilians and 10 military forces, has a had dramatic consequences. Shortly after the attack there were numerous suicide, car, and roadside bombings against the military forces and civilians; three in one day, and not only in the NWFP but also in other parts of Pakistan.

AFGHANISTAN

In Afghanistan in 2005 President Karzai's government offered amnesty to armed Taliban militia.[53] However, several former Taliban officials have taken advantage of the amnesty, including a senior member of the ousted Taliban government. Mofti Habibu-Rahman, chief of the criminal department at the Taliban's interior ministry, took advantage of the amnesty offer and surrendered to the Afghan government on April 23, 2005. His defection came two days after two other senior Taliban surrendered—Mullah Mohammad Naseem, the Taliban governor of Zabul province, and Haji Mohammad Akhtar, the former police chief of Farah province. The Afghan government amnesty offer does not extend to the 150 senior Taliban leaders who have been accused of militant violence or of having links with *al-Qa'ida*.[54]

Interestingly, on January 20, 2005, a rare statement purportedly by fugitive Taliban leader Mullah Mohammed Omar was released for the start of the Muslim holy festival Eid ul-Adha, in which he urged Afghanis to make further sacrifices against American "imperialists." The statement, faxed to the Associated Press in Pakistan by a spokesman claiming to represent the Taliban, also rejected claims by U.S. and Afghan officials that many former Taliban are ready to embrace a proposed reconciliation program. The faxed message said, "We [Taliban] consider jihad [holy war] as the only means for the salvation of Muslims."[55]

The majority of the Militant Islamists involved in the September 11 attacks were Saudi Arabian and apparently of the upper-middle class, as is the case in many other terrorist groups whose founding members and leaders come from educated backgrounds. In contrast, the majority of the group's members come from poorer segments of society. The educated Militant Islamists believe they act on behalf of their impoverished, uneducated brethren. Educated leadership of radical movements and groups is not a new phenomenon. The majority of the Afghan *Mujahideen* (fighters) are recruited from among very poor and rural backgrounds.

A number of developments have emerged in Afghanistan since the invasion of Iraq. Such developments occurred slowly, but they continue to have direct violent impact on the government in Kabul and the U.S. -led coalition forces. The introduction of suicide and car bombings in Afghanistan, Pakistan, and Iraq have changed the nature of Militant Islamist attacks, as has the use of improvised explosive devices (IEDs, referred to as roadside bombs). Neither suicide bombings nor IEDs were used in the Afghan-Soviet war or when the U.S.-led forces invaded Afghanistan in retaliation for the September 11 attacks. In Iraq, these modes of attack are used daily against the security and military forces and sometimes against civilian targets. Since the invasion of Afghanistan in October 2001, the country has become more dangerous instead of becoming safer. In the past five years, 284 American soldiers have died, including 99 in 2005 alone, which was the deadliest year since the arrival of the International Security Assistance Force (ISAF) in December 2001. A total of 1,600 Afghans were killed in terror attacks in 2005. In the first four months of 2006, hundreds of people lost their lives in increased attacks by the Taliban forces.[56]

Clearly, in countries where Islam dominates the social and political environment and is sometimes encouraged by the ruling elite, conditions exist for the growth of Militant Islamists. A large number of these countries are poor, with a wide division between the business, political, military, and security elite and the majority poor. The gap between the rich and poor is widening. The dominant political, social, and economic systems are concentrated in the capital cities and in the hands of the minority elite, where corruption and cronyism is the norm. Afghanistan, Algeria, Egypt, Indonesia, Iraq (since the U.S. invasion), Jordan, Morocco, Pakistan, Somalia (a failed state), Sudan, Tunisia, and Yemen can all be characterized in this way.

One of the direct impacts of the U.S.-led invasion of Iraq and the responses of the opposition forces, particularly Militant Islamists, has been indiscriminate suicide and car bombings. Such tactics, which never existed in Afghanistan before, have been adopted by the Taliban and *al-Qa'ida* fighters, not only against the NATO-led forces but also the civilians. Taliban, *al-Qa'ida*, and the Militant Islamist fighters in Afghanistan do follow and exploit the developments in other Islamic nations, and particularly in Iraq. A close look at the rhetorical and threatening declarations, either by the spokesmen or posted on Web sites, highlight the everyday killings in Iraq.

SEARCHING TO CONTROL DAMAGES THROUGH DIPLOMACY

The invasion of Iraq and its persisting violent consequences in Muslim and Western European nations (see Chapter 9) led to a 2004 conference, "Forum for the Future," which brought together the foreign ministers from North African, Middle Eastern Arab countries, and the Group of Eight industrialized democracies to formulate ideas and approaches to deal with the backlash of the invasion.

Foreign ministers and other government officials from Arab and other Muslim countries met with leaders from the West in Rabat, Morocco.. Although the conference was supposed to be dedicated to advancing political change in the Middle East, Arab foreign ministers vented their frustration with America's support for Israel. Secretary of State Colin L. Powell, in an opening statement to the group, spoke of efforts to make "participation in political and public life more inclusive." Nonetheless, representatives of 20 Arab states talked largely about the ever-present thorn of the Arab-Israeli conflict and economic development. "For too long," said Prince Saud al-Faisal, the Saudi Arabian foreign minister, "the Arabs have witnessed the Western bias toward Israel." In the public session, Amr Moussa, secretary general of the Arab League, set the tone when he asked, "How can this partnership (between the Middle East and the West) be achieved without settling the Palestinian issue?"[57]

German Foreign Minister Joschka Fischer, speaking in a session closed to the press, was quoted as saying "progress in the Middle East peace process will lend all reform and modernization efforts unprecedented momentum." Libya's deputy foreign minister, Hassaouna al-Shawish, also complained about the fighting in Iraq, saying the "continued bloodshed makes it difficult for us to go forward." The conference was the culmination of two years of effort by the Middle East states friendly to the West and the Western Europeans to advance President Bush's vision of bringing democratic change to the Arab world. The United States and Western Europe had been planning and talking about the event since the Group of Eight Summit meeting in June 2004.[58]

Ironically, the United States criticized the 2004 U.N. Development Program report, prepared by leading Arab intellectuals and specialists, concerning the issue of democracy in the Arab countries. The chair of the group said Washington had specifically objected to criticism of the U.S.-led occupation of Iraq and Israel's treatment of Palestinians in the Palestinian territories. "They (the United States) threatened to considerably reduce their financial contribution to the United Nations' development budget...The report...will be published with the sole endorsement of its authors and not that of the UN, after the United States and Egypt voiced reservations over its contents." The Egyptian government had also expressed displeasure over certain aspects of the report, including references to the "inheritance of power in Egypt," a thinly veiled allusion to the alleged grooming of President Hosni Mubarak's son, Jamal, to take Mubarak's place when he steps down. The chief author said Cairo had also objected to the assessment of freedoms in Egypt and demands for improved freedom to establish political parties.[59]

In connection with the invasion of Iraq and the U.S. "war on terrorism," the U.N. Secretary General Kofi Annan in a British television interview broadcast on October 17, 2004, said, "I cannot say the world is safer when you consider the violence around us, when you look around you and see the terrorist attacks around the world and you see what is going on in Iraq. We have a lot of work to do as an international community to try and make the world safer." He has previously described the American-led invasion of Iraq as "illegal."[60]

President George W. Bush declared a "war on terrorism" shortly after the September 11 terrorist attacks. The Bush administration has made numerous claims regarding its achievements against the Militant Islamists, including the fact that two-thirds of the key *al-Qa'ida* key figures have been neutralized or killed. However, terrorism has grown since the invasion of Iraq, and Militant Islamists have become active in more than 60 countries. According to the United States government, the number of significant terrorist attacks almost tripled worldwide in 2004, from 175 in 2003, to 650, with close to one-third of them taking place in Iraq. In particular, the war in Iraq and the loss of civilian lives and daily destruction have allowed the Militant Islamists, Iraqi nationalists, and former Ba'thists to direct the anger of grieving families toward the coalition forces and exploit their losses for recruitment purposes.

The statements made at the White House in a joint press conference with President Bush and Prime Minister Blair on May 25, 2006, sums up the problems and the consequences of the invasion of Iraq. Bush said, "No question that the Iraq war has created a sense of consternation here in America...I mean, when you turn on your TV screens and see innocent people die day in and day out, it affects the mentality of our country...Not everything since liberation has turned out the way we had expected or hoped. We've learned from our mistakes, adjusted our methods, and have built on our successes." Bush regretted his rough and tumble rhetoric, such as saying he wanted Usama bin Laden "dead or alive" and taunting terrorists to "bring 'em on" when referring to the opposition in July 2003 as the attacks on U.S. troops in Iraqi civilians mounted. He also cited the shameful abuse of Iraqis at the hands of American captors at Abu Ghraib. President Bush said the world could not abandon Iraq: "Make no mistake about it: What you're seeing in Iraq could happen all over the world if we don't stand fast and achieve the objective...The decision to remove Saddam Hussein from power was controversial. We did not find the weapons of mass destruction that we all believed were there, and that's raised questions about whether the sacrifice in Iraq has been worth it...Despite setbacks and missteps, I strongly believe we did and are doing the right thing."

Blair also acknowledged errors, but insisted there should be no regrets: "I think it's easy to go back over mistakes that we may have made. But the biggest reason why Iraq has been difficult is the determination by our opponents to defeat us. And I don't think we should be surprised at that. I know the decision to remove Saddam Hussein was deeply divisive for the international community...And there's no point in rehearsing those arguments over and over again...I think that probably in retrospect, though at the time it was very difficult to argue this, we could have done de-Ba'thification in a more differentiated way than we did...What is important now is to say that after three years, which have been very, very difficult, indeed, and when at times it looked impossible for the democratic process to work...then it is our duty, but it is also the duty of the whole of the international community, to get behind this government and support it."[61]

Both Bush and Blair ultimately agreed that they made many mistakes in connection with the invasion of Iraq,and the two have been shocked by the strength of the opposition to the invasion and the extent, depth, ferocity, and consequences of the violence.

The U.N. Secretary General Kofi Annan, after a two-week tour of the Middle East region, told a news conference on September 13, 2006, that most of the regional leaders had told him that the invasion of Iraq and its aftermath had been a "real disaster for them. . .They believe it has destabilized the region. . .Many leaders think the U.S. has to stay in Iraq until things improve, and that, having created the problem, they cannot walk away." However, he added, "Iran believes the presence of the U.S. is a problem and that the U.S. should leave. And if the U.S. were to decide to leave, they would help them leave." Annan concluded by saying, "So in a way, the U.S. has found itself in a position where it cannot stay and it cannot leave. . .And I believe, if it has to leave, the timing has to be optimum and it has to be arranged in such a way that it does not lead to even greater disruption or violence in the region."[62]

The U.S.-led invasion of Iraq has had a direct impact on the terrorist activities in the Middle East, specifically in the Arab countries and Turkey, but also in other countries such as Afghanistan and Pakistan. Rather than ending quickly as the Bush administration had planned, violence has escalated in a manner that the military planners in Iraq have been unable to resolve. Death and injury in Iraq, Afghanistan, and Pakistan have become part of daily life.

CHAPTER 11

The U.S. Non-Military Campaign: Influencing Muslims' Mind to Win Their Hearts

Most Militant Islamist groups vehemently oppose U.S. foreign policy and military involvement in the Middle East and the Muslim world. Militants strongly believe U.S. foreign policy and action to be anti-Islam and anti-Muslim—and this is the most serious issue facing U.S. foreign policy in the Muslim world. Militant Islamists propagate such views throughout the Muslim world via electronic and other forms of communication. To counter such activities, particularly after the invasion of Iraq, the U.S. Congress, with a strong push from the White House, took steps to counteract such perceptions and promote democracy by using what Joseph S. Nye refers to as "soft power." He describes soft power as "the ability to get what you want by attracting and persuading others to adopt your goals...Both hard and soft powers are important in the war on terrorism, but attraction is much cheaper than coercion, and any asset needs to be nourished."[1]

The administration has used this approach through communicative, diplomatic, and cultural tools. One of the most well-established tools of soft power are the radio international networks, *Voice of America* (radio and television networks) and Radio Free Europe/Radio Liberty (radio and an Internet newsletter). Through these channels, the Bush administration attempts to influence the minds of the Arab and non-Arab public in the Middle East. The U.S. government also established an Arabic-language FM radio station, *Sawa,* and *Hi* magazine, both of which are directed at young Arab audiences. In December 2005, the U.S. State

Department suspended the publication of its Arabic language magazine, *Hi*, which began publishing in July 2003 a few months after the invasion of Iraq, to develop a dialogue with a young, Arabic-speaking audience (18 to 35 years) on topics that affect them and their American counterparts. Monthly distribution of *Hi* was 55,000 copies in 18 countries, at a cost of $4.5 million a year, and 95 percent of the press run was given away for free. It was part of the U.S. government's effort to improve public relations with the Muslim world, part of the same strategy that generated the *Sawa*, radio station and *Al-Hurra* (The Free One) television.[2]

The U.S. government started a new satellite television service called *Al-Hurra*, which began airing programs on February 14, 2004. Tailored to an Arab audience, the network was launched to compete with the Arab networks, and Al Jazeera specifically, and to reach the Arabs. *Al-Hurra* has 150 reporters and is based in Springfield, Virginia. According to its Web site, it is a commercial-free, Arabic-language satellite television network for the Middle East devoted primarily to news, talk shows, and information programs. In addition to reporting on regional and international events, the channel broadcasts discussion programs, current affairs magazines, and features on a variety of subjects, including health and personal fitness, entertainment, sports, fashion, and science and technology. The channel is dedicated to presenting accurate, balanced, and comprehensive news. However, the Arab public is skeptical about the goals and intentions of the channel because of the U.S. foreign and military policies and actions in the region. *Al-Hurra* endeavors to broaden its viewers' perspectives, enabling them to make more informed decisions. The network, set up with a $62 million grant from the U.S. Congress, was launched with the aim of promoting democracy and shifting public opinion in the Arab world toward the U.S. point of view.[3] As part of this campaign to influence the Arab mind, the White House also made some changes in its diplomatic corp. Longtime presidential adviser Karen P. Hughes was named to a top post at the State Department, with the priority of improving the image of the United States in the Arab world as well as focusing on President Bush's plan to spread democracy in the Middle East. Her title is undersecretary of state for public diplomacy, and she has the same rank as an ambassador.

Hughes, who for years had a major voice in crafting President Bush's domestic ideas, is a former counselor to the president who left the White House in 2002 to move her family back to Texas. A former Texas television reporter, she continued to advise the president from her home in Austin. Although not a diplomat by training, she had a hand in several foreign policy initiatives during Bush's first term, including efforts to promote democracy and improve the lives of women and children in Afghanistan. Hughes was also close to the secretary of state, Condoleezza Rice. Her deputy is Dina Powell, Bush's former personnel director. Powell is an Arabic speaker who came to the United States as a child when her parents emigrated.

In 2005 Hughes made a carefully orchestrated trip to several Muslim countries, such as Egypt, Jordan, Indonesia, Saudi Arabia, and Turkey. For each visit her audience was handpicked; however, she nevertheless had difficulty dealing with the questions that are the crux of Muslim complaints about U.S. policy actions, such as the invasion of Iraq, the Palestinian-Israeli conflict, and America's support of nondemocratic governments while promoting democracy in Muslim countries, particularly the Arab nations. There were mixed reviews for Hughes's first Middle East trip, where she repeated talking points, introduced herself as "a mom," and unsuccessfully confronted criticism of the war in Iraq and American support for Israel. Some regional commentators described her as patronizing.[4]

The Brookings Institution sponsored a conference in Doha, Qatar, in February 2006 to encourage a practical understanding between Muslims and the Bush administration. American policy analysts as well as Hughes met with carefully selected prominent Muslims from all Muslim nations. For the American participants, promotion of democracy in the Middle East—albeit selectively—was one of the principal goals. Unfortunately, the conference viewed Muslims as a monolithic community, which it is not. Thus, the conference's discussions approached the subject in the same way. However, nothing came out of the meeting because the conference was held shortly after the HAMAS majority election victory in the Palestinian Parliament in January 2006 and the publication of inflammatory Danish cartoons of the Prophet Mohammad as a suicide bomber, which were reprinted by several European newspapers and resulted in outrage and violence directed toward the West by both radical and moderate Muslims.

Shortly after, tens of thousands of Palestinians, Indonesians, Malaysian Muslims, Pakistanis, and Syrians demonstrated against the cartoons and burned the Danish flag. During demonstrations held on February 6 and February 7 at least eight people were killed in Afghanistan by security forces. On February 9, *Shi'a* Muslims used the al-Ashura processions to condemn the cartoons, particularly in Lebanon where an estimated 700,000 *Shi'as* participated, and Sheikh Hassan Nasrallah, the leader of *Hizbullah*, criticized Europeans and President Bush and the U.S. Secretary of State by name.[5] Further, the U.S. response to the HAMAS victory—not to deal with the new Palestinian government unless it recognized Israel, among others—made it unthinkable that the conference and the White House's goal of promoting democracy would diminish Islamist militancy and anti-Americanism.

Moreover, the persistent pressure by the United States and European governments on the democratically elected HAMAS leaders to either recognize the state of Israel or face cuts in financial aid to their government would further the poverty and social problems in the territories. In connection with the imposition of financial aid sanctions on the Palestinian government, U.S. Secretary of State Condoleezza Rice made a visit to the friendly and "liberal" Arab governments of Egypt, Jordan, and Saudi Arabia in February 2006 to urge them not to support HAMAS by continuing to send aid money to the Palestinian Abbas government. However, the Muslim reaction to the Prophet cartoons, the war in Iraq, and the regional conditions made her visit to Saudi Arabia unsuccessful.

Although Saudi Arabia is a key Arab ally of the United States, withholding aid to HAMAS is politically impossible for the kingdom because of popular support for the Palestinians, especially when HAMAS won the election. Moreover, the kingdom has traditionally championed Muslim causes, such as backing the Afghan *Mujahideen* (fighters) against the Soviet Union (with the blessing and support of the United States), the Bosnian Muslim fighters in the Balkans war of 1992 to 1995, and the Chechen rebels in Russia. On March 11, 2006, a HAMAS delegation of five headed by their leader-in-exile Khaled Meshaal met with Saudi Foreign Minister Prince Saud al-Faisal and Prince Muqrin bin Abdul-Aziz, the Saudi intelligence chief, to solicit financial support.

The Bush administration's true quest to promote and sponsor democracy in the region surfaced in the outcome of the 2006 Palestinian parliamentary elections. The United States classifies HAMAS as terrorist organization. According to the *Washington Post*, on the eve of the January 2006 election in the Palestinian territories, the Bush administration spent foreign aid funds to promote the Abbas' Fatah party against HAMAS candidates, who were popular. HAMAS had also won a number of local municipal elections, and HAMAS candidates took the majority of seats in Palestinian Parliament (76 seats of 132) in the January 25 election.[6]

On February 9, 2005, Abdel Hussein Khazaal al-Basri, a correspondent for the American-funded *Al-Hurra* television station, was gunned down as he left his home in the al-Maaqal district, in the southern city of Basra, 340 miles southeast of Baghdad. Khazaal also worked for the Basra governor's press service and was a member of the *Shi'a* Islamic political party ad-Dawa, an influential movement among the *Shi'as*. Due to the conditions in Iraq, anyone connected with the United States, in this case the reporter for *Al-Hurra*, automatically became a target. Journalists have come under fire repeatedly in Iraq since the U.S.-led invasion. Questionable interrogation practices and allegations of torture at the Abu Ghraib and Guantánamo prisons and reports that U.S. troops had deliberately desecrated copies of the *Qur'an* make it very difficult for these propaganda measures to achieve their intent. The reported desecration of the *Qur'an* led to riots in Afghanistan, Egypt, Pakistan, the Palestinian territories, and Sudan. At least 15 rioters were killed. In wake of the riots and killings, several U.S. senators joined former U.S. President Jimmy Carter in calling for the closure of the camps.

The Qatari-based Al Jazeera (The Island) television network also created a dilemma for the Bush administration. This network is very popular with the Arab-speaking audience, but it is also controversial because it criticizes Arab governments, especially those friendly to the United States. Many of the states criticized by Al Jazeera are also autocratic, completely suppressing expression and any form of dissent. Shortly before the invasion of Iraq, the President's administration contended that a democratic political system would serve as a dramatic and inspiring example for other nations in the region. Ironically, however, the administration, which spends millions of dollars to promote independent and free media, became directly involved in clamping down on Al Jazeera.

The paradox and contradiction in U.S. foreign policy surfaced when the *New York Times* revealed, as suspected by many in the Arab world, that the White House pressured the U.S.-friendly government of Qatar to do something about Al Jazeera's unfriendly editorial content and programming. The Al Jazeera network was established in 1996 to present an Arab view of national, regional, and international developments rather than depend on the Western news services and networks, which are perceived as biased against the Arabs. It is financed by the Qatar government and also by advertising. Because of Al Jazeera's editorial orientation, however, Saudi Arabia established the Al-Arabiya (the Arab) network as a competitor, but it has not been able to have any impact on Al Jazeera's popularity.

Al Jazeera is a major source of news in Arab-speaking nations and communities throughout the world. The network has been a source of annoyance for the Bush administration and Arab governments. Vice president Dick Cheney, Secretary of Defense Donald Rumsfeld, Secretary of State Condoleeza Rice, former Secretary of State Colin Powell, and other Bush administration officials have complained heatedly to Qatari leaders that the network broadcasts have been inflammatory, misleading, and occasionally false, especially on Iraq. Thus, the content and the nature of the reporting have become a point of contention for both the Bush administration and Arab governments throughout the Middle East.

In April 2004 U.S. Secretary of State Colin Powell publicly complained about Al Jazeera to the government of Qatar. Powell had "very intense" discussions about the network with the Qatari foreign minister, Hamad Bin Jasim Thani, who said he would pass the information to the right people in his country. Jihad Ali Ballout, spokesperson for Al Jazeera, said that the criticism of the network by senior U.S. officials was unprecedented and that, far from being biased, Al Jazeera had explored taboo topics and provided an independent platform for diverse views that had been missing from the Arab media. Rami Khouri, executive editor of *The Daily Star* of Lebanon, notes that Al Jazeera's reporting and editorial approach is not the root of anti-American sentiment; instead, this sentiment is the direct consequence of U.S. foreign policy in action. He then observed that promoting American values might merely highlight the gap between those values and U.S. policy in the Middle East.[7]

The program of promoting democracy in selected Middle Eastern countries highlights the central challenge facing the White House in the region. Free elections in the Arab world, where most countries are still governed by unelected autocracies or unchallenged parties like Palestinian *Fatah*, often result in strong showings by radical Islamic movements opposed to the policies of the United States and to its chief regional ally, Israel. In attempting to manage the results, however, the administration risks undermining the democratic goals it is promoting.

Another contradiction of the program has been the Bush administration exerting tremendous pressure on Qatari officials such that in 2006 it discussed selling Al Jazeera. However, the administration countered that a privately owned station in the region may not be better in terms of editorial policy. Thus, the Bush administration clearly wants the network to change so that it will address the complaints about content and programming of all those involved, both the United States and Arab governments, and particularly Egypt and Saudi Arabia. Al Jazeera is not only pressured by the United States but also by advertisers and Arab governments. Because of its critical approach and editorial policy toward the Middle East states—from Morocco to the Persian Gulf—Al Jazeera is banned from operating in numerous Arab countries, including Saudi Arabia. Such pressure from the United States and Middle Eastern governments amounts to direct editorial control of content and is a form of censorship, which presents the irony of the Bush administration's efforts to promote its program of democracy in the Middle East and its policy problem with the Muslims in general.

The Al Jazeera audience ranges from 30 million to 50 million in the Middle East, but through cable television it also reaches a large audience among the Arab-speaking populations of Europe, North America, and elsewhere. Thus, it leaves the competitors, such as Al-Arabiya, far behind. Al-Arabiya is a Dubai-based television station owned largely by a member of the Saudi family, Prince Walid bin Talal. Al-Arabiya supports the Saudi government and is intended to be a less strident competitor to Al Jazeera. Al Jazeera's large audience also has been a major concern of the Bush administration.[8]

Publications such as *Hi* magazine and broadcast networks such as *Al Hurrah* or programming on Voice of America are some of the Arabic-language public relations efforts that the United States has directed toward the Middle East. Younger Arabs are the target audience because U.S. officials believe they are future of these countries, but an older audience, too, is pursued. The administration has also attempted to promote "reformist Islam" to counteract the teachings of militant Muslims. However, this step could turn out to be a double-edged sword if those involved are not well in tune with the local environment where "reformist Islam" ideas or teachings are presented and promoted.

Many influential officials in the administration believe that the U.S. government should develop a broader soft power strategy that goes beyond telecommunications and print approaches. Such a program, for example, could include efforts to discredit and undermine the influence of mosques and religious schools that have become breeding grounds for Muslim militancy and anti-Americanism across the Middle East, Asia, and Europe. It might include setting up schools with covert American financing to teach a moderate Islamic position, with lessons that include sympathetic depictions of how the religion is practiced in America. The aim would be to rectify the negative view of America held in many Muslim countries.[9]

The United States has a number of soft power resources, including foreign aid, that could be used to produce more positive results rather than relying on television and radio broadcasts such as *Al Hurrah.* The above approaches are based on the "positive results" of Voice of America and Radio Free Europe-Radio Liberty in connection with the "war on communism." The U.S. administration needs to realize that the Middle Eastern nations are different in many ways from the former communist nations. Importantly, in many Muslim nations their institutions of higher learning, specifically curriculum development and teaching, are in dire need of change.

In the communist states, developing countries, and particularly in Muslim and Arab countries, education continues to be regarded as a way to train technicians, physicians, nurses, engineers, lawyers, and so forth, not for becoming educated in the liberal meaning of the word; that is, to become critical thinkers and gain a broad perspective of subject matters. Memorization of information is highly emphasized in these educational institutions. Curriculum comes directly from the ministry of education (which is the same as communist systems), thus preventing any form of local educational autonomy in the institutions. It is important to underscore that a significant number of militants and radicals come from the educated sector of the young people; among many names that stand out are Dr. Ayman al-Dhawahiri, Dr. Mahmoud Zahar, Dr. George

Habash, and Dr. Abdel Aziz Rantisi, and many others are engineers and scientists.

The nonviolent means to counterterrorism is also expressed at the global level. The U.N. Secretary General Ban Ki-moon in a two-day meeting of the Alliance of Civilizations, a U.N.-backed initiative held in Madrid, Spain, said there is an urgent need for direct dialogue between Western and Muslim nations as a way to combat terrorism. "Never in our lifetime has there been a more desperate need for constructive and committed dialogue, among individuals, among communities, among cultures, among and between nations."[10] Turkey later became a cosponsor of the project, which is backed by 80 nations.

The forum was attended by dozens of government members, representatives of international organizations, civil society, the media, and philanthropic foundations from across the world. This showing presents a clear indication that there is room for the use of nonviolent means to bridge the divide. However, one should not expect that conferences alone can either bridge—or for that matter solve—the ever serious underpinning problems that are the root causes of the Militant Islamist's adoption of terrorism. At the same, it is clear that military responses to the terrorism alone cannot bring about change and eliminate the evil of violence and terrorism.

To assist in the development of democracy and openness in the Arab and Muslim world, there is a widespread need for an immediate and long-term program to promote educational progress and economic development by expanding existing U.S. economic aid and programs, such as the Fulbright scholarship and similar educational programs, rather than politicizing the process by the U.S. government. The emphasis on the use of television and radio not only may not assist in democratization, but in fact presents the Militant Islamists and other critics of the U.S. policy with ammunition to attack native reformers as U.S. proxies and even agents whose principal missions are anti-Islamic. The Brussels-based International Federation of Journalists reported in January 2005 that Iraq was the deadliest place in the world for journalists, where 49 of them were killed in 2004. This is a clear indication of the shortcomings of the supposedly calm environment in that country. Moreover, elections are not a good indicator of democracy because many of the elections held in the Arab and Muslim world are controlled and orchestrated by elite (*nukhba*) members of society, whose intention is to please global powers, specifically the United States.

For the United States to influence the mind and win the heart of the Muslim nations, and particularly the Arab world, it needs to develop a genuine policy and plan to use soft power to promote the democracy that the administration views as the cornerstone of U.S. security. The use of hard power and military might alone cannot promote democracy. The more that death and destruction are inflicted on Muslim nations, the more reasons exist for Militant Islamists to recruit and to carry out their terrorist plans.

Former U.S. president Bill Clinton called for the United States to sharply increase foreign aid, suggesting it was important in fighting terrorists and "cheaper than going to war." Saying the U.S. government gives a little more than $10 billion annually in real aid—excluding funds like military aid and aid to Egypt and Israel under the Camp David accords. "We should be giving about $60 billion a year," Clinton said. "And in a budget that's what, over $2 trillion, it's no money, really...And it's much cheaper than going to war. We've already spent over $300 billion in Iraq alone. So spending this money to be in a world with more partners and fewer terrorists and more possibility for growth and more prosperity for Americans is a very inexpensive thing to do...In the Cold War we gave less farm aid because we spent more on the umbrella defense of the rest of the world...But now that the world is much more complicated, we need to do our part. And we ought to hit that 0.7 percent aid target...Most Americans believe we spend far more of our federal budget and far more of our national income on foreign assistance than we do. If Americans knew how much we spent and knew that we could get good value per dollars, I think they would strongly support this." He said the United States should be giving aid at the target level set by the United Nations of 0.7 percent of gross national income. While few developed countries come close to meeting the 0.7 percent target, according to figures from the Organization for Economic Co-operation and Development, the United States has one of the lowest levels. In terms of private aid abroad, however, the United States is recognized for being one of the world's most generous, with donations by private citizens and organizations each year surpassing government aid by some estimates.[11]

CHAPTER 12

Conclusion

Human history is replete with events involving militancy and violence for the purpose of achieving religious and secular objectives. As for the use of violence and "terrorism" in Islam, the first known group that involved suicide and assassination were the *Hashishins*, or the Assassins referred to in the West, who existed between eighth and fourteenth centuries. However, national and regional conflicts, along with global political and military actions and interventions, presented opportunities to the Militant Islamists to become active in the war against communism in Afghanistan. Furthermore, their success in defeating the Russians increased their stature on a global scale.

Shortly after, it became apparent that suicide bombing by Militant Islamists was a weapon that could not be predicted or defended against. It was the September 11 attacks on the United States that put Militant Islamists on the radar screen as a new violent, Islamic, nonstate phenomenon. Militant Islamist terrorist campaigns pre and post-September 11 resulted in the burgeoning declaration of the existence of Militant Islamist groups and organizations (see Table 3.2).

The invasion of Afghanistan resulted in the disruption of *al-Qa'ida* networks as an epicenter of Militant Islamism and forced them to flee to their principal home nations, where they began to establish new, highly secretive, and autonomous cells while using national grievances to further their aim of global Militant Islamism. Shortly, the U.S.-led invasion of Iraq gave the Militant Islamists not only a new source of regional and global *casusas belli* against the enemies of Islam, the United States and the West, but also a training camp.

There has been a steady increase in the indiscriminate use of violence in Iraq since the U.S.-led invasion, and suicide bombing especially (e.g., cars, trucks, fuel tankers, and individual explosive belts)—in other words, human bombs— have been deployed as the principal terrorist tactic. Some of the attacks have had devastating effects, such as the bombing of the dome of the *al-Askari Shi'a* shrine on February 22, 2006, as well as bombings in open markets and bus stations, among others. Attacks on the Green Zone and the parliament building cafeteria provide evidence of insider cooperation and information regarding the whereabouts of would-be targets. There has also been an increase in the infiltration and direct participation of "foreign Militant Islamists" in the indiscriminate use of violence in the country.

At the same time, suicide bombings were adopted and utilized by the Militant Islamists and Taliban fighters in the Afghan war. Since then there has been an increase in its use, specifically in 2006 and 2007. There were at least 99 suicide bombings in 2006, compare to at least 21 in 2005, and at least 60 suicide bombings as of June 28, 2007. Moreover, the use of suicide bombings spread to other Muslim nations, such as Algeria, Morocco, Saudi Arabia, Somalia, Turkey, and Qatar, in addition to the London bombings in July 2005 and the Glasgow Airport car attack by two Muslims in late June 2007. However, the spread of Militant Islamist terrorist cells and operations continue to be the major concern of the security authorities throughout the Muslim and Arab nations as well in those that are perceived to be supporters of the repressive governments in those countries. Conflict areas such as Palestine-Israel, Kashmir, Chechnya, southern Philippines, southern Thailand, and the northwestern and Baluchistan regions of Pakistan are sources for the establishment of terrorist cells, with the aim of carrying out terrorist campaign in their home bases. One may hardly read about the Militant Islamists in southern Thailand, but in fact every month in southern Thailand, bombs are detonated, gunmen open fire from passing motorbikes, and some victims are beheaded, but no one admits responsibility.

Militant Islamists monitor media and other sources of information and use the Internet to communicate and inform the "field operators or activists" about new developments and discussions that take place in those countries and societies that are the established targets or would-be future targets of their terrorism. Posted audiotapes, videotapes, and other messages reveal their knowledge of recent or current occurrences. Thus, they disseminate information for the purpose of recruitment, to express "grievance or justification," and ultimately to commit violence against civilians, businesses, and government targets.

CHALLENGES AND PROSPECTS

Evidence throughout the Islamic world points to the existence of extensive underground Militant Islamist movements that are not allowed to function openly—from extreme groups to those who advocate integrating Islamic tenets and *Shari'a* in the state constitution and daily life.. In countries and regions such as Bangladesh, Indonesia, Malaysia, Pakistan, Afghanistan, the Persian Gulf, Turkey, and North Africa, it is not difficult to observe the presence and actions of Militant Islamists.

Bangladesh, similar to Pakistan, is founded on Islam. One of the signatories to the famous 1998 "Declaration of the World Islamic Front for Jihad against the Jews and the Crusaders" (see Chapter 2), along with Usama bin Ladin and Ayman Al-Dhawahri, was Fazlul Rahman, a radical Muslim closely associated with the Harkat ul-Jihad al-Islami (HUJI) of Bangladesh. The HUJI became active in Afghanistan by the early 1990s. Bangladesh is one of the world's poorest countries, and education is a luxury. It is estimated that Bangladesh has 64,000 *Madressah*s, all of which would not be considered as Islamic seminary schools, as this term is also used for school in general. Most of these *Madressah*s receive substantial funding from other Muslim countries, particularly Arab nations in the Persian Gulf. Most of these schools follow the teachings of Abdul A'la Mawdudi (1903–1979), who taught Deobandi Islam in Pakistan (see Chapter 2). This school of thought was dominant in the Pakistani Islamic *Madressah*s that gave rise to the Taliban, which then went to Afghanistan.

On October 29, 2004, a video by bin Ladin was delivered to the Al Jazeera network office in Islamabad, Pakistan, an event that is likely to have embarrassed Pakistan's president, Pervez Musharraf, one of the United States's closest allies in the war against the Taliban and *al-Qa'ida*. The United States has invested some of its best resources in trying to capture bin Ladin, using satellite tracking systems and sophisticated spying systems. Pakistan has deployed at least 80,000 troops in the area who, along with the U.S. forces, regularly carry out raids on the Afghan side of the border.

Contrary to the popular view that most Militant Islamist recruits in Pakistan come from Islamic seminaries, they, in fact, attend all types of public and private schools. Rather, economic disparities, widespread poverty, and economic and political desperation have created circumstances that have led to anger and disaffection among Pakistani youth, and it is these feelings on which radical Islamists have capitalized to gain new recruits. In Pakistan, however, poverty, religious orientation, and political desperation alone are not necessarily enough for young Muslim men to become Militant Islamists. Rather, Pakistan's relations with its neighbors and its relations with the United States are also factors. The Pakistan border, which stretches from China to Iran and covers thousands of miles, is an area that is very difficult, if not impossible, to control, and not coincidently it is the region where bin Ladin and those close to him appear to be hiding.

The area is dominated by Pakistani Pashtuns whose tribal cousins live across the border in Afghanistan, an artificial divide the British created when Pakistan was established. The Pashtuns continue to support the Taliban, especially in the Pakistani province of Baluchistan. Also, the involvement of Pakistani civilians, the military, and the government intelligence service in the region makes it impossible for the military to eradicate the Militant Islamists and the Taliban in Pakistan and Afghanistan. As long as Afghanistan remains chaotic, has little economic and social development, and anti-Indian Militant Islamists actively persists in Kashmir, the Pakistani government will be able to do little to eliminate the militants.

The situation in Afghanistan since the invasion, particularly in the past four years, clearly indicates that a military campaign alone is unlikely to defeat the Taliban and Militant Islamists in the country. Soaring violence in the form of suicide bombings—a rarity in Afghanistan— and roadside bombings, an increasing number of new Militant Islamist recruits, persisting poverty, and ever-growing corruption remain, despite years of a NATO-led military campaign and million of dollars being spent in the country. The government's power hardly extends beyond Kabul.

Despite its official pronouncement, the United States is reluctant to establish democracy in Iraq and the Middle East. To do so would mean that political systems in these countries would have to change drastically and that existing regimes would have to change, most likely through force. Such transformation could easily bring democratically elected groups to power that have strong anti-U.S. views regardless of whether those groups are, for example, Islamists or secular nationalists. Furthermore, any change in regime that is encouraged or supported by the U.S. government would be construed locally as being directed by the United States rather than as a popular rejection of the government. In such a case, Islamist and nationalist sentiments may only be reinforced.

Like Bangladesh, Somalia is a Muslim country (it has about 10 million Muslims) that has become a potential breeding ground for Militant Islamist movements and terrorism. It is a failed state and extremely unstable because of poverty and more than a decade of warlord rivalry. Since 1991, it has been carved into fiefdoms run by rival warlords. The ensuing instability ultimately gave rise to the radical militant Union of the Islamic Courts (UIC), which has taken over Somalia's interim government in the small town of Baidoa. The strategic location of the country, plus poverty and chaos, make it attractive for recruitment and the establishment of autonomous Militant Islamist cells. Further complicating the situation is that weapons continue to pour into the country despite a 1992 U.N. arms embargo, threatening efforts by Europeans and the United States to install a new government.[2]

For those reasons, the United States established the Combined Joint Task Force-Horn of Africa in Somalia in June 2002. The group is responsible for combating terrorism in the nine countries of the region: Djibouti, Eritrea, Ethiopia, Sudan, Kenya, Tanzania, Uganda, Somalia, and Yemen. (Although Yemen is located in the southwest Arabian Peninsula, it also is considered as part of the Horn of Africa.) The impoverished and conflict-ridden region has a sizable Muslim population and has been used by Militant Islamists to recruit operatives. The region has suffered four attacks either claimed by or attributed to Militant Islamists, including *al-Qa'ida*. In August 1998, car bombs destroyed the U.S. embassies in Kenya and Tanzania; in October 2000, suicide bombers attacked the USS Cole while it was refueling in Yemen; and in November 2002, attackers tried to shoot down an Israeli airliner minutes before a car bomb destroyed an Israeli-owned hotel on Kenya's coast.

Somalia has been ravaged by violence and anarchy since the overthrow of Mohamed Siad Barre in 1991. The current government was formed in 2004, but it has struggled to assert any real control. A radical Islamist group tied to the Militant Islamists ruled the capital city and much of southern Somalia for six months in 2006 until it was driven out with the direct intervention of Ethiopian forces, assistance from U.S. special operation troops, and U.S. air support. The former Militant Islamists and other opposition groups then launched an insurgency, vowing to defeat both the Ethiopians and the interim government. Daily indiscriminate killings and crimes have become the dominant feature of the capital city Mogadishu. The fighting has decimated the capital, already one of the most violent and gun-infested cities in the world. Thousands of civilians have been killed since December 2006, and one-fifth of Mogadishu's 2 million residents have fled. The United States has repeatedly accused the Somali Islamic group of harboring Militant Islamist terrorists linked to *al-Qa'ida* and alleges that it is also responsible for the 1998 bombings of the U.S. Embassies in Kenya and Tanzania. The United States is concerned that Somalia could be a breeding ground for Militant Islamists, particularly after the Islamists gained power briefly in 2006 and the *al-Qa'ida* leaders declared their support for them.

Somalia is facing its worst humanitarian crisis in a decade, and the situation is deteriorating, an international aid agency said on June 4, 2008. Worsening armed conflict, rising global prices of food and fuel, and severe drought in central Somalia are the main factors contributing to the humanitarian crisis in the Horn of Africa nation, said Pascal Hundt, head of the International Committee of Red Cross (ICRC) delegation for Somalia. "When you put all these factors together this is explaining why we are in front of an acute humanitarian crisis in Somalia," Hundt told journalists in neighboring Kenya, where the ICRC bases its operation because of insecurity in Somalia. "We have no reason to be optimistic in the short term." Somalia is experiencing its "worst tragedy of the past decade," he added. The ICRC will triple its budget this year due to the worsening humanitarian situation in Somalia, Hundt said, declining to give the figure because of concern for staff safety. In the past when the aid agency has made public the financial details of its Somalia operation, the ICRC staff had been threatened with robbery.

The most severely affected areas are in central Somalia, which has suffered from poor rainfall and harvests for more than two years, the statement said. It said food shortages in central Somalia are severe, and livestock, a major source of sustenance, are weakening as pasture land dries up.

On June 3, 2008, a group representing a range of Somali organizations warned members of the U.N. Security Council of a worsening humanitarian crisis in Somalia. These groups called for the withdrawal of Ethiopian troops who have been in the country since 2006 to back up Somali forces fighting Somali Militant Islamists, saying the departure of Ethiopian forces would accelerate a political settlement of the country's 18-year conflict.

The U.N. Security Council members were in Djibouti to encourage direct talks between Somalia's transitional government and an opposition alliance. "The presence of Ethiopian troops is exacerbating the crisis, and their withdrawal will accelerate all-inclusive political settlement," the Somalis said in a joint statement. The ICRC's Hundt said there is no safe place in Somalia, either for Somalis or foreign aid workers: "The best place, as I'm speaking now, can be the worst place tomorrow."[3]

Somalia, a poverty-stricken nation of 7 million people, has been in anarchy since warlords overthrew dictator Mohamed Siad Barre in 1991 and then turned on one another. A transitional government was formed in 2004, but it remains fragile. Islamic insurgents who seized the capital and much of the south in 2006 before being ousted by troops backed by Ethiopian forces remain a disruptive presence and a continuing threat to Somali President Abdullahi Yusuf's government. Thousands of Somalis have been killed, and hundreds of thousands have been forced from their homes.

The existing political, economic, and social conditions in the Muslim and Arab world, direct international intervention in the Muslim nations, along with regional problems, will continue to produce Militant Islamists. Moreover, *Ikhwan al-Muslimoon* (Muslim Brothers) has followers in many Islamic nations. Like many other Militant Islamists, the Brothers seek to establish the Islamic Umma, or Muslim community as it existed during the time of the prophet Mohammad and his four immediate successors, the *Khalafa*. Some in the Brothers promote nonviolent approaches to achieving the Umma, but others advocate that violence is the only way to bring down the existing governments to establish the Umma. The contemporary concept of Umma is to argue for a perpetual theocracy and the position of *Valayat-i Faqih* (Islamic Theocratic Political Leadership, or government by an Islamic Jurist in canon law). Iran is not the only country in which the Islamic government has gained strength. In Muslim nations and communities throughout the world, Islamist leaders are strengthening their grip. Both clerical and nonclerical rulers are using Islamic teachings to persuade their populations to adhere particularly to the Islamic tenet of submission to the will of God, and they have exploited this idea to encourage and perpetuate widespread gender discrimination, among all other restrictions and inhibitions.

The security situation in Iraq is unlikely to improve anytime soon, and the U.S. forces would remain in Iraq in one form or the other for some time to come. The official assessments are more pessimistic than the Bush administration's portrayal of the situation to the public. The classified cable sent in November 2004 by the CIA's station chief in Baghdad after completing a one-year tour of duty painted a bleak picture of Iraq's politics, economics, and security, and it reiterated points in briefings by senior CIA official Michael Kostiw. The cable, described as "unusually candid," cautioned that security in the country was likely to deteriorate unless the Iraqi government made significant progress in asserting its authority and building the economy. On December 5, 2006, U.S. Defense Secretary Robert Gates told the Senate Armed Services Committee that the United States is not winning the war in Iraq. "Our course the next year or two will determine whether the American and Iraqi people and the next president of the U.S. will face a slowly but steadily improving situation in Iraq or...the very real risk and possible reality of a regional conflagration," Gates said. His statement came on the day that suicide bombers, car bombings, and shootings killed at least 30 people in Baghdad and more than 30 others in north and southwestern Iraq.

The local Militant Islamist cell is structured so that members have minimal, or if any, contact with other militants. Thus, the individual cells are very hard to trace and destroy. Although Militant Islamists have their own local agendas, they are united in their opposition to the U.S. military and nonmilitary campaigns in Muslim regions and countries that are carried out under the "Global War on Terrorism" campaign, which is nothing more than dealing with the symptom rather than the actual cause.

Importantly, the Militant Islamists may support and assist each other at the regional and even global level without leaving concrete evidence of direct contacts, except possibly when they access Web sites, send mass e-mail messages, and use couriers for financial transfers. Although the cells are small, they can carry out massive attacks. Only 19 young men carried out the attacks of September 11, 2001, but their attacks changed history. The attacks led within two years to an American-led invasion and military occupation of two Muslim countries, Afghanistan and Iraq. These actions, in turn, damaged Muslim perceptions of the United States and Western Europe.

Al-Qa'ida was founded as a decentralized coalition of Militant Islamists, led by bin Ladin and al-Dhawahiri, but without any further direct chain of command. Since the invasion of Afghanistan, the command structure has been dismantled, but local Militant Islamists cells have spread and been inspired and energized by the invasion of Iraq, U.S. support of Israeli policies and action in the occupied territories, and the war with *Hizbullah* in July 2006. This decentralization and growth of local groups has made it very difficult to have a direct impact on Islamist extremists. Moreover, the September 11 attacks and the invasion of Afghanistan and Iraq unleashed events that removed what control *al-Qa'ida* had over the Militant Islamist groups. However, *al-Qa'ida*'s ideology still remains the paramount world view for the Militant Islamists while tactical approaches are developed to achieve local objectives. Terrorist attacks in Indonesia, Philippines, southern Afghanistan, Pakistan, Indian-administered Kashmir, Thailand, Chechnya, North Africa, Kuwait, Saudi Arabia, Yemen, Europe, and Iraq clearly show that numerous independent cells exist.

In fact, since 2004, specifically after the Thai government forces attacked demonstrators, which resulted in the suffocating of at least 78 Muslims in army truck, the increased number of attacks by Militant Islamists have resulted in the loss of at least 3,000 lives in southern Muslim-dominated provinces of the country. The Militant Islamists have one clear demand, and that is independence for the four southern provinces populated by 1.3 million Mali-speaking Muslims. In a stark contrast to other Militant Islamists, the Mali-speaking Militant Islamists remain anonymous, and do not claim any responsibility and demands for their attacks. However, similar to other Militant Islamists they do carry out assassinations and beheadings and bomb structures, including schools. All these forms of violent attacks are carried out despite an extraordinary Thai military presence, with fortified checkpoints and indiscriminate arrests and tortures throughout the southern provinces.

One of the major features of the "Global War on Terrorism" is to remedy the sources and the wrongs that feed terrorism. As noted earlier, however, it is clear that the global effort has a major shortcoming:the absence of a direct and honest assessment of the causes, a dilemma that would be around for some time to come, specifically with the problems generated by the Iraqi invasion and the Israeli war on the Lebanese *Hizbullah*. Both of these problems, in addition to the Israeli-Palestinian conflict, have weakened the credibility of the Arab governments such as Saudi Arabia, Egypt, and Jordan specifically, if not their legitimacy. The predecessors of militants and the current Militant Islamists have succeeded in de-secularizing social, political, and economic grievances in addition to the regional and global problems that directly touch Muslims, thus allowing them to characterize any action taken by the governments in Muslim nations, the United States, and Western Europe as "War against Islam."

Militant Islamists are changing their approaches and strategies in regard to recruitment for local cells and the violent campaigns against their national, regional, and international targets. These changes are being introduced because the current young Militant Islamist recruiters are different from those who founded the ideological base of radical Islam and those who founded *al-Qa'ida*. The current young Militant Islamists have many common characteristics and more information and knowledge of the present-day political, social, and economic systems. Changes in the Militant Islamist propaganda and recruitment are having an effect on the composition of new members in the Militant Islamist cells, both in Muslim regions and in Western European countries and elsewhere.

Militant Islamists perceive all Muslims to be victims of the actions of other nations. Specifically, a "monolithic center" in the West is seen as responsible for poverty among Muslims in their countries as well as for the ills afflicting poor Muslims worldwide. Their grievances against Muslim nations focus on high unemployment, poverty, and repression (see Table 3.1). However, these problems are not comparable to those that Muslims experience in Western countries, specifically Western Europe. Muslims suffer greatly due to the widespread repression and poverty in the Muslim nations. Consequently, the Militant Islamist argument that the West is responsible for the suffering of Muslims worldwide makes a little sense. This sense of victimization is exacerbated because Muslims today also have greater awareness of regional conflicts that pit Muslims against non-Muslims and the West—the Israeli-Palestinian conflict, Afghanistan, Algeria, Morocco, Chechnya, the Philippines, southern Thailand, Indian-administered Kashmir, Somalia, Sudan, Darfur, and especially the death and destruction in Afghanistan and Iraq.

In Western Europe, Muslims are alienated and experience widespread job discrimination. For Muslim youths in Western Europe, these very real discriminations have led to disillusionment, and they may become vulnerable to militant messages on the Internet or may be swayed by a Militant Islamist acquaintance. Unlike the generation of bin Ladin, Muslim youths are savvy users of information technology and so often have direct access to militant propaganda through the Internet, making them more vulnerable to recruitment. Militant Islamists in Europe are not fighting solely for national causes, but rather for such ones as the invasion of

Afghanistan and Iraq, the Israeli-Palestinian conflict, and against the oppressive Muslim and Arab governments.

The Militant Islamists and *al-Qa'ida* are not sitting still when it comes to the use of the available information technology as means to recruit and mobilize Muslims toward their ends. In fact, *Al-Sahab,* the media wing of the *al-Qa'ida* and the Militant Islamists, posted an announcement in January 2008 on the Web site frequently used by the Militant Islamists that the video messages of bin Ladin and al-Dhawahri can now be downloaded to cell phones. A day later, eight of the previously recorded videos were made available, including one that was a tribute to Abu Musab al-Zarqawi, the former *al-Qa'ida* leader in Iraq who was killed by U.S. forces in June 2006. *Al-Sahab* has promised to release more of its previous video messages in cell phone formats. Videos playable on cell phones are increasingly popular in the Middle East, as files are transferred from phone to phone using Bluetooth or infrared wireless technology. Clips showing former Iraqi leader Saddam Hussein's execution in December 2006 showed up on cell phones soon after his death. In Egypt, images showing police brutality have been passed around via cell phones, including one video that showed an arrested bus driver being sodomized with a stick by police in the fall of 2006.

Video and audiotapes of *al-Qa'ida* and various Militant and non-Militant Islamist organizations and groups are widely available on Islamist Web sites. The Militant Islamists and the *al-Qa'ida* network have been growing more sophisticated in targeting international audiences. Videos are always subtitled in English, and messages this year from bin Ladin and al-Dhawahri focusing on Pakistan and Afghanistan have been dubbed in the Urdu and Pashtu languages used in Afghanistan and Pakistan. Both men have been prolific in broadcasting their messages over the Internet, and they are likely to continue to use the Internet in their war against the West. Both have delivered a number of audio and video messages in the past 12 months.

The heavyhanded U.S. foreign policy toward the Middle East, the Arabs, and Muslim states in general has further widened the gap between the governments of these countries and their populations. The governments of most Arab countries ignore the needs and wants of the populace while the Western European and American governments support, and in some cases protect, these Muslim governments. The Arab governments do represent the people because of their dictatorial political system but are friendly to the West, while the public maintains and expresses, whenever opportunity arises, its strong anti-Western sentiments. With a certain exception, the West views the Arab governments in a positive manner and, in fact, Egypt, Jordan, and Saudi Arabia are presented as "moderate." This division between the Arab governments and the attitudes and actions of their populations has produced greater and deeper sympathy and support for the Militant Islamists among the public, from Morocco to Pakistan to Indonesia. Such a development is very alarming in light of the U.S. government's continuous announcements of "democracy" for the Middle Eastern nations, starting with Iraq.

Current Militant Islamist violence and terrorism will not crumble like communism or fascism; it cannot be defeated by containment, force, economic sanctions, or free and fair elections. Moreover, the Western intelligence agencies have not been able to penetrate the Militant Islamists, whether in Europe or any Muslim nations. To adopt the Cold War tactic, such as waving cash in front the East European or any nationalities of the former Soviet Union, will not work to recruit Muslim spies. Militant Islamists who are willing to carry out suicide missions, partly because of religious dedication, cannot easily be recruited. Those who are knowledgeable about Islam or are practicing Muslims know that physical threat to Islam (e.g., the Mongolian invasion, the Crusaders, colonialism, and communism) has never been viewed as a true danger; rather, the penetration and popularization of genuine Western philosophy and ideology, along with a fair and open political environment, are considered to pose the most legal threat to Islam. Western colonialism, along with many decades of the Western hypocrisy under the banner of anticommunism of the Cold War, generated widespread cynicism among the Muslims who were the victims of those policies and actions.

However, combining both physical invasion and the constant underscoring of the importance of the Western world views as the true salvation are what fuel Islamic radicalism. Militant Islamists, in fact, view the physical aggression—the use of media, military, and financial prowess—and the aggrandizement of the Western world view as a direct assault and insult on Muslims and Islam by characterizing Islam as a backward, antihuman rights, and antidemocratic religion. Indeed, it is possible that the greater attacks and threats to Islam by Western ideas and practices may only intensify the desire and commitment of Militant Islamists.

The Militant Islamists who adhere to the *al-Qa'ida* ideology advocate and promote the use of violence against governments in Muslim nations and the international "enemies of Islam." The Militant Islamists often accompany their written, audio, and video messages with direct quotations from the *Qur'an* or slogans that advocate or call upon the believers, and especially youth, to join the Jihad in places such as Afghanistan, Chechnya, Indian-administered Kashmir, Aceh, southern Philippines, Pakistan, and Iraq specifically—regions where Muslims are directly targeted by the so called "enemies of Islam."

Muslims are as diverse as all other religious and ethnic communities in the world and should not be characterized as a single, homogeneous group, and neither should Militant Islamists. Even though Militant Islamists throughout the world do believe in jihad—struggle or the holy war—to bring about change, they too do not think alike, each being the product of his or her social, economic, and regional political circumstances. Militant Islamist groups have different agendas, but when possible they will support each other to help achieve local goals. There is a strong tendency among observers, analysts, scholars, politicians, and government authorities to regard Militant Islamists as not diverse, an attitude that makes them much easier to analyze and thus makes it easier to devise a response. However, this approach does not result in an accurate evaluation, and any response based on such an inaccurate assessment will fail.

Terrorist attacks, specifically human bombs, and widespread casualties have increased, contrary to the expectation that the "war on terrorism" would result in a decline in terrorism. In particular, the wars in Afghanistan and Iraq have directly contributed to this rise. Violent terrorist attacks and kidnappings worldwide exceeded 10,000 for the first time in 2005, propelled in part by a rapid increase in such activities in Iraq, which accounts for at least 60 percent of the total casualties.

The numbers are a striking reminder that all forms of violence by the Militant Islamists have dramatically increased in the more than four years of the war on terror. In August 2004, the National Counterterrorism Center was established as the U.S. government's new hub for monitoring terrorism. The Center counted 3,192 terror attacks in 2004, and in 2005 the number exceeded 10,000 attacks and kidnappings, according to a federal official familiar with the Center's work on the subject. Terrorist violence in Iraq increased in every category in 2005, including armed attacks and kidnappings. The official said Iraq represents more than 50 percent of the total increase in terrorist incidents. The year before, the center reported 866 terror attacks against civilians and other noncombatants in Iraq. These numbers were formally released in May 2006 in a broader report from the State Department, called the Country Reports on Terrorism.[4]

A number of *al-Qa'ida* key figures in Afghanistan, Algeria, Indian-administered Kashmir, Indonesia, Pakistan, Philippines, Saudi Arabia, and Somalia have been either eliminated or arrested following the September 11, 2001, attacks. In the past seven years, however, the spread of *al-Qa'ida* ideology and subsequently the recruitment of Militant Islamists throughout Muslim nations and Europe have been on the rise. Of course, Afghanistan, Iraq, and Pakistan are the frontline of the direct confrontation between the U.S.-led Western forces and the Militant Islamists, who continue to cause heinous casualties and the death of large numbers of people through the use of suicide bombings and other forms of attack. In fact, the suicide attacks have increased at an alarming rate and have spread to other parts of target countries. The evidence clearly underscores the spread of the Militant Islamists cells, influenced by the *al-Qa'ida* ideology. The failure of the U.S.-led allies in their military and political campaigns in Afghanistan and Iraq will embolden the Militant Islamists, further their recruitment, and increase their activities in the Persian Gulf and North African countries, where governments remain autocratic and supported by the United States and Western European governments.

The Militant Islamists, the new nonstate actors and clearly a new phenomena, are very difficult, if not impossible, to defeat in a conventional military campaign, not only in conflict areas but also in the larger arena of the "Global War on Terrorism." The U.S. and NATO forces in Afghanistan and Iraq may have all the latest military technology at their disposal, but Militant Islamists and other radical Islamist forces are not visible targets and are invulnerable to conventional military targeting systems, being as they are scattered throughout cities, towns, and villages. Although the United States implemented various counterinsurgency campaigns during the Cold War because of known targets, these approaches most likely will not be effective against Militant Islamist terrorist campaigns. Thus, the Militant Islamists will require innovative political and military approaches that include the support of the local governments where these militants are active.

Notes

CHAPTER 1

1. M. G. S. Hodgson, "The Order of Assassins," in *Encyclopedia of Islam* (S'Gravenhage, Holland: 1955), 133–7; Olivier Roy, *Globalized Islam, The Search for A New Umma* (NY: Columbia University Press, 2004).42, 178–179; Mia Bloom, *Dying to Kill: The Allure of Suicide Terror* (NY: Columbia University Press, 2005); Diego Gambetta, ed., *Making Sense of Suicide Missions* (NY: Oxford University Press, 2004); Anne Marie Oliver and Paul Steinberg, *The Road to Martyrs' Square: A Journey Into the World of the Suicide Bomber* (NY: Oxford University Press, 2004); Nadia Taysir Dabbagh, *Suicide in Palestine: Narrative of Despair* (UK: Hurst and Company, 2005); Robert A. Pape, *Dying to Win: The Strategic Logic of Suicide Terrorism* (NY: Random House, 2005).

2. Anarchists in the late 19_{th} century and early 20_{th} century assassinated several key state leaders. Irving L. Horowitz, ed., *The Anarchists* (NY: Dell, 1964); Scott Atran, Genesis and Future of Terrorism, http://www.interdisciplines.org/terrorism/papers/1

3. *Associated Press*, June 17, 2002.

4. http://www.defenselink.mil/news/Oct2001/n10162001_200110164.html. "A more secure world: our shared responsibility," Report of the U.N. Secretary General's High-Level Panel of Threats, Challenges and Change, 2004. http://www.un.org/secureworld/. Bruce Hoffman, *Inside Terrorism* (NY: Columbia University Press, 1998), contends that the affiliation of the terrorist is an important factor rather than the nature of the act.

5. *New York Times*, March 6, 2005.

6. Ron Steel, in his review of the book by Michael Ignatief, *The Lesser Evil: Politics in an Age of Terror* (Princeton University Press), 212; *New York Times Book Review*, July 25, 2004.

7. *Guardian Weekly*, October 15–21, 2004.

8. Reuters, February 16, 2005.

9. *Economist*, January 10, 2004; *Associated Press*, April 25, 2006; *Agence France Presse*, January 7, 2006; *Reuters*, June 26, 2006; *Agence France Presse*, October 18, 2006; Robert A. Pape, *Dying to Win: The Strategic Logic of Suicide Terrorism* (New York, NY: Random House, 2005), especially, 4 and 79–80. On February 3, 2008, a female suicide bomber killed at least nine and wounded 100 at a train station in

Colombo, Sri Lanka (BBC, February 3, 2008). On April 6, 2008, a suicide bomber killed at least 11 and a government minister near Sri Lankan capital city Colombo. (*Associated Press*, April 6, 2008).

10. *Agence France Presse*, December 3, 2004.

11. Oliver Roy, *Globalized Islam*, 43.

12. Naim Qassem, *Hizbullah: The Story from Within*, Translated by Dalia Khalil (London, UK: Saqi Books, 2005), 45 and 74–75.

13. John A. Nagl, *Learning to Eat Soup with Knife: Counterinsurgency Lessons from Malaya and Vietnam* (Chicago, IL: University of Chicago Press, 2005).

CHAPTER 2

1. Nadav Safran, *Egypt in Search of Political Community* (Cambridge, MA: Harvard University Press, 1961), 63; Kemal H. Karpat, ed., *Political and Social Thought in the Contemporary Middle East* (New York, NY: Praeger Publishers 1982), especially 3–26; Juan R. I. Cole, *Colonialism and Revolution in the Middle East: Social and Cultural Origin of 'Urabi Movement* (Princeton University Press. 1993).

2. Malcom H. Kerr, *Islamic Reform: The Political and Legal Theories of Mohammad Abdu and Rashid Rida* (Berkley, CA: California University Press, 1996).

3. Malise Ruthven, *Islam in the World* (Oxford University Press, 1984), 309–313.

4. Ruthven, *Islam in the World*, 313–314, 327.

5. John Esposito, *The Islamic Threat: Myth or Reality*, 3_{rd} ed. (NY: Oxford University Press, 1999), 47–48.

6. James Pavlin, "Sunni Kalam and Theological Controversies" in S. H. Nasr and O. Leaman, eds, *History of Islamic Philosophy* (London: Routledge, 1996), 105–18. James Pavlin presents an overview of Tamiyya's views in a Routlege copyright of 1998: http://www.muslimphilosophy.com//ip/rep/H039.htm.

7. Sohail H. Hashmi, ed., *Islamic Political Ethics* (Princeton University Press), especially 48–49, 185–187, and 208.

8. Nozar Alaolmolki, *Struggle for Dominance in the Persian Gulf: Past, Present and Future Prospects* (New York, NY: Peter Lang, 1991), 235–6.

9. Mahmood Mamdani, *Good Muslim, Bad Muslim* (NY: Pantheon Books, 2004), especially 51–60.

10. *Reuters*, July 22, 2005.

11. Oliver Roy, *Globalized Islam* (NY: Columbia University Press, 2004), 41–57.

12. *Al Jazeera*, January 27, 2005; http://www2.gwu.edu/~nsarchiv/NSAEBB/NSAEBB147/index.htm.

13. *Agence France Presse, Al Jazeera*, January 16, 2005.

14. *Jihad Against Jews and Crusaders*, http://www.fas.org/irp/world/para/docs/980223-fatwa.htm; www.secularislam.org/visitors/guest114.htm (hard copy is in possession of the author).

15. *Reuters*, March 11, 2005. Al-Dhawahiri, second in command of al-Qa'ida, criticized Iran for cooperating with the United States in its 2001 invasion of Afghanistan that helped oust the Taliban. "Iran's aim here is also clear—to cover up its involvement with America in invading the homes of Muslims in

Afghanistan and Iraq," he said. This is the second verbal attack on Iran, a predominantly Shi'a Muslim country. In an audiotape marking the fifth anniversary of the U.S.-led invasion of Iraq, al-Dhawahiri accused Iran of planning to annex southern Iraq and the eastern part of the Arabian Peninsula. Such messages appear to play on Sunni fears throughout the region of growing Iranian influence and to present al-Qa'ida as the best bulwark against Islamic Republic government. *Al Jazeera*, April 22, 2005.

16. *The Economist*, August 30, 2003.

17. Rohan Gunaratna, *Inside Al Qaeda, Global Network of Terror* (Columbia University Press, 2002); Mariam Abou Zahab and Olivier Roy, *Islamist Networks: The Afghan-Pakistan Connection* (Columbia University Press, 2004); *Agence France Presse*, November 30, 2005.

18. *Agence France Presse*, September 13, 2003; *New York Times*, December 7, 2003.

19. Giles Kepel, *The War for Muslim Minds: Islam and the West* (Cambridge: Belknap, 2004).

20. Mahmood Mamdani, "Wither Political Islam?" *Foreign Affairs* (January/February 2005).

21. *Al Jazeera*, February 10 and 20, 2005.

CHAPTER 3

1. *The Economist*, April 3, 2004; *Arab Human Development Report 2003* (AHDR 2003) http://www.undp.org/rbas/ahdr/english2003.html.

2. *Arab League/UNICEF Report*, http://www.unicef.org/media/media_25968 .html; *Agence France Presse*, April 12, 2005.

3. *The 2004 Arab Human Development Report*, http://cfapp2.undp.org/rbas/ahdr_2004/1PR; *Washington Post*, April 6, 2005.

4. "Those who eat [take] Riba (usury) will not stand (on the Day of Resurrection) except like the standing of a person beaten by *Shaitan* (Satan) leading him to insanity. This is because they say: 'Trading is only like *Riba* (usury),' whereas Allah has permitted trading and forbidden *Riba*. So whosoever receives an admonition from his Lord and stops eating [taking] Riba shall not be punished for the past; his case is for Allah (to judge); but whoever return [to Riba], such are the dwellers of the Fire—they will abide therein." *Qur'an, Al-baqarat*, 2: 275. Principles of Islamic Banking: 1) All money must be invested in purely ethical industries; 2) The giving or receiving of interest is forbidden; 3) Money cannot be simply traded for money; 4) Money can be used to buy goods or services, which can then be sold for a profit.

5. *Al Jazeera*, November 29, 2004.

6. *Al Jazeera*, June 17, 2005; *Associated Press*, June 17, 2005; *Agence France Presse*, December 18, 2005.

7. *New York Times*, December 12, 2004; University of Maryland Annual Arab Survey, November 11–16, 2006.

8. *Associated Press*, April 23, 2006.

9. *Associated Press*, April 21, 2006.

10. *Associated Press* and *Agence France Presse,* June 4, 2006; *New York Times,* June 19, 2006; *Al Jazeera,* October 9, 2006.

11. *Al-Sharq al-Awsat,,* June 6, 2006; *Agence France Presse,* June 7, 2006; *BBC,* December 29, 2006, and January 4, 2007.

12. *Arab News,* February 5, 2005.

13. *Arab News.*

14. *Reuters,* February 5, 2005.

15. *UN News,* September 20, 2006.

16. *Al Jazeera,* August 4, 2005; *New York Times,* September 5, 2005.

CHAPTER 4

1. http://www.interpol.int/Public/FinancialCrime/MoneyLaundering/hawala.

2. Mohammed El-Qorchi, *IMF,* http://www.imf.org/external/pubs/ft/fandd/2002/12/elqorchi.htm.

3. *New York Times,* December 12, 2003.

4. *New York Times,* April 10, 2005, August 27 and 31; *Financial Times,* August 27, 2004.

5. *Radio Netherlands International,* July 23, 2005.

6. *Reuters,* April 20, 2006.

7. *Agence France Presse,* May 14, 2005.

8. *Washington Post Weekly,* December 20, 2004–January 2, 2005; *New York Times,* February 27, 2006

9. *Reuters,* December 9, 2005.

10. *International Crisis Group,* September 27, 2005.

CHAPTER 5

1. *Agence France Presse,* November 30, 2005.

2. *Agence France Presse,* October 20, 2006.

3. *Agence France Presse,* February 5, 2005; *Associated Press* and *Reuters,* February 4, 2006.

4. *Christina Science Monitor,* December 13, 2002.

5. *Associated Press,* November 28, 2003; *Reuters,* March 7, 2005.

6. *Washington Post,* December 3, 2002; *New York Times,* November 20, 30 and December 3, 2002; *Globe and Mail,* December 9, 2002.

7. *BBC,* December 6, 2002.

8. *Jakarta Post,* January 15.2006.

9. Zachary Abuza, http://www.jamestown.org/publications; *BBC,* October 29, 2005.

10. *Washington Post,* January 5, 2005.

11. *The Jakarta Post* and *Associated Press*, December 27, 2005; *The Jakarta Post*, August 26, 2005. http://www.thejakartapost.com/yesterdaydetail.asp?fileid=20050826.E02.

12. *New York Times*, September 2, 2003; *Washington Post*, September 2, 2003; *Reuters*, December 2, 2004.

13. *Reuters*, March 3, 2005; *Al Jazeera*, August 18, 2006. The author is in the possession of the full text.

14. *Washington Post*, March 3, 2005; *Reuters*, March 3, 2005.

15. *Associated Press; BBC*, June 14–15, 2006; *Reuters*, June 15, 2006.

16. *Associated Press*, November 16, 2005.

17. *Reuters*, November 26, 2005; *Reuters*, January 31, 2006.

18. *Agence France Presse*, April 12, 2005.

19. *Reuters*, February 14, 2005.

20. *New York Times*, June 30, 2004.

21. *Agence France Presse*, August 28, 2005 and December 30, 2006.

22. *Voice of America*, November 4, 2004; *Reuters*, November 8, 2004; *Agence France Presse*, February 12, 2005; *BBC*, November 15, 2004 and February 14, 2005.

23. Arnab Neil Sengupta, "Eye on Thai PM as he tours south," *Al Jazeera and News Agencies*, February 15, 2005.

24. *BBC*, February 17, 2005.

25. *Agence France Presse*, February 18, 2005.

26. *Agence France Presse*, February 24, 2005 and March 1, 2005; http://hrw.org/press/htm and http://hrw.org/english/docs/2005/01/13/thaila9858.htm.

27. *BBC*, July 15, 2005.

28. *International Herald Tribune*, February 27, 2007.

29. *BBC*, February 28, 2005.

CHAPTER 6

1. *New York Times*, December 11, 2004.

2. *BBC*, December 10, 2005.

3. *U.S. State Department* Web site, 2004; http://fpc.state.gov/documents/organization/48610.pdf; http://www.state.gov/p/inl/rls/rm/62413.htm; *Reuters*, March 1, 2006.

4. http://www.unodc.org/unodc/index.html 2003.

5. *The Economist*, November 20, 2004.

6. *The Economist; BBC*, March 4, 2005.

7. *BBC*, November 18, 2004.

8. http://web.worldbank.org/wbsite/external/countries/southasiaext/afghanistan/, February 10, 2003; *Associated Press*, August 30, 2005 and March 8, 2006.

9. *Associated Press*, September 2, 2006.

10. *BBC*, June 4, 2008.

11. *Al Jazeera*, June 2, 2008.

12. *New York Times,* February 4, 2005.

13. *Washington Post,* March 18, 2005.

14. *Reuters,* December 21, 2004.

15. *Reuters,* February 21, 2005.

16. *Reuters,* March 8, 2006.

17. *Associated Press,* December 31, 2007.

CHAPTER 7

1. The northern Caucasus republics consist of seven autonomous republics and are located north of Azerbaijan and Georgia: Adygeia; Chechnya, the second largest North Caucasus republic; Dagestan, the largest North Caucasus republic; Ingushetia; Kabardino-Balkaria; Karachai-Cherkessia; and North Ossetia, its majority people ethnically related to the South Ossetians, who are Iranian-speaking Muslims and Christians in the region. South Ossetia is struggling to join the Russian Federation. http://www.iwpr.net/index.php?apc_state=henocrscaucasus_map.html&s=o&o=caucasus_profile_northcau.html.

2. *Associated Press,* December 27, 2002.

3. *BBC,* October 29, 2004.

4. The above quotation is not exact because the verse that parallels those in Matthew and Mark verses is Luke 6:38 (or one could say 6:36-38); www.kazkovcenter.org; *Guardian,* September 10–16, 2004; *The Economist,* January 15, 2005; *Agence France Presse,* April 15, 2005.

5. *Agence France Presse,* January 23, 2005.

6. *Associated Press,* October 9, 2004.

7. Tamil women also have carried out suicide bombing missions as part of the Tamil Tiger Liberation Front's campaign for independence against the Sri Lankan government. In 1969, a Palestinian woman, Lyla Khalid, carried out the first airline hijacking. *AP,* May 5, 2003; *NYT,* June 6, 2003.

8. www.kavkazcenter.org and *Guardian Weekly,* September 10-16, 2004. Turkish women began suicide bombing in 1996.

9. *Associated Press,* December 4, 2004.

10. *Associated Press,* January 17, 2005.

11. *IWPR,* February 3, 2005; http://www.iwpr.net/caucasus_index1.html.

12. *ISN Security Watch,* October 10, 2005; "http://www.isn.ethz.ch/news/sw/details.cfm?ID=13142".

13. *Reuters,* February 20, 2005.

14. *ISN Security Watch,* http://www.isn.ethz.ch/news/sw/details.cfm?id=11065.

15. *Washington Post,,* March 8, 2005; http://www.kavkazcenter.com/eng/article.php?id=3599.

16. *Agence France Presse,* March 8, 2005.

17. kavkazcenter.com; *Agence France Presse,* March 10, 2005.

18. *The Economist,* July 9, 2005; *Christian Science Monitor,* July 25, 2005; *ISN Security Watch,* September 3, 2005; http://www.isn.ethz.ch/news/sw/details.cfm?ID=12707

19. *Associated Press,* October 13, 2005.

20. http://www.kavkaz.org.uk/eng/content/2005/10/14/4147.shtml

21. http://www.kavkaz.org.uk/eng/content/2005/10/14/4147.shtml

22. *Human Rights Watch and Human Rights in China,* April 10, 2005; http://hrw.org/reports/2005/china0405/; *Reuters,* January 20, 2006.

23. *Reuters,* November 9, 2005; *Associated Press,* July 10, 2008.

24. http://www.state.gov/r/pa/prs/ps/2002/13403.htm; *New York Times,* January 8, 2006.

25. *Associated Press,* January 15, 2003, June 9, 2003, and February 16, 2004; *RFERL,* October 26, 2004. *Hizb ut-Tahrir* is not the same group known as *Hizb-ut-Tahrir al-Islami* (Islamic Liberation Party).

26. *CBS/Associated Press,* March 25, 2004.

CHAPTER 8

1. *Washington Post,* December 20, 2004.

2. http://www.isn.ch/news/sw/details.cfm?ID=10810.

3. *Reuters,* March 11, 2005.

4. www.dw-world.de, May 4, 2006; *ISN Security Watch;* http://www.isn.ethz.ch/news/sw/details.cfm?id=10923http://www.isn.ethz.ch/news/sw/details.cfm?id=10923

5. For the religious-political views of *Hizbullah,* see: John J. Donohue/John L. Esposito, Ed., 2nd Ed., *Islam in Transition: Muslim Perspectives* (NY: Oxford University Press, 2007), 444–448; *Al Jazeera, Associated Press,* and *Reuters,* March 16, 2005

6. *Al Jazeera; Associated Press.*

7. *The Economist,* August 19, 2006.

8. *Guardian Weekly,* July 21–27, 2006

9. Two days later, the Egyptian weekly *El-Destour* headline read, "To Arab leaders get off our backs." *Al-Ahram Weekly,* August 17–23, 2006. http://weekly.ahram.org.eg/2006/808/re601.htm.

10. *BBC,* July 25, 2006.

11. *Al-Ahram Weekly.*

12. *BBC,* August 15, August 28, and August 30, 2006; *Associated Press,* August 16 and August 29, 2006; *Agence France Presse,* August 19, 2006; *The Daily Star,* August 29, 2006; July 12, 2007.

13. *Associated Press,* and *Al Jazeera,* September 5, 2006.

14. *Reuters,* August 26, 2006.

15. For the HAMAS Covenant and Islamic world views, see *The Avalon Project at Yale Law School,* HAMAS Covenant 1988 http://www.yale.edu/lawweb/avalon/mideast/hamas.htm; Jean-Francois Legrain, "The Islamic Movement and the *Intifada,"* in Jamal R. Nassar and Roger Heacock, ed., *Intifada: Palestine at the Crossroads* (NY: Praeger, 1990) 175–189; John J. Donohue/John L. Esposito,

433. Jean-Francois Legrain, "HAMAS: Legitimate Heir of Palestinian National-ism?" in John L. Esposito, Ed., *Political Islam: Revolution, Radicalism, or Reform?* (Boulder, CO: Rienner, 1997), 163–174.

16. Scott Atran, "Genesis of Suicide Terrorism," *Science* 299, March 7, 2003, 1534–1539; Shaul Mishal and Avraham Sela, *The Palestinian Hamas* (NY: Columbia University Press, 2000); Hala Jaber, *Hezbollah* (NY: Columbia University Press, 1997); For a time line of HAMAS bombings and suicide bombings since April 6, 1994 bombings, http://www.mfa.gov.il/MFA/Terrorism-%20Obstacle%20to% 20Peace/Palestinian%20terror%20since%202000/Suicide%20and%20Other% 20Bombing%20Attacks%20in%20Israel%20Since

17. *BBC,* April 17, 2004 and February 18, 2006.

18. Mohammed Abdulrahman, based on an interview by Reina Frescó, "Hamas: one hand on power, weapons in the other," *Radio Netherlands,* August 30, 2005; http://www2.rnw.nl/rnw/en/currentaffairs/region/middleeast/ pal050830; *Associated Press,* December 28, 2002; *New York Times,* December 2002; *Al Jazeera,* March 22, 2004; *BBC,* March 22 and November 12, 2004.

19. *Reuters* and *New York Times,* November 25, 2004; *Guardian,* November 25, 2004.

20. *BBC.*

21. *Agence France Presse, Reuters,* and *Associated Press,* March 12, 2005.

22. *Associated Press,* June 16, 2005. Militant operations carried out by HAMAS's underground Izzedine al-Qassam Brigades.

23. *Washington Post,* January 22, 2006.

24. *Radio Netherlands,* August 30, 2005; http://www2.rnw.nl/rnw/en/curren taffairs/region/middleeast/pa1050830.

25. *Radio Netherland.*

26. http://www.state.gov/r/pa/ei/rls/22520.htm.

27. *BBC,* January 27, 2006; *Associated Press,* February 12, 2006.

28. *Al Jazeera,* and *New York Times,* December 15, 2007.

29. *Al Jazeera,* January 5, 2008.

30. For HAMAS's view of the recent developments, see Ahmed Yousef (senior political advisor to the dismissed HAMAS-led prime minister Ismail Haniyeh), "Engage With Hamas:We Earned Our Support," *Washington Post,* June 20, 2007; *New York Times,* June 20, 2007.

31. *Agence France Presse,* January 5, 2005; *Al Jazeera,* June 9, 2005.

CHAPTER 9

1. *Independent,* April 1, 2003.

2. *Agence France Presse* and *Al Jazeera,* January 18, 2009.

3. The grandfather breaks the usual stereotypes. As with the cases of a 64 years old Palestinian grandmother Fatima Omar an-Najar—mother of 9 and grandmother of 41—in northern Gaza and also Muriel Degauque 38 years old, the first white European woman convert to Islam who attacked the US soldiers'

check point in Iraq, the grandfather's case casts further doubt on the practice of profiling.

4. *Al Jazeera,* January 5, 2008.

5. http://www.bt.cdc.gov/agent/ricin/facts.asp; AP, January 29, 2003. http://www.msnbc.com/modules/wtc/wtc_globaldragnet/custody_uk.htm

6. *Associated Press,* November 8, 2004; *Telegraph,* September 8, 2002 and *Independent,* January 25, 2003.

7. *Agence France Presse,* November 23, 2004.

8. *BBC,* August 10-11, 2006.

9. *BBC.*

10. *Guardian Weekly,* August 25-31, 2006; *AP*; *AFP* and *BBC,* September 2, 2006; *Reuters* and *AP,* September 5, 2006.

11. *NYT,* July 9, 2005; *Reuters,* September 12, 2005.

12. *Independent*; *AFP*; *NYT,* July 17, 2005.

13. *Al Jazeera,* September 1, 2005.

14. http://www.homeoffice.gov.uk/documents/7-july-report.pdf; *AP,* May 11, 2006.

15. *Associated Press,* January 6, 2006. There are more than 15 million Muslims in Western Europe countries and the majority are in following: Austria 339,000 (4.1% of the population); Belgium 400,000 (4%); Denmark 270,000 (5%); Finland 20,000 (4%); France approximately 5 to 6 million (8 to 9.6%); Germany 3 million (3.6%); Greece 450,000 (4%); Ireland 19,000 (4.5%); Italy 825,000 (1.4%); Luxembourg 6,000 (13%); Netherlands 945,000 (5.8%); Spain 1 million (2.3%); Sweden 300,000 (3%); Switzerland 310,000 (4.2%) and United Kingdom 1.6 million (2.8%). Compiled from BBC website, January 20, 2006. http://news.bbc.co.uk/2/hi/europe/4385768.stm

16. *BBC,* July 1-7, 2007. British court jailed three Muslim men, Tariq al-Daour 21 (sentenced to six-and-a- half year), Younes Tsouli 23 (sentenced to10 years) and Waseem Mughal 24 (seven-and-a-half year), who tried to encourage people to follow the ideology of *al-Qa'ida* via emails and websites. Compact discs with instructions for making explosives and poisons were found among their possessions and documents showing how to use a rocket-propelled grenade and make booby traps and a suicide vest. Films of hostages and beheadings were also discovered. Sentencing them, Judge Charles Openshaw said the men had engaged in "cyber jihad," encouraging others to kill "Kuffar [plural for Kafir nonbeliever]." *BBC & AP,* July 5, 2007.

17. *New York Times,* January 25, 2003; *Independent,* January 25, 2003.

18. *Associated Press,* February 1, 2005; *Reuters,* April 11, 2006.

19. *Associated Press,* May 28, 2007.

20. *Associated Press,* March 9, 2004.

21. *Associated Press.*

22. *BBC,* March 11, 2005; http://news.bbc.co.uk/2/hi/europe/4340315.stm *AP,* January 13, 2006.

23. *Agence France Presse,* March 10, 2005.

24. *The Observer,* December 5, 2004.

25. *BBC,* November 9, 2004; *Reuters; Associated Press* and *Agence France Presse,* November 10, 2004; *Telegraph,* November 10, 2004; *Guardian,* November 12–18, 2004.

26. *Reuters,* November 11, 2004; *Associated Press,* November 13, 2004.

27. *Associated Press,* December 23, 2004.

28. *Reuters,* December 23, 2004.

29. *Washington Post,,* February 1, 2005. The Dutch court ordered prosecutors to put the Member of Parliament, Geert Wilder, on trail for inciting hatred with his "offensively anti-Islamic film *Fitna,* and discrimination against Muslims." The court, in a written statement, said, "By attacking the symbol (Qur'an) of the Muslim religion, he also insulted the Muslim believers . . . In a democratic system, hate speech is considered to be so serious that it is in general interest to . . . draw line." (*BBC,* January 21, 2009.)

30. *Washington Post,,* July 13, 2005. http://www.radionetherlands.nl/current affairs/ned060331mc-a, March 31, 2006. http://www.radionetherlands.nl/current affairs/ned060428mc-a; April 28, 2006.

31. *Radio Netherlands.*

32. *Radio Netherlands.*

33. http://www.radionetherlands.nl/currentaffairs/mus060609, June 9, 2006.

34. *Deutsche Welle/AF,* December 3, 2004; *Agence France Presse,* December 5, 2004. *Reuters; New York Times,* December 3, 2004.*AP,* January 12, 2006.

35. *Associated Press,* January 12, 2005.

36. Spiegel ONLINE, June 16, 2008.

37. *New York Times,* January 25, 2005.

38. *Agence France Presse,* September 19, 2005; *Reuters,* September 14, 2006.

39. *Reuters,* September 14, 2006

40. BBC, September 15, 2006.

41. *Agence France Presse,* September 15, 2006.

42. *Reuters; BBC,* September 18, 2006.

43. *Agence France Presse,* April 19, 2006.

44. *Associated Press,* and *Reuters,* January 25, 2005; *NYT,* January 27, 2005

45. *Associated Press,* January 23, 2005.

46. Hans de Vreij, "At least 15 foiled terrorist attacks in Europe since 9/11" Transcript from *Radio Netherlands website:* http://www2.rnw.nl/rnw/en/current affairs/region/westerneurope/ter050218 February 18, 2005.

47. *BBC,* November 12, 2004.

48. The report 'Muslims in the European Union: Discrimination and Islamophobia,' *Europa* and *AP,* December 18, 2006.

49. *Reuters,* July 4, 2006.

50. Peter Levene said, "The research shows that boards are spending an increasing amount of time discussing terrorism and political violence risks. However, there appears to be a significant gap between this growing risk awareness and tangible actions actually taken by many companies driven by a lack of understanding of the dynamics of political violence." *Reuters,* May 9, 2007

51. *Washington Post,,* April 20; September 12, 2005 and December 8, 2006; *Amnesty International Press Release,* December 15, 2005; *AP,* November 23, 2005; *Le Figaro,* December 2, 2005 and *Guardian,* December 1, 2005.

52. *New York Times,* March 17 & 30, 2005 and *Washington Post,,* July 21, 2005.

53. *Washington Post,,* July 21, 2005.

54. *Washington Post,,* December 4, 2005 and *Agence France Presse,* December 18, 2005.

55. *Associated Press,* December 6, 2005; www.dw-world.de, December 6, 2005 and *AFP,* January 9, 2006.

56. *Washington Post,,* July 21, 2005.

57. *Washington Post,,* March 13, 2005; http://www.chrgj.org/docs/Off Record/Off_the_Record_PR.pdfhttp://www.chrgj.org/

58. *Reuters,* March 11, 2005; *AP,* March 12, 2005.

59. Radio Netherlands, May 2, 2008.

CHAPTER 10

1. *BBC,* September 29, 2004.

2. Table 3.2, and *Agence France Presse,* April 2, 2006; *BBC,* April 4, 2006; *Associated Press,* April 25, 2006 and June 16, 2006.

3. *Guardian,* September 17–23, 2004.

4. *Agence France Presse,* January 20, 2005.

5. *Agence France Presse,* January 3, 2004; *Associated Press,* January 5, 2005; *Financial Times,* January 28, 2005; *Times of London,* September 15, 2005.

6. *Associated Press.*

7. *New York Times,* January 9, 2005.

8. *Guardian,* January 5, 2005; *Radio Nederland,* January 4, 2005.

9. *Reuters,* January 4, 2005.

10. Interview with *Radio Nederland,* January 4, 2005; *Associated Press,* April 12, 2007.

11. *Washington Post,* January 5, 2005; *BBC,* March 19, 2006. For certain responses to the Shi'a-Sunni in Iraq, see *Reuters,* April 8, 2006; *Associated Press,* April 12, 2006.

12. http://www.un.org/News/.

13. *Associated Press,* December 24, 2004.

14. *Al Jazeera,* October 29, 2004.

15. *Christian Science Monitor,* March 15, 2002.

16. *New York Times,* December 23, 2004. The Jaish Ansar al-Sunnah Web site is used for recruitment; *Associated Press,* December 25, 2004.

17. *Reuters,* December 26, 2004.

18. *Associated Press,* January 3, 2005.

19. *Associated Press,* September 2, 2003.

20. *Agence France Presse,* December 5, 2004.

21. *Associated Press,* December 24, 2004.

22. *Associated Press,* March 31, 2003.

23. *Washington Post,* January 14, 2005.

24. *Washington Post,* January 11, 2005.

25. *Reuters,* January 15, 2005.

26. *Reuters,* January 15, 2005; *Agence France Presse,* January 11, 2005.

27. *Reuters,* January 30; *Agence France Presse,* February 9, 2005.

28. *Associated Press,* February 6, 2005.

29. *New York Times,* May 12, 2003; *Associated Press,* May 13, 2003.

30. *Associated Press,* December 6, 2004.

31. *Associated Press,* June 5, 2003.

32. *Arab News,* December 6, 2004; *International Herald Tribune,* December 6, 2004.

33. *Christian Science Monitor,* December 7, 2004.

34. *Al Jazeera,* December 29, 2004.

35. *Al Jazeera,* December 6–7, 2004; *Arab News,* December 8, 2004.

36. *Agence France Presse* and *Al Jazeera,* January 16, 2005.

37. *Associated Press,* January 20, 2005.

38. http://www.isn.ethz.ch/news/sw/details.cfm?id=14080; *Arab News,* December 29, 2005.

39. *Al Jazeera,* January 24, 2005.

40. *Arab News,* May 22, 2006.

41. *Associated Press,* April 15, 2006.

42. Ahmed Rashid, author of *Taliban and Jihad,* made the above observations, in an interview with Mohsin Hamid, "Reinventing Pakistan," *Smithsonian* (July 2004), 91–95; *Associated Press,* October 13, 2005.

43. *Guardian,* October 1, 2004.

44. *Agence France Presse,* January 11, 2005; *Associated Press,* January 11, 2005.

45. *INS Security Watch,* December 17, 2004.

46. *Washington Post National Weekly Edition*, October 4-10, 2004.

47. *Reuters,* February 26, 2005.

48. *Guardian,* May 27, 2006.

49. Examples of attacks in Baluchistan: December 31, 2005; January 22, 2006; February 4 and 15, 2006; March 10, 2006; April 12 and 28, 2006; May 11, 2006.

50. *Guardian,* March 21, 2005; *Agence France Presse,* August 26, 2006.

51. *Reuters,* February 24, 2005; *INS Security Watch,* January 21, 2005.

52. *Washington Post,* June 20, 2006.

53. *The Economist,* January 13, 2005.

54. *Associated Press,* January 20, 2005.

55. *Reuters,* April 23, 2005.

56. *Der Spiegel,* April 20, 2006; *Associated Press,* May 23, 2007.

57. *Washington Post,* December 6, 2004; *New York Times,* December 12, 2004.

58. *New York Times.*

59. *Agence France Presse,* December 21, 2004; *New York Times,* December 16, 2004.

60. *ITV*, October 17, 2004.

61. The de-Ba'thification program was issued by *Coalition Provisional Authority (CPA) Order Number 1* on May 16, 2003, by L. Paul Bremer III, the chief of the U.S. occupation in 2003–2004. *Associated Press* and *Agence France Presse*, May 26, 2006; http://www.whitehouse.gov/news/releases/2006/05/20060525-12.html.

62. *Reuters*, September 13, 2006.

CHAPTER 11

1. Joseph S. Nye, "Propaganda Isn't the Way: Soft Power," *The International Herald Tribune*, January 10, 2003; Joseph S. Nye, *Soft Power: The Means to Success in World Politics* (Public Affairs, 2004).

2. *Washington Post*, February 9, 2005; http://www.state.gov/r/pa/prs/ps/2005/58401.htm AFP, December 27, 2005; http://www.dailystar.com.lb/home2.asp.

3. *BBC* and *Agence France Presse*, February 9, 2005; *Washington Post*, February 9, 2005.

4. *New York Times*, December 26, 2005.

5. Time line of the publishing and reprinting the cartoons: September 30, 2005: Danish Jylands-Posten newspaper published commissioned cartoons for the first time; January 10, 2006: Norwegian publication reprints cartoons (Magazinet, Evangelical Christian); January 26: Saudi Arabia recalls its ambassador; January 30: Gunmen raid European Union's Gaza office demanding apology; January 31: Danish paper apologized; February 1: Newspapers in Belgium (*De Standaard*); France (*France Soir*; *Charlie Hebdo*), Germany (*Die Welt*), Italy, and Spain (*El Mundo*) reprinted cartoons. February 3:*Associated Press*; *CBC*; *BBC*, February 9, 2006.

6. *Washington Post*, January 22, 2006.

7. *Washington Post,*, January 31 2005 and January 22, 2006; *New York Times*, March 6, 2005.

8. *New York Times*, January 30, 2005.

9. *New York Times*, December 16, 2002.

10. *New York Times*, January 15, 2008.

11. *Agence France Presse*, September 4, 2006.

CHAPTER 12

1. *Reuters*, March 14, 2005.

2. *Associated Press*, June 4, 2008.

3. *Associated Press*, April 22, 2006.

Glossary

Al-Harakat: Movement
Al-Hurra: Free One
Al-Jaiysh or Al-Jayish: Army
Al-Jihad: Struggle and armed struggle
al-Akbar: Greater struggle
Allahu Akbar: God is Great
al-Asqar: Minor struggle
Al-Jema'a, Al-Jama'at or Al-Gama'a: Islamic society
Al Jazeera: The Islad, the TV network
Al-Mujahid (singular): Islamic (Holy) fighter
Al-Mujahidoon and Al-Mujahideen (Plural): Minor struggle
al-Nafs or Fard al-'ayn: Personal obligation or struggle
Al-Qa'ida: The Base
Al-Rafidha: Those who reject the faith, a derogatory term used by the Militant Sunnis for the Shi'ites
Al-Shura: Council
Al-Takfir: (Excommunication), To Accuse a Muslim of committing Kufr (irreligious act)
Ansar: Supporters
Azzam: Great or Grand

Dar al-Harb: House of War
Dar al-Islam: House of Islam or Peace
Deobandi School: Islamic liberation school of thought

Eid al-Adha: Feast of Sacrifice

Emir: Prince, commander, or leader

Fatwa: Specific theocratic "legal" ruling

Hadith: Unauthenticated prophetic sayings and deeds
HAMAS: Zeal, is an acronym of the first letters of the Arabic words
Harakat: Movement
Haram: Forbidden, unclean, or sinful
Hawalla: Transfer of Funds
Hawalladar: Hawalla or fund operator
Hizb: Party
Hizbullah or Hiz-Allah: Party of Allah or (Party of God)
Hizb ut-Tahrir: Liberation Party

Intifada: Uprising

Jahiliyya: Ignorance
Jamiat al-Ikhwan al-Muslimoon: Literally, Society of Muslim Brothers
Jhangavi: Fighters
Jihad: Struggle and Armed Struggle

Kafir (singular): Infidel, irreligious, nonbeliever
Khalafa, Khalifah (Calipha): Successor of Prophet Mohammad
Kifayaa: Enough
Kufar (plural): Infidels, nonbelievers

Lashkar: Army

Mahroomeen (plural): Dispossessed or deprived
Masrif: Disburse
Moqawama: Resistance
Munafiq: Traitor

Nukhbah: Elite

Riba: Usury; interest

Sepah: Corp or army
Shi'a or Shi'it Islam: Followers of Khalifa Ali
Shoura: Council
Sirf: Pay or spend
Sunna or Sunnah: Tradition
Sunni: The largest Muslim sect

Takfir: Excommunication; see Al-Takfir

Taliban: Plural for Talib meaning one who inspires to learn
Tandhim: Organization
Tawheed: : Affirmation of the One-ness of God
Tayyba: Righteous
Tehrik: Movement

Ulema: (plural of Alim): Muslim scholars
Umma or Ummah: Community of Muslims worldwide

Valayat-e Faqih (Arabic Walayat al-Faqih): Islamic theocratic leader or government by an Islamic jurist in canon law

Zakat: Alms

Bibliography

Abou, Zahab, and Mariam and Olivier Roy. *Islamist Networks, The Afghan-Pakistan Connection.* New York: Columbia University Press, 2004.

Abuza, Zachary. http://www.jamestown.org/publications.

Alaolmolki, Nozar. *Struggle for Dominance in the Persian Gulf: Past, Present and Future Prospects.* New York: Peter Lang, 1991.

Al-Sharq al-Awsat. June 6, 2006.

Arab Human Development Report 2003 (AHDR 2003). http://www.undp.org/rbas/ahdr/english2003.html.

Arab League/UNICEF Report. http://www.unicef.org/media/media_25968.html and AFP. April 12, 2005.

Bloom, Mia. *Dying to Kill: The Allure of Suicide Terror.* New York: Columbia University Press, 2005.

Chechen Web site. http://www.kavkazcenter.com/eng/article.php?id=3599, October 1, 2005.

———. http://www.kavkaz.org.uk/eng/content/2005/10/14/4147.shtml.

Cole, R. I.,. *Colonialism and Revolution in the Middle East: Social and Cultural Origin of 'Urabi Movement.* New Heaven, CT: Princeton University Press. 1993.

Dabbagh, Nadia Tavsir. *Suicide in Palestine: Narrative of Despair.* London: Hurst & Company, 2005.

Deutsche Welle. www.dw-world.de. May 4, 2006.

El-Qorchi, Mohammed. *IMF.* http://www.imf.org/external/pubs/ft/fandd/2002/12/elqorchi.htm, December 2202.

Esposito, John. *The Islamic Threat: Myth or Reality,* 3rd ed.. New York, NY: Oxford University Press, 1999.

Gambetta, Diego, ed. *Making Sense of Suicide Missions.* New York: Oxford University Press, 2004.

Gunaratna, Rohan. *Inside Al Qaeda, Global Network of Terror.* New York, NY: Columbia University Press, 2002.

Hamid, Mohsin. "Reinventing Pakistan." *Smithsonian*: July 2004.

Hashmi, Sohail, H., ed. *Islamic Political Ethics.* Princeton, NJ: Princeton University Press.

Hodgson, M. G. S. "The Order of Assassins." *Encyclopedia of Islam*, S'Gravenhage, Holland, 1955.

Hoffman, Bruce. *Inside Terrorism.* New York: Columbia University Press, 1998.

Horowitz, Irving L., ed. *The Anarchists.* New York: Dell, 1964.

Human Rights Watch. http://hrw.org/english/docs/2005/01/13/thaila9858 .htm. January 13, 2006.

———. http://hrw.org/reports/2005/china0405/ 2005.

Ignatief, Michael. *The Lesser Evil: Politics in an Age of Terror.* Princeton, NJ: Princeton University Press, 2004.

International Crisis Group. September 27, 2005.

Interpol. http://www.interpol.int/Public/FinancialCrime/MoneyLaundering/ hawala.

ISN Security Watch. http://www.isn.ethz.ch/news/sw/details.cfm?id=11065.

IWPR. http://www.iwpr.net/caucasus_index1.html. February 3, 2005.

Jihad Against Jews and Crusaders. http://www.fas.org/irp/world/para/docs/ 980223-fatwa.htm; www.secularislam.org/visitors/guest114.ht

Karpat, Kemal, H. ed. *Political and Social Thought in the Contemporary Middle East.* New York, NY: Praeger Publishers 1982.

Kepel, Giles. *The War for Muslim Minds: Islam and the West.* Cambridge, MA: Belknap, 2004.

Kerr, Malcom, H. *Islamic Reform: The Political and Legal Theories of Mohammad Abdu and Rashid Rida.* Berkeley, CA: California University Press, 1996.

Mamdani, Mahmood. *Good Muslim, Bad Muslim.* New York, NY: Pantheon Books, 2004.

———. "Wither Political Islam?" *Foreign Affairs.* January/February 2005.

Nagl, John, A. *Learning to Eat Soup with Knife: Counterinsurgency Lessons from Malaya and Vietnam.* Chicago, IL: University of Chicago Press, 2005.

Oliver, Anne Marie, and Paul Steinberg. *The Road to Martyrs' Square: A Journey Into the World of the Suicide Bomber.* New York: Oxford University Press, 2004.

Pape, Robert A. *Dying to Win: The Strategic Logic of Suicide Terrorism.* New York: Random House, 2005.

Pavlin, James. *"Sunni Kalam and Theological Controversies,"* in S. H. Nasr and O. Leaman, eds. *History of Islamic Philosophy.* London, UK: Routledge, 1996.

Qassem, Naim. *Hizbullah: The Story from Within.* Translated by Dalia Khalil, (London, UK: Saqi Books, 2005.

Radio Netherlands International. July 23, 2005.

Roy, Olivier. *Globalized Islam, The Search for A New Umma.* New York: Columbia University Press, 2004.

Ruthven, Malise. *Islam in the World.* New York, NY: Oxford University Press, 1984.

Safran, Nadav. *Egypt in Search of Political Community.* Cambridge, MA: Harvard University Press, 1961.

Sengupta, Arnab Neil. "Eye on Thai PM as he tours south." *Al Jazeera and News Agencies.* February 15, 2005.

The 2004 Arab Human Development Report. http://cfapp2.undp.org/rbas/ ahdr_2004/1PR.

University of Maryland Annual Arab Survey. November 11–16, 2006.

U.S. Department of State Web site. http://www.state.gov/p/inl/rls/rm/ 62413.htm.

———. http://www.state.gov/r/pa/prs/ps/2002/13403.htm.

World Bank Web site. http://web.worldbank.org/wbsite/external/countries/ southasiaext/afghanistan. February 10, 2003.

Index

About the Author

NOZAR ALAOLMOLKI is Chair of the Political Science Department at Hiram College. He has been a Fulbright Scholar in Kyrgyzstan and Kazakhstan and has published a number of books, including *Life After the Soviet Union: The Newly Independent Republics of Transcaucasus and Central Asia, The Persian Gulf Region in the 21st Century: Stability and Change,* and *Struggle for Dominance in the Persian Gulf: Past, Present and Future Prospects.* He is a native of Iran.